ALL BLACK LIVES MATTER

BONDAGE, VIOLENCE, SUBJUGATION

KEN MENON

authorHOUSE

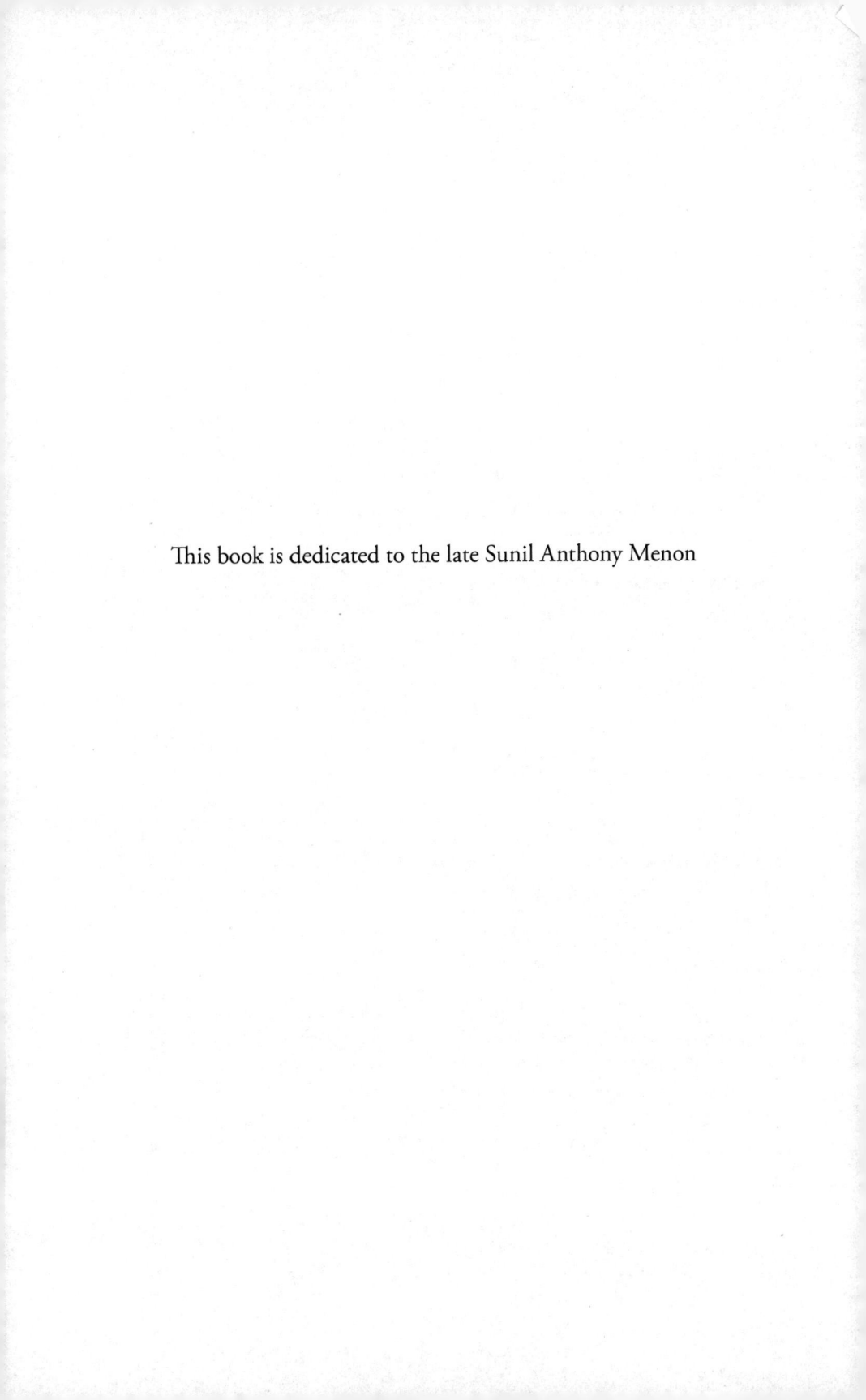

This book is dedicated to the late Sunil Anthony Menon

AuthorHouse™ UK
1663 Liberty Drive
Bloomington, IN 47403 USA
www.authorhouse.co.uk
Phone: UK TFN: 0800 0148641 (Toll Free inside the UK)
UK Local: (02) 0369 56322 (+44 20 3695 6322 from outside the UK)

© 2023 Ken Menon. All rights reserved.

No part of this book may be reproduced, stored in a retrieval system, or transmitted by any means without the written permission of the author.

Published by AuthorHouse 06/26/2023

ISBN: 979-8-8230-8325-6 (sc)
ISBN: 979-8-8230-8326-3 (hc)
ISBN: 979-8-8230-8327-0 (e)

Print information available on the last page.

Any people depicted in stock imagery provided by Getty Images are models, and such images are being used for illustrative purposes only.
Certain stock imagery © Getty Images.

This book is printed on acid-free paper.

Because of the dynamic nature of the Internet, any web addresses or links contained in this book may have changed since publication and may no longer be valid. The views expressed in this work are solely those of the author and do not necessarily reflect the views of the publisher, and the publisher hereby disclaims any responsibility for them.

CONTENTS

Slaves and Slavery 1

Of Africa, by Africa, for Africa 29

'a moment of madness' 63

Stompei, Nkosi, 'Dr.Beetroot' 87

'We Are Not Your Boys' 114

Iconoclasm, Wokeism 140

Reparations 186

Rise of the Phoenix 213

White Crocodile, Black Crocodile, New Slavery for Old ... 227

SLAVES AND SLAVERY

The word slave derives from 'Slav' where Slavs became slaves when the Holy Roman Empire was involved in battle in the German –Slav border in the 9th century. The German King, Henry the Fowler (Heinrich der Vogler or Heinrich der Finkler (876 – 936) and his son Otto 1, defeated and conquered the Slav people who lived east of the Elbe river, between it and the Baltic coast. The Slav people were converted to Christianity by Otto 1 who became Holy Roman Emperor. However the Slav people have a better meaning for the word 'Slav'. It means 'famous' or 'renown'. Hence the name 'Stanislav' means a person who achieves glory or fame in resisting enemies or opponents. Similarly, the capital of Slovakia, Bratislava, comes from the Czech word 'brat' meaning brother and 'slav ' meaning glory or fame. The female version of the word is Bratislava.

The word slave first appeared in English usage around 1538.

Alexander Hamilton (1755 – 1804) an American politician and one of the Founding Fathers of the United States, said 'The only distinction between freedom and slavery is this: In the former state, a man is governed by the laws to which he has given his consent; in the latter, he is governed by the will of another.'

In his 1998 book, *Slaves and Slavery*, Duncan Clarke defines slavery as 'as the reduction of fellow human beings to the legal status of chattels, allowing them to be bought and sold as goods'. This is a useful definition of human slavery as it happened then and in respect to what is witnessed now in acts of 'modern slavery'.

A slave is a person owned by another and therefore in complete servitude to the latter. The word slave also has non –human meanings for e.g. being a slave to work or being under the control of and dependent on an object like the saying 'he is a slave to alcohol'. The word may also be used to describe a component of machinery that is controlled and operated by another part of the machine cycle. Therefore a robot in a car manufacturing plant may be seen as a slave.

But in the use of the word related to human slavery, the word 'slave' is one who is not only owned by another, but is devoid of rights, and is used and controlled in virtually every aspect of life by the owner of the slave. It is an experience of total surrender and of dehumanisation. Slavery is extreme servitude with no ability to exercise any freedom of action or of opinion.

Duncan Clarke's description of a slave encompasses what it is to be one. A near-inanimate 'object' devoid of feeling, emotions, a voice to articulate views and freedom of action and thought. Everything about the word 'slave' implies ownership by another, who decides what a slave may or may not do. It is the most degrading state to be reduced to and above all to subject another to. It exceeds by a great magnitude the suffering for e.g. of the black people in apartheid South Africa. Nelson Mandela, on release from incarceration in Robben Island off the coast of South Africa said 'Never, never and never again shall it be that this beautiful land will again experience the oppression of one by another'. But the oppression he was referring to was subjugation and was so different to the conditions of slavery that it would have been a welcome relief to a slave.

Slavery is probably as old as humanity. For example, the Book of Exodus in the Bible states that slaves were to manumitted after six years. In Islamic society too, slaves were to me manumitted after six years. This practice was no doubt a relief for most of the slaves, to be released from captivity. But this placed a burden on society, due to a need to find a continuous supply of slaves that were needed.

Peonage or debt slavery was the practice where a person offered his services in repayment of a debt. It was a form of servitude. There is no contract and therefore the person is under servitude to the master for an indefinite term in time and under ill-defined conditions, which in most cases never existed. In its first Global report, 'Stopping Forced Labour -2001' The international Labour Organisation (ILO) estimated that globally, there were at least 12.3 million people in forced labour. The 2020 UK Annual Report on Modern Slavery, calls it an abhorrent and despicable crime.

Eshnunna, which is modern Tell Asmar in Iraq, was one of the earliest states in Mesopotamia. In about 2000 BC the Laws of Eshnunna were set out inscribed in two tablets which were discovered in Tell Abū Harmal, Baghdad, Iraq in 1945 and 1947. The Eshnunna Laws fell into five groups- theft, false seizure of a person's property in lieu of money or other items owed, bodily injury, sexual offence and damages caused by ox and related causes. The Laws had a section on slavery for e.g. a slave woman and silver owed shall be of equal value. When a slave owner 'brings the silver, he shall retrieve his slave woman'. And it stated that 'If a man should deflower the slave woman of another man, he shall weigh and deliver 20 shekels of silver, but the slave woman remains the property of her master.'

In about 2250 BC was the Code of Hammurabi which set out rights of slaves and of slave owners. For e.g. Code 15 states 'If a man should enable a palace slave, a palace slave woman, a commoner's slave, or a commoner's slave woman to leave through the main city-gate, he shall be killed.' And Code 17 says that 'If a man seizes a fugitive slave or slave woman in the open country and leads he back to his owner, the slave owner shall give him 2 shekels of silver.'

However the various ancient Codes that were inexistence did not always make life easier for those in slavery. For e.g. the Codes of Middle Assyrian of 1076 B.C. stated 'If either a slave or a slave woman should receive something from a man's wife, they shall cut off the slave's or slave woman's nose and ears; they shall restore the stolen goods; the man shall cut off his own wife's ears. But if he releases his wife and does not cut off her ears, they' shall not cut off (the nose and ears) of the slave or slave woman, and they shall not restore the stolen goods'.

While affording some protection to slaves, Codes favoured owners of slaves. But slave owners were responsible for providing food and shelter for slaves in their ownership.

The Hebrew Bible had two sets of laws – one for Canaanite slaves and another for Hebrew slaves. The latter laws were lenient in comparison to those applied to Canaanite slaves. 'Cursed be Canaan; lowest of slaves shall he be to his brothers'.

The Canaanites were a group of people, who lived in Lebanon, Syria, Israel and Jordan. They spoke the Semitic language. The Semitic language is a Syro-Arabic language that is spoken by over 300 million people living in the Middle East, North Africa, Malta. The word Semitic comes from Shem, who was one of the three sons of Noah. It has been shown and written that most Lebanese are descended from Canaanites.

The Book of Joshua is the sixth book in the Hebrew Bible and in the Old Testament of Christianity. The Book of Joshua states *'Joshua turned back at that time and took Hazor, and struck its king with the sword, for Hazor was formerly the head of all those kingdoms. And they struck all the people who were in it with the edge of the sword, utterly destroying them ... Then he burnt Hazor with fire.'*

This appears to tell the story of how the ancient Israelites reached the promised land of Canaan. However, archaeologists who have excavated relevant sites in Canaan find no evidence to support this description. Israelites followed the Canaanites in Canaan. In its time Hazor appears to have been a thriving Canaanite acropolis.

It is currently accepted that around the 13th century BC a terrible catastrophe befell Caanan. Archaeologists describe a 'violent conflagration'. The heat was so intense that for eg. bricks turned to glass. That there was a fire is generally accepted. It is therefore possible that the Israelites laid siege and destroyed Canaan in pursuit of their Promised Land. After the conquest of Hazor, it is written in the Book of Joshua that the Israelites took all of the land between the Dead Sea and the Sea of Galilee. However the Book of Judges, which is the seventh book in the Hebrew Bible and the Old Testament of Christianity, paints a gradual encroachment on Canaan with some peaceful co-existence between the Israelites and the local Canaanites.

Richard Dawkins, philosopher and atheist claimed that the God of the Old Testament was "a vindictive, bloodthirsty ethnic cleanser ... a genocidal ... megalomaniacal, sadomasochistic, capriciously malevolent bully". The Canaanites were perceived as sinful and God had ordered the slaughter of them by the Israelites. As was written in the Book of Joshua 'thus Joshua struck all the land, the hill country and the Negev and the lowland and the slopes and all their kings. He left no survivor, but he utterly destroyed all who breathed, just as the Lord, the God of Israel, had commanded.... He left nothing undone of all that the Lord had commanded Moses.'

However it is known, as stated before, that the people of Canaan were not totally exterminated. Some survived and their descendants are in Lebanon and in the Levant. It is said that 90% of the genes in Lebanese are from their forebears of ancient Canaan.

The foregoing brief history may explain why the Canaanite slaves were considered the 'lowest of slaves.' Here one sees not only ancient slavery but also one of the first descriptions of discrimination between people. The Hebrew bible had two sets of laws- one for Canaanite slaves and the other for Hebrews. The reason for the differential treatment of Canaanite slaves is complex and has been interpreted and re-interpreted several times. What is probably without doubt is that Ham, son of Noah, saw his father in the nude following consumption of wine from his vineyard. Looking at another's genital was a serious offence at the time. Some have suggested that Ham was wrong to a much greater extent than just seeing his father's exposed genitals. He was accused of talking about his father's nude, drunken state with other persons in the street. In the Babylonian Talmud of 500 it is claimed that Ham either castrated his father or sodomised him. But Ham had been blessed by God and therefore could not be cursed by his father. Others write that Noah's nakedness was first noted by Ham's son, Canaan, who proceeded to tell his father and also to talk about it with others. So Noah cursed Ham's son, Canaan and thereafter it would appear that Canaanites were considered inferior and Canaanite slaves were treated worse than Hebrew slaves.

And here is where one arrives at as interesting and as controversial a part of the story. The descendants of Ham are supposed to have populated Africa. They were said to be black. Now one sees a biblical justification for slavery – the black man was cursed by Noah. For a curse to be binding, the person had to be cursed by God. But in this case it was only Noah who had cursed his grandson. The late Martin Luther King claimed that any such theory is 'blasphemy'. However for slave owners of the Southern United States the bible provided ample justification for continuing with the ownership of slaves. There also emerges a racial explanation, as the bible apparently provided a narrative relating to the origins of blacks and a distinction of races.

The blackness of descendants of Canaan was not only the view of the Jewish community of the time. It was shared and expounded by Christian and Islamic scholars.

The land area that is currently recognised as the state of Israel was the original biblical land of Canaan. It bears the name of Noah's grandson and Ham's son. Some describe Canaan having left Africa after the curse on him and settling in the land of Canaan. It is the land that God promised to Abraham. Some would claim that Ham is the father of all black people.

Were Canaanites black or white? This is central to an understanding of slavery in the region and in respect of the religions of the region, especially Judaism and Christianity. Eurocentric Christian churches speak of a white or light coloured Canaanite people. Mormons teach that Canaanites were black; this accords with the Book of Moses – 'For behold, the Lord shall curse the land with much heat, and the barrenness thereof shall go forth forever; and there was a blackness came upon all the children of Canaan, that they were despised among all people.'

The views of Mormonism and its attitude to slavery and redemption make interesting reading. Morons taught that righteousness was related to whiteness. They believed and taught that 'by righteous living, the dark-skinned races may again become 'white and delightsome'. The righteous black man could become white in the image of God. The white Mormon who became an apostate and relinquished Mormonism would see their skin becoming darkened!

But Mormons were largely opposed to slavery and were sympathetic to the abolitionist cause. However, due to conflicting pressures of the time, the Mormon Church took a neutral position and maintained that having a slave was a private matter between the slave owner and God. In 1852 Brigham Young, Governor of Utah, legalised slavery involving Black Americans and their Native American compatriots. The laws were different in Utah compared to the strict laws of the Southern States and represented a liberal form of slavery, like being an indentured worker for a master. It was helped by the law requiring that slaves came to Utah 'of their own free will' and that they could not be traded without the prior consent of the slaves. Slaves were to be freed if they were abused by their owners or masters.

When the law stated that slaves came to Utah of their free will, it was implied that slavery was an accepted practice by some persons. Slaves probably recognised that it was their way of life. The reasons for this choice are not clear. Could it have been a better standard of living, care, safety or a combination of a multitude of reasons? However slavery was an accepted form of life of the times; accepted by both slave and slave owner. This questionable conclusion needs to be viewed in the context of the times.

The Greek philosopher and polymath Aristotle (384BC-322BC) believed that all men but particularly African men were hypersexual. He thought, obviously, that Greeks were superior to non-Greeks. As such, Puritans were thought to be superior to Native Americans, Africans, and all non-Puritans.

Aristotle viewed slavery as being beneficial to the slave. He thought that some societies practised slavery if they believed that there were some people in society who would be natural slaves. Who are these people who would be natural slaves? Aristotle provided an explanation in that there are people whose judgement is not as effective as it should be for their good. Such a person he thought would be a slave because he does not have the capacity to regulate his life and would benefit from being a slave. As such he opined that slavery would be just and it would be helpful to the slave. In modern parlance one would consider some persons as having a learning disability or not mentally competent and therefore in need of guardianship. Since the twentieth century and even earlier, one would not treat such a person as a slave. On the contrary, society would provide them with the care they need and assist them in leading normal independent lives. On the other hand treating such persons as slaves would be a breach of their fundamental human rights and would be an affront to society and its values.

But in Roman times Aristotle was a beacon of moral thinking. Morality, ethics and human values evolve and change.

People in the antebellum American south may have shared Aristotle's views and even taken succour from them. But given the two vastly different eras in which these events occurred, it is reasonable to question why the slave owners of America could not see nor could they confront their own sense of injustice towards other human beings.

Aristotle's philosophy on slavery was used by the Puritan, John Cotton (1585 – 1652) in his first constitution for New England in America. Slavery was legalised and blacks and Indians 'could be sold'.

What is most worrying is whether this 'blindness ' to the injustice of inequality exists today in some sections of the population. Or worse still there is justification for considering the black man as being inferior.

Greeks believed that people were divided into 'slaves and 'non-slaves'. Greeks thought that slavery was necessary and slaves were often captured after war. Race was not the basis of this division of people, rather it may have been influenced by colour, religious and ethnic prejudices. There were supposed to be about 80,000 slaves in the 5th and 6th century BC in Athens. It was not uncommon for most households to have slaves. Slaves could do any type of work in ancient Greece except that they could not enter into politics, which was reserved for citizens. There was also an international trade in slaves and persons captured during piracy were used as slaves.

From most accounts it appears that slaves in Greece were treated well and even welcomed into the house of the owner. Manumission also existed in ancient Greece.

The great Muslim philosopher and sociologist, Ibn Khaldun also known as Abū Zayd 'Abd ar-Raḥmān ibn Muḥammad ibn Khaldūn al-Ḥaḍramī (1332 – 1406) wrote that black people were genetically inferior and were 'submissive' to slavery'.

Prince Henry of Portugal or Dom Henrique of Portugal was also known as Prince Henry the Navigator (1394-1460). He has the reputation of being the first slave trader in the Atlantic slave trade. He dispatched expeditions to the west coast of Africa. Two mariners, Nuno Tristao and Antao Goncalves brought back to Portugal captured Africans in 1441. It is said that one of the captured men negotiated his release and sailed back to Africa, with the promise of providing more Africans to the Portuguese. Thus became the European involvement in the African slave trade. One also sees here the beginning of the involvement of the African in slavery, for the Europeans. This led to the establishment of the Atlantic slave trade in 1444.

The Portuguese historian and chronicler, Gomes Eanes de Zurara (1410 – 1474) described black Africans as 'beasts' and gave the impression that Prince Henry was freeing them.

In the nineteenth century the study of phrenology came to the fore. It was not a science as much as a series of observations. It started on the basis that the brain is an important organ. It controls vital functions and serves as the site of human thought. It was accepted that various sections of the brain had separate functions. This part of the origin of phrenology was based on some appreciation of human biology and was therefore to some extent grounded in the science of the time. Phrenology originated from the works of the German neuro-anatomist Franz Josef Gall (1758-1828) who studied the mental functions of the brain. He then added cranioscopy which was an attempt to correlate mental faculties of a person to the structure of the skull and its shape. To explain his theory Gall studied over 120 skulls which he had collected. He used the phrase ' localisation of function' to assign to parts of the brain various functions. He described twenty-seven essential function or faculties in the human brain like love of poetry and music, mechanical ability and manual dexterity, memory of and recollection of people etc. He then made a seismic jump to assume that the surface of the skull could determine a person's character and their faculties. He stated that a mature skull under fourteen inches in circumference was incapable of normal function. Well developed parts of the skull overlie well developed parts of the brain and therefore the function assigned to that part of the brain.

Localisation of function to parts of the brain received a boost from the work of Paul Broca (1824 –1880). He was a French neurologist and anatomist who localised speech and language to a part of the frontal lobe of the brain which is called Broca's area. He was interested in the physical features of humans and his work contributed to the science of anthropometry. Anthropometry as the name suggests is measurement of, in this case, facial structures and the skull and then using these findings to make judgements on brain function, especially a person's intelligence. He developed a measurement called the cephalic index which was the association between the length from the forehead to the back, and width of the head measured between the top of the ears. This gave an estimation of the size of the persons brain which was then reflected in the person's intelligence. He concluded that most intelligent Europeans were 'long headed' compared to the least intelligent *black* person whom he described as 'short headed'. Broca claimed that white Europeans had a large frontal area of the brain which he said contributed to their supposed greater intelligence.

In his 1859 book *'On the Phenomenon of Hybridity in the Genus Homo'*, Paul Broca wrote thus – 'We meet, first, with this fact, namely, the union of the *black* with a white woman is frequently sterile, whilst that of a white man with a *black woman* is perfectly fecund'. This was explained by the shape of the black woman's pelvis and the penis of the black man. Sexual intercourse between a Caucasian man and an Ethiopian woman for e.g. was described as 'easy and without inconvenience to the latter'. However intercourse between an Ethiopian man and a Caucasian woman was described as a cause of suffering for the latter, as her uterus (womb) was pressed against the sacrum (spine), causing not only pain but also was described as 'unproductive'.

However, the German physician and anthropologist, Johann Friedrich Blumenbach (1752-1840) came to the conclusion, from his extensive studies, that all human races were equal. He avoided the derogatory description used by Carl Linnaeus (1707-1778), the father of Taxonomy, who used terms like 'hopeful' Europeans', 'sad and rigid' Asiatics, 'irascible' American natives, and 'calm and lazy' Africans to describe the different types of humans that he identified. Blumenbach's book *'On the Unity of Mankind'* was a scientific description of human beings using the available evidence at the time. He used the shape of the skull, facial features and the shape of teeth to identify five human races - Caucasian, Malaysian, Ethiopian, American, and Mongolian. This helped Blumenbach to conclude that Africans were not inferior in terms of their mental capacities and natural talents.

Broca described the inferiority of the natives of Australia and Tasmania. He refers to Australian natives as savages. He wrote that natives Australians and Tasmanian were the most inferior to have come in contact with Europeans, who together with Anglo-Saxon and those of Germanic origin were described as the superior races. Broca wrote 'The English have made the most persevering attempts to instruct them, but without any success. As they could not succeed with the adult population, they tried it with children of a tender age, and educated them with European children in orphan asylums; they have there learned to mumble some prayers, even to read and write; but, with approaching puberty, the young pupils succumbed to their savage instincts, and escaped into the woods to live again with their parents whom they had never known'.

The use or rather misuse of philosophy, the Bible and human biology in the 18th and 19th centuries to justify the inferiority of black persons appears with hindsight now to have been a logical step in the quest to demonstrate white superiority and conversely black inferiority. With the advance of abolitionist thought, it was natural for slave owners and anti-abolitionists to pursue their thinking of the black man as being inferior. Even though based on questionable research and thinking of the time, the development of scientific racism evolved. It is now possible to see how flawed research and lack of rigour in the pursuit of evidence and review, contributed to erroneous conclusions. As the poet and satirist of the Enlightenment era, Alexander Pope (1688 - 1744), wrote – 'to observations which ourselves we make, we grow more partial for the observers sake'. Lack of evidence is the enemy of truth and the happy bedfellow of fiction.

As has been seen slavery is an old institution which had been interwoven into the fabric of human society from time immemorial. Therefore it is of no surprise that there were Islamic or Muslim slaves. What is important is how Islam viewed the practice of slavery and how it treated slaves. While the West African slave trade is much talked about and written of, it is useful to appreciate that there was a thriving slave trade in the East coast of Africa too. Indeed when the trade in West Africa diminished, that in the East increased. Thus, rather than being free, slaves were traded elsewhere. They were, in this respect a commodity to be traded where the market existed. In doing so the slave trade followed a basic law of commerce in that goods or in this case slaves would be traded where it was most profitable. Where there is a buyer for goods or slaves, there would be a market and they were traded.

While Islam may have contributed to improvements in the conditions for slaves, there is little evidence that Islam actively sought to abolish slavery and the trade in slaves. Islam required slave owners to treat slaves well, with compassion, and encouraged owners to free slaves. Freedom for slaves was a virtue that was preached. Despite all the good intentions slavery continued under Islam. It was illegal for a Muslim to have a Muslim as a slave.

Slaves were often not the lowest in the hierarchy of people under Islamic slavery. Slaves often served their masters in different roles and were not used only for labour.

One feature was of female slaves who were used for sexual purposes. They were kept as concubines or part of the master's harem. They were of lower social status than the owner's wife.

Slavery was included in Sharia law. When the law was written, the practice of slavery was common even in religions like Judaism and Christianity. It is easy to be critical now of the common practice of slavery then. But there were no human rights laws at the time or even a concept of what constitutes the rights of a human being. Therefore slavery was accepted and practiced in most, if not all, societies. It was not easy to abolish slavery in ancient times even though Islamic law saw it as virtuous to free slaves. Also the Quran accords primacy to human freedom and dignity. Therefore slavery continued but in an ameliorated, compassionate and tolerant from in Islamic society. However under Sharia law slavery still remains legal. Therefore it is still possible that legal enslavement can occur if a person is captured in war and comes from a long line of slaves. However such a situation is hardly likely to arise in the twenty-first century.

The word 'Saqaliba' refers to the Slavic people of Central and Eastern Europe. There was a great demand for Slavic slaves who were transported to the Arabic world. The Eastern Slavs were traded through central Asia. The Tartars of the Ottoman Empire were able, after the fall of Constantinople in 1453, to transport slaves from Europe to Arabia. The Crimean Khanate was a Crimean state that existed from the 15th to the 18th Century. It was said that it's economy depended on abducting Russians and Slavs for sale to Iranian, Ottoman and Egyptian slave markets. The Crimean Khanate ran an elaborate slave trade with raids called 'harvesting of the steppe'. The steppe refers to the southern area of Russia which separated it from the Crimea and the Ottoman Empire. The historians Gábor Ágoston and Bruce Alan Masters reflect that the rise of Istanbul to become the largest city in Europe in the 16th century would not have been possible without its abundance of Slavic slaves. Slavs were transported southwards through the Balkans. Western Slavs were transported to al-Andalus, which was that part of the Iberian peninsula which was under Islamic control. This area covered most of the states in modern Iberia and parts of southern France. The slave trade in Iberia was an important part of the economy in al-Andalus.

It is useful to look at the power of the Ottoman Empire in slavery. The

Crimean Khanate lasted from 1449 until 1783. And it was controlled by the Ottoman Empire. During this time Crimea was involved in large scale slavery and slave trading with the largest market for slaves in Europe being in Caffa. Raids by the Crimean Tartars extended northwards up to modern day Lithuania and Poland, capturing mainly Slavic and non-Slavic persons for slavery. One historian has noted that the 1500–1501 raids netted the Crimean Muslims 50,000 Slavic Christian slaves.

In his book, 'Russia's Steppe Frontier', Michael Khodarkovsky writes that in the first half of the seventeenth century 150,000-200,000 Russians were captured by the Tartars into slavery. Khodarkovsky maintains that with increasing power, Russia was able to control that land area of the Crimea and incorporate it into Russia. Russia's need to protect its southern border transformed the steppe people into Russians, in an act of expansionism and imperial might. This philosophy may be ingrained in the Russian psyche as we see to this day in its annexation of modern Crimea. However, this view is at variance with that of William H. McNeill who in his book *Europe's Steppe Frontier- 1500-1800* claims that industrialisation especially of agriculture led to the Russians acquiring control of the Crimea.

The main slave market in Crimea was in the city of Caffa. From Caffa slaves were transported overland and by boat across the Black Sea to Ottoman Turkey. In 1666 most of the people in Crimea were Christian Ukrainian slaves, who outnumbered the Turkish Tartars who were Muslims. Evliya Chelebi was an Ottoman writer who travelled extensively and estimated that there were 400,000 slaves in Crimea compared to 185,000 free Muslim persons. However, Vladimir Emmanuilovich Shlapentokh (1926 – 2015), Professor of Sociology at Michigan University and considered the father of Russian Sociology, thought that there were over 900,000 slaves in Crimea at the time. The Polish historian, Bohdan Baranowski (1915 – 1993), wrote that from 1474 to 1694 the Polish–Lithuanian Commonwealth which comprises modern day Poland, Belarus and Lithuania, lost 20,000 people yearly and almost one million in total to slavery .

The institution of slavery is unusual in its difference to the traditional understanding, where a slave is a person with no rights and held in servitude. The enslavement of white people has not received much attention but that it occurred is not in doubt. Slavery was common in the Ottoman

Empire and was an integral part of its economy. Slaves were captured in war and came from Africa, the Balkans, Caucuses and Eastern Europe. An important aspect of Ottoman slavery was that slaves could achieve a higher status than the term suggests. They could become administrators and hold other official posts in government. Some of these slaves became Janissaries, who were the household troops and body guards of the Sultan. Janissaries came through the *devşirme* system, where child slaves were converted to Islam, trained in discipline and remained fiercely loyal to the Sultan. Those persons in this service carried a higher social status that even the average citizen. They earned a salary and had the benefit of a pension on retirement. The children who were slaves in this system were non –Muslim, Christian boys from the Balkans. Jews were never included in the *devşirme* system.

Female slaves could work as slaves or become concubines for the Sultan. Only the most beautiful women would be lucky to be concubines. When slave ships arrived in Turkey, the human cargo would be inspected by officials for the prettiest females. Some would eventually become concubines while other female slaves who were also pretty were at an advantage. They would be sold to others in power or to other Muslim rulers in the region.

Women who became concubines were called 'cariye', which literally mean a lady-in-waiting. A woman who was a cariye was compelled to obey her male owner. A son born to a cariye was not a slave. But a daughter was a slave from the moment of birth. However, it became the custom that such a woman would be manumitted. Famous European women who became concubines were Hurrem, who was of Ukranian origin and the Italian, Safiye. Hurrem Haseki Sultan, or Roxelana, as she was known, became one of the most powerful women in the Ottoman Empire. Roxelana's real name was Aleksandra Lisowska. She was born in Rohatyn in the then Kingdom of Poland, which is now in Ukraine. She became the favourite of the Sultan, Suleiman the Magnificent, and married him. She was allowed to have more than one son which was in contravention of the palace customs at the time. One of her sons, Selim II, became Sultan following the death of Suleiman the Magnificent in 1566, after having been on the throne for 45 years.

Roxelana became one of the most powerful persons in the Ottoman

Empire and played a significant part during the period called the Sultanate of Women. She was at the outset, a member of the Sultan's harem and as was the custom, resided in the Old Palace in Istanbul. The Sultan resided in the Topkapi Palace, which was also the seat of government. In a break with tradition, following her marriage to Sultan Suleiman, she moved in to the Topkapi Palace which was thereafter called the New Palace. Roxelana's move in to the Topkapi Palace was very significant as Sultan Mehmet the Conqueror (ruled 1444-1446 and again 1451-1481) had decreed that the Topkapi Palace would be used for government affairs and women were not to be allowed to reside in it.

She used her influence with Suleiman in many aspects of government activities, for e.g. Suleiman chose her son-in-law Damat Rüstem Pasha to the position of Grand Vizier. Roxelana's daughter Mihrimah was married to Damat Rustem Pasha.

The unusual form of slavery in Ottoman Turkey is also shown in the rise and fall of another Grand Vizier, Pargalı Ibrahim Pasha (1495 - 1536). He had a variety of names to match his station in life - Frenk Ibrahim Pasha or the 'Westerner', Makbul Ibrahim Pasha or 'the Favourite'. But following his execution, the name changed to Maktul Ibrahim Pasha, ' the Executed' after his execution in the Topkapı Palace. He was the first Grand Vizier of the Ottoman Empire appointed by Sultan Suleiman the Magnificent.

Ibrahim was born a Christian in Venice. Sometime around 1500 he was captured by Iskender Pasha, the Governor of Bosnia, during a raid and was enslaved. While living in Iskender Pasha's estate he met the young Prince Suleiman and began to serve the latter. It is said that Suleiman and Ibrahim grew up together and became close friends. Ibrahim converted to Islam and when Suleiman became Sultan, he eventually appointed Ibrahim as the Grand Vizier of the Ottoman Empire. The post of Grand Vizier is equivalent to the current position of Prime Minister of a country. In an elaborate wedding ceremony, Ibrahim married Mushin Hatun in 1523. Mushin was the grand-daughter of Iskender Pasha who had captured Ibrahim over 20 years previously and brought him to Turkey. It appears that this was a marriage of convenience with approval of Sultan Suleiman to allow Ibrahim to become accepted within the elite of the Ottoman Empire. In the same year Pargali Ibrahim Pasha became Grad Vizier. In this position he had great power and Venetian diplomats even referred to him as 'Ibrahim the Magnificent'. Roxelana was concerned about Ibrahim's increasing power and with his arrogance. It is written that she arranged for him to be killed. So it became that after dining with the Sultan on 5th March 1536, he was killed. Following his death, Ibrahim Pasha's property was confiscated by the state. This allowed Roxelana to now become the chief advisor to Sultan Suleiman. Ibrahim had been Grand Vizier for thirteen years.

The power of Roxelana and the influence she had on Ottoman society is evident following her death. Gabriel Bounin, a French author wrote the tragedy, La Soltane, in 1561 which was three years after Roxelana's death. It was a stage play in France. Denys Sichynsky (1865-1909) who was born in Stanyslaviv, Ukraine, was a conductor and composer. He wrote the opera Roksoliana which was composed of Three Acts with a Prologue. Joseph Haydn wrote La Roxelane, The Symphony No. 63 in C major. Many novels were written about Roxelana, who also inspired several paintings.

It is generally believed that Safiye was an Albanian slave although some consider her to be of Bosnian origin. When she was only 13 years old she was presented to the young Murad III who was later to become Sultan Murad III who reigned from 1574 to 1595. She became a concubine of Murad III and on 26th May 1566 gave birth to a son by Murad III. This son became the future Sultan Mehmed III who ruled from 1595 to 1603 following his father's death in 1595.

However, these three stories are about a very small minority of slaves amidst the vast majority of them in the Ottoman Empire. Slaves were bought from Africa, Eastern Europe, the Caucuses and the Balkans. There were slave markets called 'esir' or 'yesir' in many cities. Slaves of all ages and of both sexes were brought to the market where they were displayed naked so that they may be checked by prospective buyers. Prices for slaves varied depending on age, colour of skin and virginity. European virgins aged 13-25 and young boys, commended the highest prices at market. There were taxes to be paid on the importation and sale of slaves. These taxes would be paid in cash or kind, which included other slaves. There was an agreement that Muslims, Jews and Christians would not be taken as slaves. It therefore led to pagan black people in Central Africa being captured and sold as slaves to the Ottoman Empire. These black slaves were known as

Zanj and were considered inferior to European slaves. They often helped to swell the ranks of slave soldiers but they had the opportunity to rise in the government. One way of achieving a higher status was to become a eunuch. Young back boys were castrated to render them eunuch. This was a horrifying surgical operation done without any form of anaesthesia. Bleeding was controlled by applying hot coals to the area. The patient, if one could use the word in this case, would scream and writhe in pain. Many died from the procedure; it is reported that only 10% survived the operation.

Having survived castration, eunuchs could work for the Sultan in the Palace, in the courts etc and were able to exercise much influence. As eunuchs were seen as not being a threat, there was much demand for them. Arab raids into Africa ensured a supply of eunuchs.

Mullah Ali, a black slave, was a chief judge in the Ottoman Empire in 1620. As a thinker and writer of influence he worked to reduce prejudice against black and to counter the view that Africans should be slaves.

Many millions of Europeans were slaves under the Muslim rulers of the Middle East and Africa. This period of slavery is said to have lasted almost a thousand years until the nineteenth century. Robert C. Davis in his book *'Christian Slaves, Muslim Masters: White Slavery in the Mediterranean, the Barbary Coast and Italy, 1500-1800'* describes the slavery of Europeans by Muslims from North Africa as the 'other ' slavery'. This Barbary coast slavery occurred during the time of the trans-Atlantic slave trade. A million or more slaves from Italy, France, Spain, Holland, Great Britain and even a far north as Iceland were captured and transported to the Middle East and North Africa. There were even more than 500 American slaves. Slaves were captured from ships that sailed close to the Barbary coast, by pirates. Over four hundred merchant ships from England were captured by and lost to Barbary pirates. Records suggest that Istanbul acquired two and a half million slaves from across the Black Sea between 1450 and 1700. This human piracy only ended in the nineteenth century when the United States of America, Britain, France and the Netherlands fought the First and Second Barbary Wars defeating the pirates.

The historian, Paul Lovejoy, estimates that seven and a quarter million Africans were transported as slaves from 650 AD to 1600. In the 19th century, 1.2 million African slaves were sent to Arabia.

Ken Menon

Edward Gibbon FRS (1737– 1794) was an English Member of Parliament and a historian, who wrote *The History of the Decline and Fall of the Roman Empire* in a book that was of six volumes. In this treatise, Gibbon charted the establishment of the Muslim Arabian empire following the Arabian conquests which started in the 7th century. The Sassanid Empire was the third Persian or Iranian Empire of the time and had existed for over four centuries. Its rival at the time was the Byzantine Empire or Eastern Roman Empire of Byzantium. Byzantium reached it peak under Emperor Justinian (527–565) and extended from Rome to North Africa and Italy. The Sassanian-Byzantine war of 602-608 exhausted both armies and allowed the Arabian conquests to succeed. The scholar and political thinker, Geroge Liska, in merging geo-politics with geo-history wrote that the 'unnecessarily prolonged Byzantine–Persian conflict opened the way for Islam'. James Douglas Howard-Johnston (born 1942) was a lecturer in Byzantine studies in the University of Oxford and is a historian of the era. He wrote that the Arabs who were united by Islam were easily able to take advantage of the Byzantine-Sassanid conflict and overrun the region, which he described 'can only be likened to a human tsunami'.

Following the death of Prophet Muhammad, the Islamic region was largely run by caliphs. There were four major caliphates which succeeded each other -the Rashidun Caliphate (632–661), the Umayyad Caliphate (661–750), and the Abbasid Caliphate (750–1258). The fourth caliphate was the Ottoman Caliphate. When the Arabs invade Sind in India in the 8th century, the Umayyad commander Muhammad bin Qasim, was described as having enslaved Indian soldiers and civilians in their tens of thousands. Sindh is now a province of Pakistan.

Perhaps the most famous slave in Islam was Bilal ibn Rabah who was born a slave. He became a loyal companion of prophet Muhammad. He was one of the earliest converters to Islam and was renowned for his voice, which he used to call the faithful to prayer. The sayings of Muhammad called the Hadith and the Quoran have reference to slavery as a normal part of life at the time, but that it should be exceptional. In the divine law (Sharia) only persons who were non-Muslims could be slaves. Slavery in Muslim lands took many forms and there was a varying degree of freedom given to slaves. Some could achieve high positions in civil society and in the military. Most slaves were treated well in ancient Islamic society.

Slavery existed in Arabia in pre-Islamic times. The Quran introduced the concept of manumission of slaves by the use of alms, and prohibited the use of female slaves in prostitution. The latter was common in pre-Islam Arabia.

Slavery was not confined to Arabia and Africa. Mahmud of Ghazni (971 – 1030) was the ruler of the Turkic people and was founder of the Ghaznavid dynasty, which he ruled from 998 to 1030. The Turkic are a group of people in West Asia and parts of Europe and North Africa who spoke Turkic languages. Mahmud conquered Peshawar in modern day Pakistan on 1001. In a subsequent expedition to India in 1018-1019, he returned with so many slaves that the price of a slave dropped drastically and they were said to have been sold for as low as only two to ten dirhams a slave.

Slavery existed in North America before European colonization. With the existence of several North America Indian tribes, persons captured from another tribe were treated as slaves. This was an unusual kind of slavery as there was no market and no trade in slaves. Captured persons were sometime traded for those of the same tribe. But apart from this, there was no trade in slaves as occurred with slavery in Africa.

Inter-tribal American-Indian slavery had some unusual features. Slaves may be killed but were often used for labour. They could be used in gambling where a slave was 'traded'. Often they were used in battle as replacement for those of the tribe who had fallen. Adoption and assimilation into the tribe was not uncommon as happened with Iriquoi people.

The Alaskan Haida and Tlingit tribes were somewhat unusual in that they raided for slaves and would often extend as far south as California. Those whom they captured were treated as slaves and their children continued as slaves. In the Pacific Northwest regions, more than 25% of the population were slaves. These slaves were captured in inter-tribal war or purchased at slave markets.

The arrival of Europeans changed the nature of American Indian slavery. Captured slaves were now sold to Europeans than being retained by or incorporated into the capturing tribe.

The Indian slave trade virtually ended in 1750. The arrival of African slaves made the need for Indians much less. Also, the American Indians were a force to reckon with. They knew the topography of the area and so could easily escape. They were also responsible for devastating wars with the colonialists. They were tenacious fighters who would fight to the last man, as it were, in defence of their tribes. The Yamasee war for e.g. in South Carolina was fought from 1715-1717 between the Indians and British colonialists settled in the state. Many colonialists were killed and South Carolina was nearly completely destroyed. Similarly the many Indian wars or First Nation wars lasted until the early part of the 20th century.

An interesting feature that has been described about American Indian slavery is that the American Indian considered his slave from another tribe as being ethnically inferior. The European, Spanish, French and British, considered the American Indian slave as racially inferior. Another feature in North American slavery was the status conferred on the owner of slaves. Owning 30 slaves was a status symbol and reflected the power of the slave owner, in this case the chief of the tribe.

Europeans did not introduce slavery to America; it had existed before the arrival of Europeans. But the arrival of Europeans changed the nature of slavery. Allan Gallay's well researched book *'The Indian Slave Trade'* describes the different interest of Europeans when they entered the scene. By Europeans one refer to the Spanish, French and British colonialists. His book describes the different interests of the three colonialists, each of whom appeared to have been trying to outwit the other for gain, which was of land and for plantation. They used different Indian tribes for their benefit. The arrival of Europeans changed the nature of American Indian slavery in that slaves became now a tradable commodity. American Indians who previously acquired slaves for eg at war with another tribe, now captured slaves to trade with the European for the latter's goods. It is interesting to note how American Indians adapted quickly to the new requirements of slavery, occasioned by the European. Gallay's book opens with the following paragraph:

'The savage who told me all of this is a man of the Maugoulacho nation who is living with the Mauvilla nation. He had assured me that the English were in those nations every day, and that they take pack horses burdened with clothing, guns, gunpowder, shot, and a quantity of other goods which are sold or traded to the savages for cured deer hides, for fresh deer hides with hair, and for the buffalo that are covered in a fine wool being grey in color like a moose. But the greatest traffic between the English and the savages is the trade of slaves which the nations take from their neighbors whom they war with continuously, such that the men take the women and children away and sell them to the English, each person being traded for a gun. This greatly destroys the nations which are our neighbors. —Charles Levasser, 1700'.

The European land owners tried to divide and rule. They made every effort to separate Indians from African slaves. They tried to prevent the African blacks from associating with and learning the language of the Indian tribes. They indeed even used the American Indian to track escaped African slaves. But this policy was unlikely to succeed for long. Black African slaves entered Indian communities, fraternised with them and even married into Indian tribes. It is interesting to note how blacks joined with Yamasee Indians in raiding European plantations.

The Yamasee War was in many respects a turning point in the relationship between Europeans and American Indians. Both learnt that they needed each other. The black African was therefore often in an inconsequential position.

Five Native American Nations, so called because their populations consisted of North American tribes, owned black slaves. They were the Choctaw, Chickasaw, Cherokee, Creek, and Seminole Nations who were together known as the Five Tribes. The land they occupied is modern Oklahoma. The Europeans introduced a new, almost 'industrial' form of slavery which the Five Tribes adopted and resulted in the Chickasaws becoming the largest slave-holding nation of the Five Tribes. The slave holding tribes had a vested interest in maintaining and perpetuating slavery. They contributed significantly to, for e.g. the cotton economy, and became wealthy. They were naturally resistant to the ending of slavery and many fought on the side of the Confederates in the American Civil War. However American Indians also fought on the side of the Unionists.

One discerns from the foregoing, two important aspects of slavery and involvement of Europeans. Like in Africa, slavery was pre-existing in the two continents. The European used what was already present and added a commercial aspect to the proceedings, converting traditional slavery to a transaction between seller and buyer. And again it was the Europeans and the ruling white Americans who worked to abolish slavery despite resistance from the slave owners - the rulers in Africa and the slave owning tribes in America.

China has a long history of slavery extending many thousands of years. Historically, China was governed by a succession of hereditary dynasties or regises. Dynastic rule probably started with Yu the Great around 2070 BC. Yu was a descendant of the Yellow Emperor and is credited with introducing flood control in China. Yu started the Xia dynasty. Yu's son Qi who succeeded him introduced slavery to the Xia dynasty. Slavery in China included those captured in war, those kidnapped and persons who were indebted to others. It also included, at various times, indentured labour. During the Qwin dynasty (221-206 BC) slavery was severe and entire families could be taken into slavery and were used in forced labour, often in infrastructure projects like road building. During the Han dynasty that extended from 206 BC to 220 AD there were attempts to limit slavery and at manumission of existing slaves.

Slavery was legally abolished in China in 1909 but the practice continues in various forms to this day. The Global Slavery Index showed that in 2016 there were almost 4 million people living in conditions of slavery in China. In the same year there were 1004 cases of human trafficking. China's astronomical economic rise is due to cheap production of labour intensive goods. Forced labour and the use of child labour have been reported. It was reported that vocational trainees were forced to work or to risk their degrees. The sugar cane industry was known to attract up to 50,000 illegal Vietnamese workers.

In 2013 the government of China announced that it would abolish the system of Re-education Through Labour (RTL). In RTL, prisoners are forced to work. However there is no evidence RTL has been completely abolished. Incarceration and re-education continues with the Uyghurs in Xinjiang.

The Chinese ruled over Vietnam for almost a millennium and used Vietnamese as slaves in China.

The use of African slaves by China is a seldom talked about story. Since the Tang Dynasty of 618 AD there have been commercial contacts between east Africa and China. Arab traders brought African slaves to China. They were known as 'Kunlun' and were considered ignorant and dangerous. Chinese made a distinction between the Kunlun and free Africans. Although official Chinese policy has been to support Blacks, American Indians, coloureds and other minority groups against 'white imperialists', this view was not shared by many ordinary Chinese people. In Chinese minds the African is still seen as 'inferior'.

The first Africans were boys and girls who were gifted by King Kalinga of Java to the Chinese emperor in 813 AD. They were viewed as curiosities and described as 'no different from the rhinoceros and other animals they were presented alongside.' Many Africans died during the sea voyage from the east coast of Africa to the Chinese ports. Many did not acclimatise well to the local food of rice and succumbed as a result.

In his book *'The Blacks of Premodern China'*, the author Don Wyatt concludes that the Chinese were as cruel and as oppressive to black slaves as happened in the United States.

The undercurrents of Chinese racism towards blacks manifested themselves during the initial stages of the Covid-19 pandemic in 2020. Africans were evicted from rental properties, not allowed in to shops and businesses and forcibly tested for the virus. These discriminatory actions brought protestations from many African countries. The Chinese authorities, as usual, denied that such events had occurred.

China's current involvement in Africa is another useful lesson of what may be termed an 'internal slavery'. The paper by Peter Hutchins in 2008 titled *'How China has created a new slave empire in Africa'* provides useful insight to the creeping encroachment of China in Africa and its exploitation of the continent's natural resources. To work some of the copper mines of Zambia, China uses its own workers who had been shipped from China. It is said that these are prisoners from China. When locals are used they are often young person's hardly past childhood, who toil under the scorching sun to forage pieces of copper which they sell to middlemen, who trade them to their Chinese masters. The mine workers would be lucky to earn $3 a day for their labours. Quoting Peter Hutchens one Zambian said 'They bring Chinese to come and push wheelbarrows, they bring Chinese bricklayers, and they bring Chinese carpenters, Chinese plumbers. We have plenty of those in Zambia.'

Africans and their Diasporas need to ask whether the world is witnessing another form of slavery in the 21st century, an 'economic slavery' that would deprive the continent of the just rewards of its work and of its natural resources. Yet again the ruling elites of Africa, who are acting like slave traders of old, are undoubtedly as responsible as are the Chinese exploiters. What is the difference, one may ask? In the former, people were sold into slavery by their own people; in the latter, people are selling their resources, the 'family silver' as it were, with little gain for the countries and their people. This is hardly the way forward and national and personal progress will continue to be elusive.

Chinese themselves were slaves. In a paper *'Chinese Slavery in America'* written in 1897, Charles Fredrick Holder described the horrors of Chinese held in slavery in San Francisco by other Chinese. Holder described Chinese slavery as 'obnoxious and debased as could be found in any slave-dealing country of to-day'. The Chinese community was trafficking other Chinese, with some women working in brothels. The market value of a nine to twelve year old Chinese girl was $150-$500. Women were dragged by their hair and even burnt with hot irons. Chinese girls over the age of 16 years had a market value of up to $3500. Chinese men would often capture young Chinese girls and bring them to the USA on the false promise of getting married to a rich Chinese man. Instead they were sold as sexual slaves.

In her 1923 novel, *'In The House of the Tiger,'* Jesse Juliet Knox described the whole sordid business of the buying and selling of Chinese girls. She relates the story of one girl who, having being brought to California, was housed in what appears to have been a rich person's home. She was presented with a wardrobe, ostensibly, for her wedding. In reality, the dresses were for her to become more presentable and marketable as a slave!. Life was harsh, with many Chinese girls dying within five years of arriving in the USA. Many of them were rescued by the Presbyterian Mission in California.

One may compare the foregoing with what is currently happening to the Uyghur people in Xinjiang, China. An unofficial UK tribunal, the Uighur Tribunal, was chaired by Sir Geoffrey Nice who is a prominent British barrister. The tribunal concluded that China carried out 'a deliberate, systematic and concerted policy' to cause the 'long-term reduction of Uyghur and other ethnic minority populations'. This, by definition, is genocide.

When the African slave trade ceased there was a demand for cheap labour. It is estimated that between 1840 and 1875, 135,000 Chinese men were shipped to Latin America and the Caribbean. They were described as indentured workers or coolies but they worked often with no contract. The Chinese accused owners of selling them like pigs. The Peruvian Congress compared the transport of Chinese as akin to the Atlantic trade in African slaves. It was estimated that 50-70% of the slaves died in the first years of their contract. Those who survived were often not free but had their contracts extended. These slaves petitioned their Emperor in China to help them. However it is noteworthy that many did not return to China, choosing instead to live as free citizens in Peru.

The Chinese in Peru were used for work in the guano industry. Guano is bird dropping that had been collecting for hundreds of years. Extracting guano was labour intensive, needing men and tools to chip it away from the rock. Poverty in China caused many to undertake the voyage, often on the mistaken belief that they were going to work in gold mines in California. Following a research paper in 1841 to the Royal Society of Agriculture by Professor James Johnston of the Chemistry Department of Durham University showing that guano used with traditional fertiliser encouraged growth of plants, guano took off; more workers were obviously needed.

A largely forgotten aspect of slavery is the Pacific slave trade. From about 1863, men and boys were transported from the Solomon Islands and Vanuatu to work in the sugar plantations in northern Australia. They were often kidnapped or tricked into going. Many died of disease contracted from Europeans. The process of enticing and capturing people for transport was called 'blackbirding'. When their use was completed they were transported and dumped on any island, often with which they had little or no connection.

Slave or compulsory labour was common in Australia from the time of its colonisation in 1788. Many convicts were transported to Australia and forced to work in chain gangs where they were held together by chains while working, for e.g. on a road. The extent of human greed and lack of empathy is seen in the words of William Hill, an officer on one of the convict ships who wrote 'the slave traffic is merciful compared with what I have seen in this fleet .... the more they can withhold from the unhappy wretches, the more provisions they have to dispose of at a foreign market, and the earlier in the voyage they die, the longer they can draw the deceased's allowance to themselves'.

Aborigines and Torres Island inhabitants were used as slaves. Even when they were paid for their labour, many did not receive payment and the funds were retained by the government of the day.

Tanna, in Vanuatu which even now has only about 30,000 people, lost 4,000 to 'blackbirding'. The first boat load of immigrants comprising 50,000 men, women and children arrived on board the ship, Don Juan which berthed in Brisbane. Whether they were slave or not is a debated point. Professor Clive Moore a historian from the University of Queensland mentions they were not slaves as they were paid for their work and returned to their home islands. Fifteen thousand of the 50,000 died.

People were tricked to come to the beach with promises of jewellery etc. Even to this day children are forbidden from going to the beach, and a rock called, Howling Rock, is the site where people went to mourn their lost husbands and sons.

A sad aspect of these events is that the islanders wages were retained by the Queensland government and not paid to the workers. Even worse, the government used the retained wages to pay for the deportation of the islanders in compliances with Australia' white only' policy of the time.

The most prominent and probably the first 'blackbirder' was a Scottish trader by the name of Benjamin Boyd. Boydtown in New South Wales and Ben Boyd Park are likely to be renamed.

The practice of 'blackbirding' was almost unique to Australia. 'Blackbirding' involved kidnapping or coercing people to work in places far removed from their homes. The slaves were used in plantations in Queensland and New South Wales. Some were sent to the Americas to work on plantations. Interestingly, some agreed to be transported to Australia but most were tricked in to travelling. Many died during the sailing. Their places of work were hardly habitable, with poor food and inadequate water supply contributing to dysentery. They were often beaten. Following a Royal Commission that inquired about recruitment of South Sea Islanders, the Prime Minster of Queensland said that what was done to these we people was little different to the African slave trade.

In his book '*The Stolen Island: Searching for 'Ata'* the author Scott Hamilton describes how Thomas McGrath put to sea in June 1863 for the island of Ata, which is part of Tonga. About 150 men, women and children were allowed to board the ship, ostensibly, to view merchandise, when the ship set sail for Peru. The captured people were sold in Peru, which at that time was an important staging post in the Pacific slave trade.

The words of a stockman, Roy Savo, makes for interesting reading. He said that he did not see physical money until he was 20 years old. If he needed anything that was necessary, he would go to his white superior who would address him as 'boy' and 'they'd just write us a note and say, 'Take that to the shop',….. that's how we got through life.' He continued 'They made you feel so low….. we were just no one, nothing. We had no chance against the white people, they just ruled our lives. We were one step from being an animal. In some places you were told to sit out and eat with the animals anyway, out in the wood heap.'

The historian, Ros Kidd, wrote that the disadvantages currently endured by Aborigines and Torres Strait islanders are linked to how they were treated as slaves in the past. She maintains that they were 'excluded from the capitalist society' and therefore carry with them the disadvantages of the past. She described this as being trapped by an 'engineered disadvantage' engendered by government policies of the time.

One now returns to the topic of white slavery. This is another story of silence drowned by the plethora of information and claims made in relation to the Trans- Atlantic slave trade. The extension of the Ottoman Empire westward facilitated the capture and transport of many Europeans, into slavery. For e.g. the Crimean Tatars transported 10,000 slaves annually from 1450 to 1700, to the Ottoman Empire. This is 2,5000,0000 slaves who went to the Ottoman Empire. Over a million people from Poland, Ukraine and Russia were captured as slaves in what was called 'harvesting the steppe'. For e.g. 800,000 persons were captured from Moscow. It is estimated that at least 7,000,000 Eastern European men, women and children were taken as slaves by Muslim raiders. Between the 16th century and the mid 18th century, raiders from Tunisia, Algiers and Tripoli enslaved 1.25 million white Christian persons in North Africa. It is written that the muslin pirates had a significant effect on France, Spain and England causing the loss of several thousands of ships and the decimation of the fishing industries in these countries. Large parts of the coast in these countries were depopulated and remained uninhabited until the 19th century.

One of the most significant raids is described as the 'Sack of Baltimore'. Baltimore, a small fishing village on the west coast of Ireland was attacked by pirates on the night of 19th June 1631. The raid was conducted by two ships that left Algiers. The ships were under the command of a Dutchman, Jan Janszoon van Haarlem. He was a slave himself but was pardoned when he renounced his faith. He took the name of Murad Reis the Younger. Murad Reis was led to the village by a man called John Hackett who had a fishing boat and had been captured earlier. Two hundred pirates attacked the village setting fire to the thatched houses. At the end of the raid they had sailed away with 100 persons including the young, old and children who were carried from their beds while they lay asleep. John Hackett was eventually hanged in the village for his part in the raid. This event, though small in numbers of persons enslaved, describes the modus operandi of the Barbary slavers.

OF AFRICA, BY AFRICA, FOR AFRICA

When Colin Kaepenick, an American footballer who played for San Francisco 49ers in the National Football League, took the knee in 2016 before a match, it was a gesture not of defiance but of protest. But he was not the first to have adopted that posture nor is there an universally accepted meaning of the symbolism of the act. Martin Luther King assumed the position in prayer. But the first impression of it is seen in the work of Josiah Wedgewood who used it as a means of expressing his and other abolitionists views against slavery. Wedgewood, the potter, used the original design by the Society for Effecting the Abolition of the Slave Trade, in medallions in 1787. It showed a black man in chains with the inscription 'Am I Not a Man and a Brother? Thomas Clarkson, a prominent abolitionist campaigner of the time said that gentlemen had the image 'inlaid in gold on the lid of their snuffboxes. Of the ladies several wore them in bracelets, and others had them fitted up in an ornamental manner as pins for their hair. As time went by, the taste for wearing them became general; and thus fashion, which usually confines itself to worthless things, 'was seen for once in the honourable office of promoting the cause of justice, humanity, and freedom.' Wedgewood sent a medallion to Benjamin Franklin in America who on seeing it declared that 'the medallion's effectiveness was equal to that of the best written pamphlet, in procuring favour to those oppressed People.' That was the first general awakening in the public of the abhorrence of slavery and the gathering mood of the public about the need to end the practice of slavery. This may be regarded as the moral awakening in relation to slavery. Prior to this, slavery appeared to exist in a 'moral void' which makes it difficult for those, now, to judge the action of people engaged in the slave trade then.

Many blacks lead their lives concealing a dark secret, which they may, in most cases not even be aware of. And it is this – how many of their ancestors were involved in capturing their fellow countrymen, transporting them across Africa and selling them as slaves on both the east and west coasts of the continent? Any description of slavery must confront this aspect of the slave trade. Why did they do it? And could all blame be apportioned to those who bought slaves? What about the trade on the east coast of Africa? Why did it continue when the trade on the west coast subsided? The answers to some of these complex issues are provided here. They are not the last word on the matter nor are they likely to be some form of beginning. But these questions need to be asked and answers sought. This would help in reconciliation by Africans and blacks of their painful past. It is hoped that it would also help as guidance for the future.

The reasons for those who sought to sell their fellow beings are complex. It has been suggested that those who captured slaves did not perceives slaves as one of them. Did they consider slaves as being inferior to themselves? This is an enduring question, for if this was so, one sees a level of intra- African discrimination. It is possible to understand this if one considered another tribe as inferior to one's own.

Angela Thomsell, Associate Professor of History at the College at Brockport, State University of New York, wrote that the first twelve slaves in the history of slavery were taken by the Portuguese back to Portugal in 1441. From this small beginning the slave trade grew exponentially. By 1460, 2500-6000 kidnapped slaves were transported each year by the Portuguese to Brazil. Until 1640, only the Portuguese, for the Brazilians, and the Spanish were involved in the transport of slaves.

It was not until 1641 that the British transported slaves to the sugar plantations of the Caribbean.

Thomsell believes that there was no feeling among the slave traders, of those whom they captured, as being African. They did not perceive any kinship with the slaves they were selling. There was also, from all descriptions, a paucity of any sense of humanity in the various acts involved in slavery. Were those who were captured perceived as humans? Was there any moral dimension in what the slave-catchers and traders were doing? One would never know. These aspects can equally be applied to the various slave traders who purchased, transported and employed slaves - - there were no moral considerations in any of these transactions. That slaves were transported in appalling conditions to America and the Caribbean show, at best, an extreme degree of callousness by current day reckoning. At worst one would consider those actions as demonstrating a disregard for human life, suffering and death. Why was there no degree of reflection of what was happening? No degree of morality across the entire spectrum of activities involved in slavery. It is as if the slaves, these people, and that is what they were - like any one of us, were looked upon as a sub-human, disposable and dispensable commodity.

Slavery had existed throughout the world long before the first Europeans set foot in Africa. It is important to recognise that slavery was not invented by Europeans. Of course, their entry into the business of slavery took it to a numerically higher level, driven by an overriding economic need. Slavery on the east African coast had been going on for a much longer time but little has been written about it. It appears that this aspect of African slavery is a submerged topic that has not received the attention and analysis that has hitherto been given to the Atlantic slave trade. However, any study about slavery in Africa must of necessity include the subject in its totality because of links between the two and with the sub-Saharan slave trade.

The lack of a national or pan-African identity is a powerful view that may have lent support to the practice of slavery at the time. But it begs the obvious question why? Was there a distinct Portuguese or Spanish or British identity etc? Or was this consideration ignored in the commercial heat of the time. There was a powerful need to profit from the venture that was slavery at the time, which in turn was driven by the need for labour in the plantations across the Atlantic ocean. Thomsell makes the interesting observation in writing - 'Indeed, to this day, individuals are more likely to identify as being African rather than, say, Kenyan, only after leaving Africa'. The apparent lack of African Identity is in contrast to how the native tribes of North America conducted their affairs. Bonita Lawrence wrote about indigenous people in Canada. 'Ritual adoption was a practice that frequently took place as a means of replacing individuals lost in battle and mourned. In the wars that took place in Canada between the Haudenosaunee (Iroquois) and many of the Indigenous allies of the French, Haudenosaunee clan mothers sent out warriors to capture enemies to be integrated into their society. These captives replaced those lost in war. By the 1660s, more than 60 per cent of people in the Haudenosaunee Confederacy were reportedly war captives who had been adopted into lineages and incorporated into their nations.' The Iroquois identified with those they captured. The captives were seen by the Iroquois as 'ours' and hence underlines an identity with them. That mothers wanted captives to be incorporated into the tribe also describes an intense affinity with these 'other' humans whom they saw as 'our'. Of course, not all-American Indians acted in a similar way. Some captives were held as slaves and others were sold as slaves.

But the Ashanti Empire, which is now Ghana, maintained that they treated slaves relatively well. Slavery was a tradition in the country which became one of the largest suppliers of slaves for the Atlantic trade. There are varying accounts of how slaves were treated in the Ashanti empire. Some could marry into their master's family; this marriage also helped to break with the matrilineal system which was common. Men were not uncommonly more comfortable marrying slave women so that they had control of their children, in what then became a patrilineal household. Slaves were sometimes used as human sacrifices at funerals. It was claimed that slaves were not abused by their masters. If a slave owner abused a slave, he was said to have been 'held in contempt by society'. In such a situation a slave could ask to be transferred to the ownership by a new master. However the apparently benign nature of slavery in the Ashanti kingdom is at variance with descriptions of human sacrifices.

The need to survive was a potent reason for slavery to thrive. It was possible that families protected their own. This is natural in any society. But debt could push a person to slavery. So why not make a profit from selling a prisoner than have to feed and keep him? It was now a quick and almost degradingly logical step towards capturing people for sale, especially if there was a market for slaves. This was obviously the case when the Europeans arrived on the west coast of Africa. Soon slavery became a self-perpetuating cycle which was also profitable to all concerned in the trade, except for the slave. Add the possibility of pecuniary gain into any venture and one soon sees the business escalating, with all types of persons being involved, driven by the desire for profit. This was an example of the free market operating according to what the economist Adam Smith wrote in 1776 in his book, *Wealth of Nations* - 'It is not from the benevolence of the butcher, the brewer, or the baker that we expect our dinner, but from their regard to their own interest.' There was no benevolence; on the contrary it was the worst form of malevolence. There were no inanimate goods to sell; what was on sale was one's brother. But there was money and a market and the whole horrifying edifice of slavery took off on the west coast of Africa. This view of the economics of slavery needs to be set against the background of the practice of slavery that had been going on for many centuries, before the European arrived on the continent. By their need for manpower, Europeans added commerce into the pre-existing practice of slavery.

When the Nigerian journalist Adaobi Tricia Obinne Nwaubani wrote about her great-grandfather Nwaubani Ogogo Oriaku, she described him as an Igbo businessman. He traded in tobacco, palm produce and human beings. From what was described, he had a sophisticated business model operating in the true spirit of the late Adam Smith. He had people who captured slaves and brought them to the coast. There, he had the people of the local ethnic groups, the Efik and the Ijaw, acting as middlemen or stevedores or longshoremen supplying the ships along the coast with necessities for their journeys. They also helped to load and unload ships. They sold slaves to the ships masters collecting a commission and did the same from the slave trader for e.g. from Nwaubani Ogogo Oriaku in this instance. It is interesting to reflect on the businessman, Oriaku, who was from the Igbo tribe and most of the slaves were Igbo. The handlers who dealt with sale of slaves were from the Efik and Ijaw tribes. The port of Calabar in Nigeria was the site from which 1.5 million slaves were shipped across the Atlantic. When slavery was abolished by Great Britain, it deployed the Royal Navy to enforce prohibition of the transport of slaves. The *HMS Comus* sailed to Calabar in 1815 and seized several Portuguese and Spanish slave ships. This event demonstrates the power of the Royal Navy at the time and its command of the seas, where it could enforce abolition of slavery not only by intercepting British slave ships but also vessels from other countries. *HMS Comus* was at sea off the coast of West Africa for a duration of six months as part of the West Africa Squadron. It captured ten slavers and was able to free about 1000 slaves.

Much later on, while the British were working tirelessly to eliminate slavery, Nwaubani Ogogo Oriaku defied the authorities. When some of his slaves were confiscated by the British, he went up to them and demanded his slaves be returned as he had a slave trading licence. The British authorities apologised and returned his slaves. He was seen as a hero by his fellow slave-traders.

In an apparent accommodation with her great-grandfather's active involvement in slavery, Adaobi Tricia Obinne Nwaubani said 'Assessing the people of Africa's past by today's standards would compel us to cast the majority of our heroes as villains.' Many people would be persuaded by this view. For by assessing people or actions of centuries ago by the standards of today, when such norms did not exist then, is virtue signalling which does not help in understanding events of the time. Nor does such retrospection help to fashion opinions and events of current times. As a generalisation it could be said that viewing events or statements of the past through the lens of today is more likely than not to find wrong.

None of this diminishes the extent to which the Atlantic slave trade changed the nature of, what was, traditional African slavery. The development of an effective commercial venture, the trading in humans, contributed to making the African man turn on his own kind. This is not only to blame the African for the kind of tragedy that befell the continent in the form of large scale slavery across the Atlantic. Nothing could be further from the truth. In the 'pre-moral' era of the time, the Europeans saw, what in horrible, unemotional terms could be described as, a ready supply of the 'raw material' they needed, humans who could toil on the plantations across the ocean. And they capitalised on it. As some Africans of the time said, they (the Africans) had been doing it for many centuries and what was wrong with it! Professor David Dabydeen of Warwick University said, 'It was a nasty unimaginable way of treating people as goods, with no sense of humanity'. While the Europeans acknowledged the errors of slavery and reversed it, Africans need to come to terms with their painful past and the part they played in a dark chapter in the history of the continent.

Of Africa, by Africa, for Africa

Duarte Pacheco Pereira (1460- 1533) was a Portuguese sea-captain and explorer who wrote about Benin, a country on the west African coast - 'is usually at war with its neighbours and takes many captives, whom we buy at twelve or fifteen brass bracelets each, or for copper bracelets, which they prize more.'

Europeans needed labour. If they did not have slaves they would have used cheap, white, European labour. But with the ready availability of slaves, this was the most lucrative and obvious option.

Those enslaved in communities in Africa were either prisoners, or had fallen into debt or were simply enemies of those who trapped them into slavery. The ruthless pursuit of profit is seen every day; opportunities are seldom missed. When one sees people attempting to cross the busy sea lanes in the Straits of Dover between England and the north coast of France, in overloaded boats that are nothing but 'floating coffins', it is easy to understand that for the profiteers of this dangerous venture, human life is expendable and always secondary to the monetary gain. A similar principle applied to the African slave trader where the human cargo was expendable in the pursuit of profit. So the African man sold whoever he could trap and transport to the shore and the waiting boats. As was then, so also now, profit was more important than morality. In fact morality does not appear in the considerations of the profiteers of modern day human trafficking either. However, unlike slaves, refugees and asylum seekers had paid for the risks attendant in travelling out of their homelands in search of greener pastures far afield. The slave had no choice in the matter. For the current day victim of human trafficking, were the risks minimised or the promises made extravagant to entice them? But the horrors of the Middle Passage must have been known to the slave traders. The seafarers of the time had plied the route on several occasions. The slave ships were 'floating dungeons' for most. As described by Markus Rediker, the transatlantic ships were 'floating coffins' for many, who eventually became food for sharks in the waters.

The historian and anthropologist *Zora Neale Hurston* located the last survivor of the last slave ship to reach the shores of America. In her book *'Barracoon: The Story of the Last "Black Cargo",'* which was only published in May 2018, she writes about Oluale Kossola from the Yoruba tribe in Benin who was captured by the Dahomian tribe. He and 120 others were sold as slaves and transported on the ship 'Clotilda' to America in 1860. The Clotilda was a ten masted schooner which was 86 feet (26m) long. It arrived in Mobile Bay within the Gulf of Mexico in the state of Alabama sometime between the latter half of 1859 and the summer of 1860. Despite the Act Prohibiting the Importation of Slaves having been passed by Congress on 2nd March 1807, illegal slave traders still continued with the trade, working with partners in West Africa. The slaves were hidden and the boat was set on fire. The brothers, Burns and Timothy Meaher and John Dabney were charged with illegal possession of the slaves from the Clotilda. In May 2019, the Alabama Historical Commission announced that remnants of a ship found along the Mobile River, near Twelve Mile Island and just north of the Mobile Bay delta, were confirmed as the *Clotilda*. One of the last survivors of the ship was Lewis who was born Oluale Kossola in Benin, a country on the West coast of Africa. He was only 19 years old when he was captured by the neighbour Dahomian tribe and taken to the coast to be sold as a slave. He was transported across the Atlantic in the *Clotilda*. He was probably one of the last slaves to reach America and told Hurston 'We very sorry to be parted from one 'nother.' 'We seventy days cross de water from de Affica soil, and now dey part us from one 'nother. Derefore we cry. Our grief so heavy look lak we cain stand it. I think maybe I die in my sleep when I dream about my mama.' 'We doan know why we be bring 'way from our country to work lak dis," ; 'everybody lookee at us strange. We want to talk wid de udder colored folkses but dey doan know whut we say.'

In his book, *'The Slave Ship'*, Marcus Rediker describes the awful hell that was a slave ship. Human beings were shackled and manacled, locked together by heavy chains or metal rings round their necks. They lay there in the holds of the ships and many died there. The absolute authority on board the ship was the captain who, by nature or of necessity, was ruthlessness personified. He was at the top of the hierarchy of evil and violence which descended to the crew and then on to those who worked on the African shore.

Here comes the crunch. And it is this. Close your eyes and imagine yourself as one of the scantily clad slaves on the *Clotilda*. You are in the hatch which has been buttoned down and with 120 other equally miserable

Of Africa, by Africa, for Africa

and pathetic people. Disorientated and fearful, the voyage, which is to last two and half months, begins. It s not a comfortable cruise ship but a basic, pathetic, overcrowded sailing ship. It pitches and rolls as the ship is buffeted by the waves. It crashes down on to the water after being lifted by a high wave. There is hardly any room as you are packed like sardines in the hatch. There is no light and the stench is overbearing. Your are chained to the floor. You could hardly stand and most of the time is spent seated or crouching down. You eat, urinate and defaecate on the spot where you are chained to. But count yourself lucky on this voyage as there are only 120 others with you. You are not very tightly packed, but still 120 of you in a 80 foot boat is a lot. Sometimes boats were tightly packed so that the profits would be greater. The captain of the ship was paid on the number of live slaves delivered to the eastern coast of America. Some of your fellow captives died, which was a common occurrence; but not too many die as this boat is not too over-crowded. Your dead fellow slaves are simply thrown overboard. As slaves were chained together in the hold, a dead slave may be linked to you by chain for some time before the dead body was separated from the other living slaves. Thrown overboard, the dead slave's body was food for sharks. Some others in the hold are ill, for many suffered dysentery. Sick slaves did not get any treatment; they stayed in the hold until they improved or died. However you are fed twice a day. But there are no toilets on board so the risk of contracting disease is high. In good weather you and the other fit slaves would be taken up to the deck for exercise which usually involved dancing, designed to keep slaves fit. There was no exception to exercise; refusal brought flogging by the crew. The captain had a vested interest in keeping slaves alive just until they are delivered to the American coast. Any minor altercation between slaves was dealt with severely by the crew. The crew were underpaid, drunk and violent. Markus Rediker describes a slave ship captain who enjoyed having 'a hell of my own'. Women were at risk of being sexually abused or raped. Women and child slaves suffered disproportionately more than men slaves. Devoid of any humanity and with no idea of morality, the atmosphere on board a slave ship was one of pure, unadulterated evil and degradation. It is therefore no surprise that many slaves and even some of the crew were suicidal.

Rediker describes four levels of inter-personal relationships in the slave trade. Those between captain of a slave ship and his crew, between the crew and slaves, between slaves themselves and finally between the white slave merchants and those who worked to abolish the trade. The captain treated his crew badly. He had to pay them from bis profits and so captains often sailed with the minimum numbers of crew possible. The crew were not looked after by the captain; they were poorly fed and were often treated no better than the slaves. The resulting anger which fomented in the crew was directed not only at the captain but also against each other and against the slaves. The slaves were undoubtedly the weakest on board, physically, mentally and emotionally. In a demonstration of utter degradation, the crew resented the food given to the slaves. The slave ship was a 'war zone' with many battles occurring simultaneously. The captain of the ship, as leader, had only one interest – to deliver live slaves to America and so maximise his income.

Although slaves came from different countries, regions and tribes with varying languages, they developed a kinship of their own. Confined to the same hell in the 'floating dungeon' of the slave ship and in the sub-human conditions on the sugar plantations, they found ways to communicate with each other and forge a kinship. This camaraderie, if it may be called that, lasted even after they reached landfall. The shared suffering that was continuously endured helped to build bonds between the slaves which helped them to resist their owners and to escape from the appalling conditions they were subjected to. Rebellion was used by slaves to overcome their suffering; a notable example was that which occurred on the slave ship the *Jolly Batchelor* in Sierra Leone in 1742. The slaves killed the Captain, Cutler, and two of the ship's crew before freeing other slaves that were held in the hold of the ship. They then stripped the ship of its sails and rigging before abandoning it.

The slave ship *Little George* under Captain George Scott sailed from the coast of Guinea with 96 slaves on board. A few days at sea the slaves revolted and broke onto the deck of the ship. The captain and his crew locked themselves in a cabin and attempted to make a bomb with gunpowder in a bottle. Unfortunately the bomb exploded, but the ship was not completely destroyed. The slaves sailed back to the coast of Africa with the captain and crew imprisoned in the cabin. The slaves escaped when they reached the coast of Africa. Apparently the Captain just survived to tell the tale of what happened on board his ship.

Two famous revolts happened on board ships in America in the 1800's. In July 1839, slaves under the leadership of Joseph Cinque took control of the ship *Amistad* and sailed her to Long Island in New York. The slave trade had ended in 1808. At a trial to determine the fate of the slaves, the Supreme Court determined that the slaves should be set free and allowed to return to Africa. The slaves were defended by John Quincy Adams who later became the sixth President of the United States of America, from 1825 to 1829. The second instance was on board the ship the *Creole* which sailed from Hampton Road, Virginia in October 1941 with 135 slaves on board. The slaves seized firearms and demanded that the ship sail to an English colony or that the crew would all be cast overboard. England and its colonies had emancipated slaves; hence the demand to sail to an English colony. When the ship reached Nassau, Bahamas, the slaves escaped. The British ignored a request from the US government to return the slaves.

What these examples demonstrate is that in their desperation, slaves were prepared to take any risk to free themselves from their miserable conditions and the awful fate that awaited them on the sugar plantations. Of course, there were risks and the punishments meted out to slaves were inhuman and barbaric. A slave caught running away in Antigua was likely to be killed on the order of judges or whipped or to lose a limb. In Montserrat, any slave who had runaway for a period greater than three months and was subsequently captured was likely to be executed. Any person who captured a slave was rewarded with 500 pounds weight of sugar by the owner of the slave. Sugar was an expensive and much sought after commodity at the time.

In their desperation, slaves sometimes resorted to murder. A notable uprising was in Antigua in 1736 where there was a plan to blow up slave owners who were attending a ball, by using stolen gunpowder. When the plot was foiled, 88 slaves were put to death, often by being burned alive.

In Barbados in 1816 revolting slaves burned more than a quarter of the entire sugar plantation on the island.

The punishments inflicted on slaves by their slave owners, who were almost exclusively white, were quite severe. Brandishing was used on slaves who ran away. Any part of the body would be brandished with a hot iron, like the back and even the palm of the hand. Whipping was so severe that it caused deep wounds. This was made worse when into the wounds, salt and pepper were rubbed to maximise the pain and suffering.

Slaves were hanged, sometimes upside down. The slave was suspended by metal hooks which pierced the chest and even the lungs. Some slaves were burned alive.

In his conversation with Hassan Mahamdallie, Marcus Rediker described the different functions of the slave ship. In one role it was a warship with a canon. On its journey to an African port the crew would be used to build and secure the lower deck where slaves would be held. To increase the number of slaves, platforms would be built. Barricades were erected so that the slaves could be safely secured. The word 'safety' is used here in the context of the sailors. They would also build barricades so that the slaves could not reach the sailors who would ensure that they remained safe from their captives. When the trans-Atlantic journey was completed and the slaves deposited on land, the ship would make its voyage back to England. But not before the various structures that were built to contain the slaves and ensure crew security were taken down. The ship would now be used to transport sugar back to Europe.

To the captain of the slave ship, the crew was as expendable as the slaves. He was only interested in profit. He needed the crew to ensure safety of the ship and its human cargo until it completed its westward voyage across the Atlantic. They were not as much needed on the return leg of the trip. On the outward sailing the captain and the crew were wary of their 'contents' – the slaves. They could rise up against the crew and the captain. They could also commit suicide which would reduce the earnings of the captain. The captain therefore needed the crew on the outward sailing from Africa. And the crew needed to work together and with the captain of the boat, if only to ensure their own safety. But, closer to the American coast or to that of the West Indies, the relationship between captain and crew would often change. The former did not need many of the latter who cost him in wages. So he hoped that they would desert him and the ship. One way to achieve this was to drive the crew harder. It is an interesting statistic that up to one in five of the sailors died; almost that same number or on some sailings greater that the number of slaves that perished.

Of Africa, by Africa, for Africa

Ships crews were sometimes in a pathetic situation, being poor, hungry and suffering with topical diseases like malaria. In a paradox of the sad situation, Rideker found evidence that slaves and slave women in particular would care for the sailors, their captors during the voyage. When sailors died they were buried by their African carers in their own burial grounds. The compassion shown by slaves to their previous captors and tormentors is an amazing story of kindness in adversity. In an age prior to ethical and moral considerations, slaves showed a greater degree of empathy and humanity than the sailors and the captain ever did. At these times the slaves demonstrated unequivocally what it was and still is to be human. The medallion by Josiah Wedgewood with the inscribed words 'am I not a man and a brother' finds a particular resonance in the acts of kindness displayed by slaves. Even in their pathetic state, many of the slaves retained their humanity.

Despite the foregoing Rideker describes the slave ship as a 'war zone' with the slaves trying to escape from their predicament. One in ten ships had serious insurrections on board. Insurrections and related losses made it increasingly unprofitable for investors in the slave trade. Rideker says that this may have led to reduced demand for slaves and prevented an additional one million people from being taken into slavery.

The slaves were often resigned to their fate. They were in no position to question any aspect of their treatment on board the slave ship. They often found solace and some peace in building relationships with each other. It is difficult to imagine what their thoughts were as they witnessed their fellow- slaves suffer and die. What were they thinking when they saw the bodies of dead slaves unceremoniously being thrown overboard? They may have been slaves but they had feelings, emotions, they had been forcibly separated from their own families in Africa and knew pain, suffering and grief. But this was not a time for a display of any emotions; they endured their feelings and thoughts in silence throughout the journey.

The ultimate weapon that the slave often had was to commit suicide. This desperate act was a financial loss to the captain. The captain had to deliver live slaves. For each one he lost he earned less. The slave may have been owned and shackled by another but he had the ultimate power over the captain and his earnings. In the final bizarre and painful analysis, the slave had a hold on the captain and crew by virtue of his ability to commit suicide. If he followed this path he deprived the captain of the sole purpose of the voyage. The captain of the slave ship was only too aware that he was a hostage to his captives.

These conditions are unimaginable to most if not all of us. But this was the reality of the trans-Atlantic voyage. These were much worse than the conditions in the Russian gulag. At least there was toilet paper in the gulags! The Nobel prize-winning Russian author, Alexander Solzhenitsyn continued to write while in the gulag. And the eminent Russian surgeon, Sergei Sergeevich Yudin, wrote two medical books on toilet paper while being incarcerated in the gulag in the late 1940's by Stalin.

In the 1700's, one in five slaves died on the voyage across the Atlantic. Later on, at the behest of their governments, the French and British legally ensured that a slave ship had a physician on board, although there were doubts as to whether this was for the welfare of the slaves or more importantly to care for the captain and the crew. However it is noteworthy that the deaths of slaves during the voyage had fallen to one in 1800.

With increasing opposition in Britain to slavery and following the *Zong* massacre, the Dolben Act was passed in 1788 to improve the conditions on slave ships. The *Zong* massacre was the mass killing of 142 African slaves who were on board the slave ship the '*Zong*'. As was customary practice, the ship's owners insured their cargo of slaves for the voyage across the Atlantic. Unfortunately the ship ran short of drinking water as a result of errors in navigation. As the situation became desperate a decision was taken to throw slaves overboard.

At the time of underwriting there were 244 slaves on board the *Zong*. The ship and its slaves were insured in total for up to £8000, which was below the market value of the slaves. Any other remaining risk had to borne by the owners of the ship. When the ship sailed from Accra, Ghana on 18th August 1781 there were 442 slaves on board - far in excess of that which was permitted. Usually a British ship would carry 1.75 slaves per ton of the ship's capacity. But on the *Zong*, on the day of sailing, there were 4 slaves per ton. One of the purposes of the physician or ship's surgeon on board was to ensure that the slaves that were taken on board were reasonably fit for the journey and for work in the plantations across the Atlantic. Therefore slaves were selected who had, what was euphemistically called 'commodity value'. If a person was not selected, that person had what was again, euphemistically called, a 'commercial death'. If being captured and forced on to a boat was bad enough, enduring a 'commercial death' with no 'commodity value' the person was useless to the ruthless traders on the shore and to the ship's crew. Not uncommonly the person was killed on the shore. Often 'commercial death' equated to real physical death. Such was the evil inherent in the business of slavery and of the people engaged in it.

In 1788, Sir William Dolben, and the Abolition Society in the United Kingdom were instrumental in encouraging the Prime Minister of the day, William Pitt, to order an investigation into the slave trade. William Wilberforce introduced the matter to the House of Commons. But because the Privy Council had not produced its report on slavery, William Pitt suggested that the matter be postponed for the next session of Parliament, due to shortage of time. But Sir William Dolmen argued that urgent action was needed and that any delay would have led to a further 10,000 deaths. He argued for a reduction in numbers of slaves on board and the presence of a ship's surgeon to help reduce loss of lives at sea. The Bill was finally passed on 10th July 1788. It is said that doctors on board slave ships received bonuses depending on the number of slaves that were successfully delivered across the Atlantic.

The relationship between slave trader and the slave buyer was often complex. On the surface it appeared to be a straightforward transaction between a willing seller and a willing buyer. The Europeans needed slaves to work the plantations in the West Indies and in America. The slave trader needed money and the goods that the European brought to the area. There were no fixed prices for this 'human commodity'. Bartering was not uncommon. In this respect the Atlantic trade differed from the Arabian and Indian ocean slave trades where the price paid for the 'commodity' varied depending on demand and the market price at the time.

In his book, *'Missionary Travels and Researches in South Africa'*, the late Dr. David Livingstone wrote about his encounters with slavery on the continent. He wrote 'No one can understand the effect of the unutterable meanness of the slave-system on the minds of those who, but for the strange obliquity which prevents them from feeling the degradation of not being gentlemen enough to pay for services rendered, would be equal in virtue to ourselves. Fraud becomes as natural to them as 'paying one's way' is to the rest of mankind.' He came to the realisation that slavery not only ruined the lives of slaves but changed the character of those who traded in slaves. His first encounter of slavery was in Botswana where he and his wife set up a mission among the Bakwena ('those who worship the crocodile') people in 1847. His only convert to Christianity was the King of the Bakwena, Sechele.

He travelled to the Zambezi and witnessed Portuguese slave traders transporting slaves to the market to meet the demand for slaves in Brazil. He also saw Africans in the interior of the continent selling slaves to the Portuguese, who then sold them to Arabs and Swahili traders in Mozambique. From Mozambique the slaves went to Arabia. He noted that slaves themselves followed the old foot trails to market, where they sold themselves.

The words of David Livingstone are reproduced here as they give a powerful impression of how slaves were treated by their Arab owners. He wrote in 1870, 'In less than I take to talk about it, these unfortunate creatures — 84 of them, wended their way into the village where we were. Some of them, the eldest, were women from 20 to 22 years of age, and there were youths from 18 to 19, but the large majority was made up of boys and girls from 7 years to 14 or 15 years of age.

'A more terrible scene than these men, women and children, I do not think I ever came across. To say that they were emaciated would not give you an idea of what human beings can undergo under certain circumstances. Each of them had his neck in a large forked stick, weighing from 30 to 40 pounds, and five or six feet long, cut with a fork at the end of it where the branches of a tree spread out.

'The women were tethered with bark thongs, which are, of all things, the most cruel to be tied with. Of course they are soft and supple when first stripped off the trees, but a few hours in the sun make them about as hard as the iron round packing-cases. The little children were fastened by thongs to their mothers.

'As we passed along the path which these slaves had travelled, I was shown a spot in the bushes where a poor woman the day before, unable to keep on the march, and likely to hinder it, was cut down by the axe of one of these slave drivers. We went on further and were shown a place where a child lay. It had been recently born, and its mother was unable to carry it from debility and exhaustion; so the slave trader had taken this little infant by its feet and dashed its brains out against one of the trees and thrown it in there'.

If dead slaves on the trans-Atlantic voyage were thrown overboard and became food for sharks, their dead counterparts in the trans-Saharan passage became food for the roaming animals of the jungles. Unceremonious and devoid of humanity and respect as both events were, they nevertheless served the commercial purpose of the time. This was, in modern parlance 'business continuity'.

These few heart-rending stories paint a gruesome picture of some aspects of slavery in Africa, outside any influence by the white man. Slavery was endemic and part of the culture. It was at the same time cruel as it was perceived a business venture driven by profit and personal gain. It degraded all who had any part to play in it. Its legacy is probably the continuous cycles of war and destruction which one witnesses in Africa to this day; human life is of limited value.

It is common and indeed easy to think of slavery as an exclusive European issue with slaves being conveyed across the Atlantic ocean. But the trans-Saharan slavery involved an even more severe passage across the continent. Slaves had to march along several miles of jungle and desert in the sweltering heat, with several dying on the journey. The routes were littered with the bodies and skeletons of many dead slaves. Most died from dehydration, starvation, heat and exhaustion on the way.

If Marcus Rediker implied that his book, *'The Slave Ship'* was painful to write and equally painful to read, then the florid descriptions of Livingstone paint a gruesome picture of the Trans-African passage.

During his travels, Ibn Battuta was in Mali and met Suleyman Keita who was Mansa or King of the Mali Empire. He was disturbed to see that female servants, slaves and the sultan's daughters exposed their bodies, which is against the Quran.

One of the less recognised aspects of the trans-Saharan slave trade is what Duncan Smith calls the 'forced migration of women and young girls across Africa into Islamic lands where they were used as concubines. The

Arab market sought beautiful females. Hence the so called Ethiopian 'red' slaves from the Oromo, also called Galla tribe, were particularly sought for their beauty. They also commanded a higher price. On 16th September 1888, the British gunship *HMS Osprey* commanded by Charles E Gissing intercepted three boats carrying Ethiopians to slave markets in the Red Sea port of Jeddah. It was part of the British moves to end the slave trade. Two hundred and four slaves were freed from the boats and taken on board the *Osprey* and ferried to Aden. Local Muslim families adopted Muslim children while the others were placed in the care of the Free Church of Scotland. Before these children could be relocated in another mission, Lovedale in the Eastern Cape, eleven children died from the climate in Aden.

One of the children on board the *Osprey* was Bisho Jarsa who had been sold to slaves for a small quantity of maize. Jasra eventually became a teacher in Cradock, a town in the Eastern Cape Province of South Africa, about 160 miles from Port Elizabeth. Her grandson was Neville Alexander (1936 – 2012) who was a teacher, educationist and anti-apartheid activist and who was a prisoner in Robben Island with Nelson Mandela.

Ethiopia was a country of many tribes. Emperor Menelik II, who was King of Shewa from 1869, gained control of large parts and ruled the Empire of Ethiopia from 1889 to 1913. It is written that emperor Menelik II was the 'greatest slave entrepreneur' in Ethiopia as he taxed the trade to finance purchase of guns and ammunition to help him gain control of the whole country. Prior to this the Kings of Kafa and Gibe in Ethiopia enslaved children of parents who could not pay taxes. In Gibe, a third of the population were slaves, while in some other states they comprised half to two thirds of the population. A considerable number of slaves were used in agriculture.

In 1886 the Oromo king, Abbar Jiffar, made peace with Menelik II and offered slaves, eunuchs and other material like spears and shields. Abba Jiffar had 10,000 slaves.

Ethiopia was a country that provided a large number of slaves in the first half of the nineteenth century. The Abyssinian Church in Ethiopia justified slavery on the need to civilise savages. But its main justification came from its adoption of the Curse of Ham as stated in the Old Testament.

Eventually Menelik II abolished slavery in Ethiopia although it appears that he did not enforce the law and was claimed to be unable to change a practice which was centuries old.

Another story is of the Oromo slave girl, Pauline. Born an only child, she was cared for and educated by her father. Unfortunately he was killed in battle; Pauline watched her beloved father die. She was only nine when she was kidnapped by Muslim slave traders while visiting her father's grave. Following a journey that lasted several weeks she was brought to a slave market in Sinnaar in Egypt. She was bought and sold twelve times and was finally purchased by Mehemet Ali, the Pasha of Egypt who had arrived in Cairo. She was given the Arabic name of Fatima and practised Islam as her religion.

When the German of African origin, John Baron von Müller visited Cairo, Fatima was gifted to him by the Pasha.

Ganamee or Fathime (Fatima) came to Germany with Baron von Müller, staying initially with his mother. As luck would have it, she was presented by von Müller to the mother of the King of Württemberg, Being a protestant, the Queen Mother wished to ensure that Fathime received a Protestant education. She was admitted to a Protestant girl's school. She lived in the home of a German family in Kornthal; they acted as her foster parents. She was baptised a Christian on 12th July 1852 and given the name Pauline and thus became Pauline Fathime. She died on 11th September 1855 of a lung disease. Pauline often expressed that her Oromo people were 'wild but good 'and hoped that they would convert to Christianity.

Slavery was an integral part of the rural economy in Ethiopia. As a result, Emperor Haile Sellassie who wanted to abolish slavery in 1930, had to proceed gradually. Ethiopia had been ruled by Emperors who claimed descent from Menelik I who was the son of Solomon and his wife Makeda who was the Queen of Sheba. Emperor Tewodros II who ruled from 1855-1868 tried to abolish slavery without much effect. Johannes IV who ruled from 1872-1889 also tried to outlaw slavery but this was opposed by several tribes who favoured its continuation. Also, Ethiopia was surrounded by countries where the slave trade continued. The Italians invaded Ethiopia on the pretext of abolishing slavery but again this was not effective. When Emperor Haile Sellasie returned to power he abolished slavery in 1942.

Mengistu Haile Mariam who was President of Ethiopia form

1977 to 1991 was believed to be the son of a former slave. When in power, he exterminated those whom he called imperialists and counter-revolutionaries. In 1977 the General Secretary of the Save the Children Fund said that '1,000 children have been killed, and their bodies are left in the streets and are being eaten by wild hyenas. You can see the heaped-up bodies of murdered children, most of them aged eleven to thirteen, lying in the gutter, as you drive out of Addis Ababa'.

Mengistu Haile Mariam resigned the post of President of Ethiopia in 1991 and went into refuge in Zimbabwe. He was found guilty of genocide but his friend, President Robert Mugabe of Zimbabwe, refused to send him back to Ethiopia to face justice.

African slave traders did not see slaves as Africans . They were from another tribe, not 'their ' people. This concept of 'others' drove the kidnapping of people who were not from one's area or tribe.

Madam Efunroye Tinubu (1810 – 1887) also known as Efunporoye Osuntinubu was a Nigerian aristocrat and a slave trader. She was known to sell slaves to the Portuguese and Brazilians in return for guns and ammunition. This was done despite Madam Tinubu having signed a treaty with Britain with the objective of outlawing the slave trade.

Although it was said that she eventually came to resist the slave trade, the author Oladipo Yemitan paints a different picture of her in his book *'Madame Timbu: Merchant and King Maker'*. Yemitan writes 'On one occasion, during her final sojourn in Abeokuta, she was alleged to have sold a young boy into slavery and was accused of it. When arraigned before Ogundipe Alatise over the matter, she reportedly explained: 'I have a large house-hold and I must feed them well. I need money to do that, that's why'. Additional accounts paint a more sinister picture of her, with Oladipo Yemitan describing her as 'unapologetic and profit minded'. When a slave trading deal did not work out as she had planned, Madame Tinubu was claimed to have once said that 'she would rather drown the twenty slaves than sell them at a discount'.

Abeokuta is the capital of Ogun state which is located in south-west Nigeria. A monument to Madame Tinubu is seen in Ita Iyalode Square. There are other monuments to her in Nigeria, especially the one in

Tinubu Square in Lagos. Here one sees an excellent example of Nigerians remembering and celebrating a slave trader. They are not concerned about slavery or iconoclasm in their own country. Slavery was and still is part of the fabric of the country. The vast majority of people in Africa are scarcely concerned about slavery and monuments. They understand slavery, they appreciate its historical context and its cultural aspects; they accept and live with their history. They do not see the utility of tearing down monuments or of renaming streets and squares. They are there to remind the public who Madam Tinubu was and what her history was and her legacy are.

In an essay on Madame Tinubu by Cosmic Yoruba, it is written 'every single important West African from that period of time had a part in the slave trade.' Surprisingly, Wole Soyinka has an essay on *'Africa's role in the transatlantic slave trade'* in which he mentions this; that is the power some Africans in that period got from trading slaves.

Nigerians are known to teach their children about the country's role in slavery. For eg it is taught that 'the bulk of the supply came from the Nigerians. These Nigerian middlemen moved to the interior where they captured other Nigerians who belonged to other communities. The middlemen also purchased many of the slaves from the people in the interior . . . . Many Nigerian middlemen began to depend totally on the slave trade and neglected every other business and occupation. The result was that when the trade was abolished [by England in 1807] these Nigerians began to protest. As years went by and the trade collapsed such Nigerians lost their sources of income and became impoverished.' This description helps a greater understanding of slavery and the context in which it occurred. It does not seek to apportion blame but to understand what happened at the time.

Mvemba a Nzinga, Nzinga Mbemba or Funsu Nzinga Mvemba (1456–1542), was the King of Kongo and was also known as King Afonso I. The Empire of Kongo comprises modern day north Angola, the western part of the Democratic Republic of Congo and a part of Gabon. King Afonso tried to persuade the Portuguese to cease slavery but was largely unsuccessful as he needed the help of the latter to maintain control of his Kingdom. The Portuguese made an attempt on the King's life but failed. However he was able to end illegal trade in slaves.

In Ghana, politician and educator Samuel Sulemana Fuseini, acknowledged that his Asante ancestors 'abducted, captured and kidnapped African'. In the process they became exceedingly rich.

As Jonathan Burack wrote, there is little to be gained from replacing 'old myths of African barbarism' with 'new myths of African innocence.' This is a clear statement, if one was needed, that Africa needed to confront the demons of its past. It sold its sons and daughters, the brightest and the best for the metaphorical 'thirty pieces of silver'.

Several African countries apologised for their ancestor's role in the slave trade. The reasons for these apologies may not always have been genuine remorse wrote Theodore R. Johnson in 2014. There were, according to him, various reasons for offering an apology or for refraining from doing so.

Tribal leaders in Nigeria took the view that they did not have to apologise, as their ancestors were responsible for what happened and that responsibility should not be passed to following generations. One leader said that Nigerians were 'not apologetic about what happened in the past'. His justification for this view was that his ancestors were involved in a 'very very legal' activity. Henry Bonsu, who was researching the subject of apologising for slavery said 'people aren't milling around Lagos ... moaning about why chiefs don't apologise. They are more concerned about the everyday and why they still have bad governance.'

The apology from Benin was a political act clothed in forgiveness and the need for reconciliation. In 1999 Benin's President, Mathieu Kérékou went on a worldwide apology tour. His minister for environment and housing, Luc Gnacadja, said 'We cry forgiveness and reconciliation ....The slave trade is a shame, and we do repent for it.' Cyrille Oguin, Benin's ambassador to the United States, said 'We share in the responsibility for this terrible human tragedy'.

Ghana apologised for slavery in 2006. However, this was driven by a business need to encourage tourism to Ghana and improved relations with America.

Senegal's President, Abdoulaye Wade apologised for his country's role in slavery, but he was vehemently opposed to any discussion regarding payment of reparations. He gained the moral high ground when he said he found it offensive that people were asking the West 'to give us money to forget our ancestors… I find that insulting'. He continued 'Europe did not have a monopoly on slavery. Muslim traders also exported as many as 17 million slaves to the coast of the Indian Ocean, the Middle East and North Africa.'

What does the casual observer conclude from the comments, set out in the preceding paragraphs, of some African leaders? Slave traders in Africa profited from the trade and in their acts of selling their countrymen and fellow human beings. They had an interest in and incentives to continue with the abhorrent business of slavery, in an era of an apparent moral vacuum on the matter. Current leaders have attempted to apologise but for different reasons, one of which is pecuniary; an increase in income to help with national development etc. And of course some, like those leaders from Nigeria, see no imperative in apologising for the acts of their ancestors. Seen in this light the views of President Wade on the matter of reparations appear honest; enough money has been exchanged and gained by individuals and country leaders from selling their fellow Africans, whom the slave traders knew were likely to suffer a terrible fate. Demanding and accepting even more money would be 'selling the dead' for personal gain. President Wade saw no benefit and in reality considered it an insult to dead slaves and the history of slavery by placing a monetary value on the bodies of those who suffered and died from slavery.

The late Ghanaian diplomat and poet, Kofi Awoonor, wrote: 'I believe there is a great psychic shadow over Africa, and it has much to do with our guilt and denial of our role in the slave trade. We, too, are blameworthy in what was essentially one of the most heinous crimes in human history'. Kofi Awoonor was among those killed on 21st September 2013, during an attack by Al-Shabab militants on the Westgate shopping centre in Nairobi, Kenya. He was in Kenya at the time participating in the Storymoja Hay Festival of writing and story-telling.

'Until there is an admission by Africans that they were involved in the slave trade, the healing process will be difficult to realize', according to Imakus Nzinga Okofo, a former New York City resident who now resides in Ghana's Cape Coast. 'Though the European was responsible, he could not have done as much without the cooperation of Africans.'

In his book, *'The African Slave Trade'*, the author Basil Davidson makes the case that slavery in Africa was not solely due to Europeans. Slavery has been a part of the culture in Africa and still continues to be practised in various forms. He drives home some salient views on the trade, the most important of which is that the African was 'seldom the helpless victim'. Davidson maintains that there is no historical basis to any claim that the European introduced or imposed slavery on Africa. On the contrary, he wrote that Africans 'responded to its challenge. They exploited its opportunities.' Indeed, Europeans did not invade African countries looking for captives to be taken into slavery. The black historian Zora Neale Hurston wrote 'My own people had exterminated whole nations and torn families apart for a profit before the strangers got their chance at a cut. It was a sobering thought. It impressed upon me the universal nature of greed.' That slavery was an amoral commercial venture in pursuit of profit is as compelling as it is without doubt.

Davidson describes how between the 7th and the 19th centuries, Arabs played a vital part in the slave trade and transported 14 million black slaves during that period. The third important aspect highlighted by Davidson was the lack of morality among Europeans of the time.

A brief description of powerful and wealthy black slave owners helps to place slavery in perspective. One of the most effective and probably powerful women in the trade was Bibiana Vaz de França (1630 – 1694) from Guinea-Bissau. She was married to Ambrosia Gomez, who was the richest man in Guinea. She was in Cape Verde Islands with her younger brother on charges of tax evasion and rebellion and was eventually granted a royal pardon.

The most prolific male slave owner was arguably Tippu Tipp. His real name was Hamad bin Muhammad bin Juma bin Rajab el Murjebi (1832-1905); he was a governor in Zanzibar, plantation owner and slave trader. He was the son of a slave trader and the grandson of a slave, who worked on the east coast of Africa in the Indian Ocean slave trade, especially for the clove plantations of Zanzibar. But he provided slaves to all sectors of the African slave trade. Even as a young man he was a successful slave catcher. His area of activity extended thousands of miles from inland to the East African coast of the Indian Ocean.

The stories written by Africans of the role played by their ancestors in the slave trade makes sobering reading. In 2019 Adaobi Tricia Nwaubani wrote about her great-grandfather, Nwaubani Ogogo Oriaku, who was a Igbo chief and who was held in great respect even by the white man. But he sold slaves to Europeans. It is estimated that between the 16th and 19th centuries, 1.4 million Igbo people were conveyed across the Atlantic as slaves.

The journalist Teddy Nwanunobi said that "What our ancestors did wasn't right, …. if they had thought about the consequences, they wouldn't have done those things." He too was referring to his great-grandfather who was an Igbo slave trader. He thinks that the failure of his own male relatives to have families of their own is because of their historical role in 'bringing other people's lineages to an end.' Nwanunobi does not think that reparation by making cash payments would wash away his family's' guilt over the matter. There is no doubt that guilt remains a painful and continuing feature of his life as indeed it must be for many others with similar family histories. He said that he is willing to surrender all he owns if only this 'would bring an end to this suffering.… I will do whatever it will take to appease anybody, if only I can identify the particular people we offended'. Herein lies a dilemma for those who seek reparations and those who may have to pay for it. He goes on to say that his father does not believe that reparations are due, as slavery has been a part of African culture and pre-dated the arrival of Europeans.

Many Africans domiciled in America also do not think that they should be part of any discussion regarding reparations. The Zambian pastor Saidi Francis Chishimba is quite forthright when he says "Slavery was wrong, but do I carry upon my shoulders the sins of my forefathers so that I should go around saying sorry? I don't think so." Chishimba's grandfather, Ali Saidi Muluwe Wansimba was from a tribe of slave traders who established slave markets in Zambia. Chishimba recalls his family being proud of what they did in relation to slavery. The important point made by him is that in Zambia, slavery is 'forgotten history'.

In her 2019 paper titled *'When the Slave Traders were African'*, Adaobi Tricia Nwaubani recounts other stories of the pain of guilt endured by many Africans. It is a cause of shame to many as in the case of Yunus Mohammed Rafiq who is a professor of anthropology who teaches at Dukes University in Shanghai. He said 'We speak of it in whispers'. His great-great- grandfather Mwarukere, raided Tanzanian villages to capture slaves. The slaves were then sold to Europeans or retained to work in coconut plantations in Africa. What is interesting is that he admits to his family history being hidden. This was a common practice in many families. Current descendants may not even be aware of their history in slavery or they continue with the collective practice of concealment. Rafiq says 'I thought talking about this legacy of Africans selling themselves is just piling another wound in a body that is already very shot through, fractured, broken down by other things…..knowing this legacy and what we have done, it put so much pressure on me.' Could these words open a door towards reconciliation between black and white, between those who contributed to slavery and engaged in the slave trade in its various forms and slaves? Could the narrative of the evil white slave trader and the pitiful innocent black slave, change to one that is more realistic. This is an evolving story and it would help in bridging the gap in our understanding of slavery. The continued polarisation of discussion and writings on slavery only serve to separate people rather than bringing people together to confront a painful chapter in human history.

Along with slavery, the practice of human sacrifice also gradually came to an end. For example it was a prominent custom among the Yoruba tribe who populate Nigeria and its neighbours Benin and Togo. With pressure from the British, the practice ceased in the late nineteenth century.

The writer Tidiane N'Diaye is a Franco-Senegalese anthropologist. In 2008 he published his book *'Le Génocide Voilé '*which is available in French. The title translates as *'The Veiled Genocide'* in which he describes the sub-Saharan slave trade. He writes how for centuries Arabs raided sub-Saharan Africa for slaves, who were transported to the Arab lands in the Middle East. The trade, if one may call it that, started with an agreement or more specifically an imposition by the Arab Emir and general Abdallah ben Saïd on the Sudanese, where the latter were compelled to supply the emir with slaves. The slaves were taken from Darfu. The practice continued annually until the 20th century. Associated with this forced conveyance of large numbers annually was the forced castration of many men, with disastrous short-term and long-term consequences for the slaves. Because of castration, the men who went into slavery were prevented from having descendants and their story has virtually disappeared from history. Unlike the slaves who went to America, these slaves could not have descendants.

There is hence no story to tell. It is reported that 17 million were castrated. One can barely imagine the extent of the extermination of blacks in the sub-Saharan and east African slave trades. There are in excess of 70 million descendants of slaves living in the Americas while there are very few, if at all, in the aftermath of the sub-Saharan and east African slave trade.

Tidiane N'Diaye wrote 'If horror and cruelty can neither be differentiated nor monopolized', one could say; "that the slave trade and the jihad carried out by the merciless Arab-Muslim robbers was far more devastating for sub-Saharan Africa than the transatlantic slave trade.'

While the trans-Atlantic slave trade lasted from the 1500's to the 1800's, that in the sub-Saharan and East Africa areas lasted 14 centuries, As many as 25 million slaves were transported to the Middle East and beyond.

Why is there this discrepancy in the almost singular narration of the trans- Atlantic slave trade to the almost total exclusion of what happened elsewhere in Africa and with much more disastrous consequences? Why is it that writers appear to have an interminable desire to highlight the evils of the trans-Atlantic trade while there is hardly mention whatsoever of the extremely catastrophic effects of the slave trades in the rest of Africa which continued until recently, and is probably still continuing?

John Azumah is an associate professor of World Christianity and Islam. He says that 'a dominant convention is that a critical approach is reserved for the Christian past but forbidden for the Muslim past …the net result is a romantic picture of the history of Islam, avoiding and sometimes denying such issues such as the jihadist's slaughter and massive enslavement of traditional African believers'

Bassam Michael Madan referring to the book by Tidiane N'Diaye laments the failure to acknowledge this aspect of slavery in Africa. It is as if any discussion of any other aspect of slavery would diminish the impact of the trans-Atlantic trade. But what happened elsewhere in Africa and over a greatly protracted period justifies the use of the term 'genocide' in the title of his book. An attempted explanation of the sub-Saharan and East African slave trades is provided by a sort of 'Stockholm Syndrome of the African type', where the captives feel an unusual solidarity with their captors even under the extremes of suffering that they had to endure.

How the African dehumanised his own kind is seen in the treatment of the Makua people. The Makua are Bantus from Mozambique and Tanzania. Although the Portuguese were in Mozambique there was, initially at least, a peaceful relationship between the Makua and the Portuguese. However, with slaves being captured, the Makua violently resisted not only the Portuguese but also the Arabs and the Sultans in the Kingdoms along the Indian Ocean coast of Africa. The Arabs, French and Portuguese captured Makua for slavery. The Portuguese needed slaves to work in Brazil while the French needed plantation workers for their colonies in Madagascar and in Mauritius, which was then called 'Isle de France'. With increasing demand for slaves, the Makua were seen as a ready supply.

The Yao people are another Bantu tribe. They are not to be confused with another Yao group, also known as Mien, who are an ethnic minority Chinese people. The African Ya or waYao are a tribe in southern Tanzania. They captured slaves for the trade but also to become their wives. In the matrilineal system of Yao society, men could keep their wives and all her children. This encouraged Yao men to take slaves as wives. In one instance a chief had 600 huts, one for each wife.

The Yao in the north of Mozambique captured the Makua as slaves for the Arabs in Swahili and Zanzibar. Makua chiefs also joined in the slave trade and captured their own people for slavery. The Makua were labelled as savages which provided a justification for slave traders as they perceived slavery as means of improving the lot of the Makua.

Although separated by thousands of miles, the slavery of Africa was little different from what happened in North America. The slaves of Alaska were not those people transported across the Atlantic from Africa; rather they were indigenous people who were taken in to slavery by their own. Alaska was not part of the USA when the Thirteenth Amendment came into effect on 18th December 1865. This Amendment abolished slavery from all the states of the USA. Alaska was purchased from Russia on 18th October 1867 for $7.2 million or 2 cents per acre of land, almost two years after the abolition of slavery. But slavery continued in Alaska. The treaty of purchase allowed Alaskans to return to Russia within three years, which most of them did. Those who remained had to abide by the Treaty which stated that ' The inhabitants of the ceded territory, according to their choice, reserving their natural allegiance, may return to Russia within three years; but, if they should prefer to remain in the ceded territory, they, with the exception of uncivilized native tribes, shall be admitted to the enjoyment of all the rights, advantages, and immunities of citizens of the United States, and shall be maintained and protected in the free enjoyment of their liberty, property, and religion. The uncivilized tribes will be subject to such laws and regulations as the United States may, from time to time, adopt in regard to aboriginal tribes of that country."

In the celebrated legal case in 1886 of Sah Quah of the Haida tribe of Alaska, the presiding judge in the Federal Court held that 'all in Alaska where under the governance and jurisdiction of the United States.'

Unarguably the last word on slavery in Alaska should be from Rosita Worl who is from the Shangukeidi clan of the Tlingit tribe. She is an anthropologist with a PhD from Harvard and is President of the Sealaska Heritage Institute. She said 'I want people to know about our culture. I know that we achieved great sophistication, great complexity, and I have to acknowledge that it was the slaves who helped us develop that society. ….. there was a slave pool that was doing a lot of that labor…….. I want to acknowledge our society, and to do that you have to acknowledge slavery'

She went on to describe the painful, yet relevant aspect of Tlingit culture 'although we honor our culture, we are not proud of all aspects of our history'. She maintained that denying slavery was not acceptable, as the public 'would figure out it was a lie'. Her words have much resonance with today once the monuments related to slavery have crashed down to earth. Who would tell the story of the slave catchers and slave owners of Africa who enslaved their people and sold them not only to the Europeans but also to other Africans and to the Middle East? Could it just be that the wave of iconoclasm sweeping Europe and North America may in the minds of some, serve to erase or conceal the guilt of their ancestors in Africa who were intimately involved in the slave trade for personal gain?

The curator of Alaska State Museum, Steve Hendrickson, and his wife are proud of their descent from Tlingit slavery. Through hard work, it is written, that her ancestors rose to a prominent position in the community. Not everyone wanted to talk of their slave past but that it was discussed openly had helped to heal divisions in society.

In these words one recognises the importance and the significance of acknowledging slavery and what it accomplished, in this case in Alaska. Countries like Britain, Spain, France, Portugal, the USA are doing well in accepting the contribution of slavery to their national achievements. But descendants of slaves and of African slave holders also need an imperative to accept that they contributed to slavery in a significant way and in so doing helped enrich many in Africa but simultaneously depleted and impoverished the continent. So much so that there were protests against abolition of slavery. This cannot be denied and needs to be accepted and talked about.

Ghana, on the west coast of Africa appears to have moved in a similar direction of soul-searching and contrition. The country declared a 'Year of Return' in 2019 as it was 400 years since the first Africans were enslaved and transported to the USA. The event was driven by a need to increase tourism. Be that as it may, that it occurred and encouraged people to reflect on their past and to look at their history to help them understand how they came to be where they are now, may have achieved some good.. The acclaimed historian, author and former mayor of Accra in Ghana, the late Nat Nunoo-Amarteifio, wrote 'There is a wilful amnesia about the roles Africans played in the slave trade'. He goes on to describe how the Europeans could not have caught slaves. To do so they would have needed to go deep into the interior of the continent 'without getting sick and dying from illnesses such as malaria'. It was the African tribes, who by warring among themselves, captured their own kind and sold slaves to the white man. Capture of slaves was kept at a significant physical distance from the European, who was confined to the African coast. In so doing the latter were kept unaware of the modus operandi of the slave catchers. This was a deliberate and highly organised structure to the trade according to Professor Toyin Falola, a Nigerian, of the department of African Studies in the University of Texas.

One can for a moment imagine the organisation – the slave catchers and their army to direct them to people who would be captured. Those captured needed to be transported securely to the coast or traded on the way to middlemen who would in turn have to transport and sell them on the coast to the European or to Arabs. Security was paramount as the slaves would either revolt or escape or be captured by a rival gang.

The late Dr. Alexander Falconbridge (1760-1792) was a ship's surgeon who sailed four voyages on slave ships before finally turning into an abolitionist against the slave trade. His writings show that while inter-tribal wars may have yielded some slaves, the major source of slaves was kidnapping. He wrote 'there is reason to believe that most of the *blacks* shipped off from the coast of Africa, are kidnapped...... it may here not be unworthy to remark, in order to prove that wars among the Africans do not furnish the number of slaves they are supposed to do, that I never saw any *blacks* with recent wounds; which must have been the consequence, at least with some of them, had they be taken in battle'. This description makes eminent sense as it is unlikely the hundreds of thousands of slaves shipped across the Atlantic were captured in battle. The continent would have needed to have been in a permanent state of inter-tribal or inter-state warfare!

This statement by Falconbridge is sobering and reflects events on the ground - 'I was told by a *black* woman that she was on her return home one evening from some neighbours... she was kidnapped and [even though] she was big with child, sold for a slave.'

On hearing that the Quakers in England were working to abolish the slave trade, Falconbridge wrote of the response of the African slave traders thus - 'it was a very bad thing, as they should then be reduced to the same state they were in during the war, when through poverty, they were obliged to dig ground and plant yams'.

Ottobah Cugoano (1757-1791) was a 13 year old boy living in the Gold Coast (now Ghana) when he was kidnapped and shipped to Grenada in 1772. When there, he was purchased by an Englishman and brought to England. He was freed and baptised John Stuart on 20th August 1773 in St James's Church, Piccadilly, London. He worked for the royal artist, Richard Cosway and his wife, Maria. Cugoano wrote 'I was early snatched away from my native country, with about eighteen or twenty more boys and girls, as we were playing in a field. We lived but a few days' journey from the coast where we were kidnapped... Some of us attempted, in vain, to run away, but pistols and cutlasses were soon introduced, threatening, that if we offered to stir, we should all lie dead on the spot.' He wrote further ' I must own, to the shame of my own countrymen, that I was first kidnapped and betrayed by some of my own complexion, who were the first cause of my exile and slavery'

In an interesting twist Cugoana, who worked for abolition of slavery, called William Wilberforce, a white abolitionist of the time 'a hypocrite'. Cugoana was the first African to demand abolition of slavery.

An English Heritage blue plaque in honour of Ottobah Cugoano was unveiled in 2020 in Schomberg House in Pall Mall, London, where he lived when working for the Cosways.

A similar description comes from that other renowned slave Olaudah Equiano (1745 – 1797), who as a child was sold into slavery in Benin, modern day southern Nigeria. He was transported to the Caribbean where he was purchased by lieutenant Michael Henry Pascal of the Royal Navy and brought to England. He was sold again but had a relatively quiet life before becoming an ardent abolitionist.

What these stories tell us defies description. Imagine for a moment the risks that were inherent in walking down the street, going shopping, visiting one's neighbour or as children, even playing outdoors. There was the ever present danger of indiscriminately being kidnapped. People across swathes of Africa must have lived their daily lives in perpetual fear of their fellowmen. While it may be viewed as grossly immoral to kidnap anyone for slavery, to do so with children and pregnant women shows a total absence of any morality. – an amoral people who sent their sons and daughters, fathers and mothers into slavery. Here was the anti-thesis of Cicero's dictum 'salus popluli suprema lex esto'. While individuals and groups of slave catchers may have worked independently, there was likely to be the over-arching reach of the rulers and kings who acted against the interest of their populations and in pursuit of personal enrichment. It was, what one could only describe, a form of 'malignant corporate complicity' in a heinous crime.

The Nigerian journalist Teddy Nwanunobi wrote that buying and selling human beings was a part of many African cultures and that Africans still respect their ancestors who were involved in the trade.

Anthony Hazard, assistant professor in the Ethnic Studies Department at Santa Clara University, spoke how the slave trade In Africa degenerated into an arms race as African rulers and kingdoms sold their people for European weapons and other merchandise.

Of Africa, by Africa, for Africa

Nat Amartefio wrote that the African role in the slave trade was deliberately submerged in the 1870's – 'The chiefs and peoples decided, 'All right, we will not talk about it.' They created a mythology that we were innocent bystanders whose land was raped by Europeans.' Now one may attempt to appreciate the words of President Abdoulaye Wade who found any talk of reparations deeply offensive. One cannot forget the role of the African; one can even conclude that the African was the prime mover in the entire African slavery project. Remove the African and the slave trade would not have evolved as it did. Europeans needed labour for the plantations in the West Indies and America. It would have been a daunting task, risking large scale war, for them to have invaded the continent from the coast of West Africa where they were with their ships, guns and merchandise. They needed the locals; they could not have done what they did without the support of the African – call it 'contributory culpability' on the part of the African.

It is useful to understand where the slaves from Africa originated and where they went to. From the Trans-Atlantic Slave Trade Database in Emory University in USA, the historian David Eltis has shown that most slaves to the US came from Senegal, Congo, Gambia and Eastern Nigeria. They also came, in relatively lesser numbers, from Sierra Leone, Ivory Coast, Guinea Bissau, Liberia etc. In total they constituted only 3% of the Atlantic slave trade who went to the USA. The vast majority of slaves from the Atlantic slave trade went to Brazil and the Caribbean. Half the population of Brazil is black and about 55% of the population has African ancestry. Brazil accounted for about 40% of slaves from Africa while the British were responsible for 18.5 % who ended in the Caribbean. 14.4% or 1.8million slaves died en route . But it remains important to appreciate that even the Portuguese did not introduce slavery to Brazil; it existed in the country prior to the arrival of Portuguese.

Compared to the 12.5 million slaves transported across the Atlantic ocean, it is estimated that 80 million slaves were transported by the Arabs over 1200 years. A little known fact is that this aspect of slavery carried a mortality rate of 85% during transportation ; 85 in every 100 slaves died or 60 million slaves.

It has been claimed that Africa was depopulated by Muslim slave hunters. This is what prompted the anthropologist Tidiane N'Diaye to claim that their activities were 'tantamount to genocide'. It is also not infrequently asked why there is silence on the subject while there is active discussion amounting to accusation of Europeans as being wholly responsible for the plight of Africa. One is compelled to ask why this is so as it is also tantamount to a from of discrimination and wilful blindness, considering the extent of slavery across Africa and in the East coast of the continent, where the European had no or little influence on slavery. While one would agree with Haklem Nankoe and Margo Ramlal- Nankoe that 'Slavery is historically one of the most oppressive relationships, and is widely considered the ultimate form of human deprivation', one would disagree that slavery was predominantly a phenomenon among, what they call, 'dominant western empires'. No – African slavery existed for millennia and exists to this day in one from or another. In the book *'Debating the Contesting Memories of Slavery Between the Continental Africans and the Africans of the Diaspora',* author Ousseynou Sy writes that there is a 'memory décalage' based on how slavery is lived and taught across the Atlantic. The author makes a plea for better dialogue and the need to accept shared responsibility for slavery. And what is particularly worrying while being enormously relevant today is the view that Africa has 'unlearned many of the lessons of that tragedy'.

'a moment of madness'

Prior to Robert Mugabe becoming leader of Zimbabwe, the country was run by the white supremacist, Ian Smith, as Prime Minister in what was then called Rhodesia. He unilaterally declared independence (UDI) from Great Britain in 1965 and maintained white minority rule. This was a process that was doomed to failure and was at odds with what was happening elsewhere in the world. Other nations were progressively moving away from colonial rule by becoming lawfully independent with in the Commonwealth of Nations. The last time a similar situation happened was the American Declaration of Independence in 1776. To try and overcome UDI, a bitter and bloody liberation war was fought against the regime of Ian Smith by Robert Mugabe and Joshua Nkomo. It is estimated that 27,000 people die during the conflict.

In the two decades of 1960-1980, preceding Mugabe's ascent to power and during the time of UDI, Zimbabwe, which was then called Rhodesia, still produced significant amounts of wheat and maize and contributed to 6% of Africa's total maize production. This was about 400,000 tons more than was consumed by the country. Hence Rhodesia was a net exporter, despite the liberation struggles of the time.

Africa has some of the most fertile, arable land in the world and is capable of becoming the bread basket of the world. Zimbabwe is no exception to this generalisation and has a proven track record of agricultural productivity. But when white minority rule ended it was noted that 4000 white farmers owned 70% of the land in the country. Mugabe's policy was to redistribute the land to the local population on the declared premise that the white man had stolen the land. But it appears that redistribution was done without a coherent plan to retain and even enhance existing food production.

Winter in Zimbabwe is from June to August. Temperatures are in the low 20's centigrade and there is seldom a frost at night. Freezing temperatures do not occur. It is the time of the year when farmers are preparing for the harvest of wheat in September. After the wheat harvest they prepare the soil for growing maize, which is the main crop and staple diet. But in the winter of 2002 the government of Robert Mugabe passed a surprising order. Farmers were ordered to stop farming forthwith. People were starving, but harvesting wheat was banned immediately. About 3000 white farmers had to cease work immediately. Any work carried with it the risk of imprisonment for two years. Farmers were ordered to leave their farms. In a peculiar act of generosity, farmers were allowed to stay in their homes for 45 days, after which they had to leave with the minimum of their possessions. When they eventually left their farms and homes there were police and local militia manning roadblocks. This was to ensure that the farmers left with the bare minimum of their possession and without taking away anything of value.

War veterans went on the rampage seizing and setting fire to farm buildings and assaulting white farm owners. This was one of the fastest national land reforms in history. The result was that white farm owners with knowledge and skills were largely eliminated from the food production process in the country. Not only did they suffer but also black workers on the farms lost their jobs and often their homes and only source of income. Many on both sides died in the process. In the end Zanu – PF supporters, the political party of Robert Mugabe, took control of land, farms, machinery etc with limited or no knowledge of commercial farming methods. The result was the wholesale collapse of food production. The economy of the country plummeted by 50% of what it was in 1980. However, some would claim that the 250,000 smaller farms that followed from the land grab became successful small producers, although this view is not shared by many and this remains the subject of much scrutiny. Prior to colonisation, Rhodesia was historically a land of subsistence farming - smallholdings by people living on the land. Colonialism introduced commercial farming practices, bringing in skills and market techniques to help increase productivity. When seed was distributed to farmers, much of it was not sown but consumed. Failure of crops were then blamed on drought and this became the dominant excuse for the failure of agriculture across large tracts of the country. Hunger and the overwhelming need of people to feed themselves was not recognised by those in power.

Zimbabwe produces wheat and maize which are major staple foods in the country and in Africa generally. Information from the Food and Agriculture Organisation (FAO) of the United Nations shows how production of these two commodities have declined. Wheat production in 1981 in Zimbabwe was about 2.5% of the total wheat produced by Africa. This figure declined significantly to less than 0.25% of Africa's total production in 2010 and stayed at that level until 2013, the period for which data was available. In the case of maize where Zimbabwe produced almost 7% of Africa's production, this dropped to 5% in 2001 and to the even lower level of 1% in 2013. Two significant events are important during this period- the late President Robert Mugabe won elections in 1980 and remained in power for thirty-seven years. The second event was land reform which was instituted in 2001. Land reform is acknowledged as having accelerated the decline in food production. From being self-sufficient in food, Zimbabwe has become a net importer of staple foods. Land reform was brought in largely to placate war veterans who were seen as a threat to the government of Mugabe.

No country has deliberately destroyed its most productive sector and thereby delivered its population to poverty. While this was happening those close to the ruling ZANU-PF party were enjoying the trappings of power. It did not seem that politicians and assorted party functionaries were working for the benefit of the population, but only for themselves.

Many would claim that the single largest tragedy that befell Zimbabwe was the policies enacted by the late Robert Mugabe. At the outset and soon after he came into power, Mugabe welcomed whites and promised to work together for a better and more inclusive Zimbabwe. This policy did not last long. He was, in retrospect, interested in consolidating power, and creating a single party state. To this end the differences between him and his co-revolutionary, Joshua Nkomo, worsened. Mugabe was from the Shona tribe while Nkomo was from the Ndebele tribe. The history of Rhodesia and Zimbabwe is littered with mistrust between Shona and

Ndebele. Despite much effort by Nkomo to bridge any differences between him and Mugabe, he was ultimately unsuccessful. It was largely due to Mugabe's first wife Sally Mugabe (nee Sally Hayfron) that Joshua Nkomo was appointed to the cabinet of Robert Mugabe as a minister without portfolio. It was said that when Robert Mugabe was offered a seat in the office of Tanganyika's Prime Minister, Julius Nyerere, Mugabe refused saying 'If you think I'm going to sit right where that fat bastard just sat, you will have to think again'. Things appeared to have come to a head in 1982 when Nkomo was accused of plotting a coup against Mugabe and the government. Mugabe said that 'ZAPU and its leader, Dr Joshua Nkomo are like a cobra in a house. The only way to deal effectively with a snake is to strike and destroy its head.'

Despite having worked together to bring an end to white rule in Rhodesia, Robert Mugabe had a deep mistrust of Joshua Nkomo and other dissidents who were a threat to his rule. His goal of a one-party state with him as leader for a long period of time was not assured, as he saw it, unless dissidents and especially the Ndebele were effectively dealt with. Nkomo's revolutionaries belonged to ZAPU while Mugabe's support was from ZANU. Both sides collaborated in the bush war against the regime of Ian Smith. ZANU were from the Shona tribe while ZAPU were predominantly Ndebele. It was not possible to assimilate the armies of both factions under a single command structure.

The fierce rivalry between the two communities dates back over a century when the Ndebele people were pushed north by what is now the northern part of South Africa. This resulted from action by Boers and Zulus. The Ndebele settled in what is now Matebeleland. The Matabele kingdom was founded by Mzilikazi. The Ndebele pushed and encroached on the Shona tribe and their lands. This is a remembered series of historical events. History has generated a deep rooted hostility that is still strong and accounts for the frictions in society, which were accentuated and taken advantage of by Mugabe. Joshua Nkomo for his part tried to talk down the tribal divisions that were later to play a part in the violence that occurred in the early 1980's.

Joshua Nkomo who was a member of the Cabinet of Robert Mugabe was removed from office in February 1982. Nkomo was accused of trying to overthrow Mugabe.

'a moment of madness'

In early 1983 the government of Robert Mugabe launched a war against Ndebele civilians. The word 'Gukurahundi' comes from the Shona language meaning 'the early rain which washes away the chaff before the spring rains'. There is little doubt that this operation was instigated by Robert Mugabe and conducted with help from the North Korea trained Fifth Brigade of the army. The historian Dr Stuart Doran claims that the operation against Ndebele was conceived of by Mugabe as early as 1983 i.e. within 3 years of majority rule and the Lancaster House agreements that were held in London. There appears to have been a need and a desire to eliminate all opposition to Mugabe 'within five years of independence'.

Elections were due to be held in 1985 and ZANU -PF wanted to eliminate any real or imaginary opposition on its way to election victory and the eventual creation of a single party state. The International Association of Genocide Scholars (IAGS) concluded that more than 20,000 people were killed in the years of the war, although others would put the figure at a much higher level. This figure does not take account of the thousands who ran away in fear and those who went into exile.

It is interesting to know what the Fifth Brigade was and where their loyalties were. In 1980, Mugabe arranged with the then President of North Korea, the late Kim Il Sung, to train a brigade with the purpose to 'combat malcontents'. The outfit was almost exclusively made up of people loyal to ZANU. The first commander of the Fifth Brigade was Perrance Shiri, who was a cousin of Mugabe. The unit had its own uniform, communication equipment etc. and was separate from the army. The Fifth Brigade was directly accountable to the Prime Minister, Robert Mugabe. It is therefore difficult to accept any view other than Mugabe being aware of and intimately involved in what the Fifth Brigade was doing. Training of the brigade was completed in September 1982 when it was then apparently ready for action. Time was not wasted by Mugabe in following up on what he had earlier said ' dissidents should watch out'.

The aim of the 'Gukurahundi' was to root out those who were supporters of Joshua Nkomo, the Party ZAPU and its armed wing, ZIPRA- Zimbabwe Peoples Liberation Army. These organisations were supported by the Ndebele- who were therefore the perceived 'malcontents'. People were indiscriminately seized and either sent to re-education camps or executed. Executions were held in public with the victims being made to dig their own graves in the presence of their families. Some were marched to a local place for e.g. a school or to a hut where they were burned alive. It became easy for the government to divert attention from these atrocities by claiming them to be lies or stories circulated by foreign agencies. Shona civilians were also killed in reprisals by dissidents, although in much smaller numbers.

Mugabe had denied any involvement with 'Gukurahundi' except to say in 1999, after the death of Joshua Nkomo, that what happened in the early 1980's was a 'moment of madness'. One may interpret in this comment a faint admission of responsibility, but Mugabe never repeated it. In an interview with South-African TV, Mugabe blamed 'Gukurahundi' on armed bandits and members of ZAPU with involvement of a few soldiers from the Fifth Brigade. But his colleagues have said that 'not only was Mugabe fully aware of what was going on but the Fifth Brigade was acting under Mugabe's explicit orders.' In 1987, the Zimbabwean Defence Minister at the time, Enos Nkala, who was involved in the operation, described it as an 'eternal hell'. He was clear in placing responsibility squarely on Robert Mugabe. However, regretting his own role in the pogrom he admitted that he would never do it again.

Moven Mahachi who was Defence Minister of Zimbabwe in 1997 was the first government official to apologise for the torture and killing of civilians by the Fifth Brigade during the 'Gukurahundi'.

Some would claim that the Gukurahundi was probably the worst stain on the rule of Robert Mugabe. At his inauguration as Prime Minister of the new Zimbabwe in 1980, the then President of Tanzania, Julius Nyerere said to Mugabe 'You have inherited a jewel in Africa. Don't tarnish it.' Mugabe who was a teacher, placed great emphasis on primary and secondary education which was not only available free but was also made compulsory. There was much hope in the air as he preached racial harmony and respect for the law. Unfortunately events in the following decades of his rule were anything but fair and harmonious. Not only did he not achieve what he aspired to, but he destroyed the foundations that would have helped him accomplish what he set out for his country. He destroyed the hopes and lives of all but a select few in Zimbabwe – those of his inner circle and loyalists. As Fadzayi Mahere, a Zimbabwean lawyer and politician wrote – 'It will take many years to undo the system of

'a moment of madness'

repression that he created and which continues under his successor today'. It will also take many years to return to a semblance of pre-Independence national and personal prosperity.

Another less murderous but nevertheless notorious project was Operation Murambatsvina or 'Move the Rubbish'. It was given a respectable name by the government – 'Operation Restore Order'. While it was portrayed by the government as a scheme to eliminate illegal housing, overcrowding and the spread of disease, one cannot ignore that it occurred in 2005 after elections. It was seen as a way to punish the urban poor who dared to vote for the opposition, the Movement for Democratic Change(MDC). Because of the extent of upheaval that followed, Zimbabweans refer to the project as 'Zimbabwe's tsunami'. About 750,000 people were rendered unemployed and about 350,000 people were displaced. People lost land which they had bought after Independence. About $15 billion of assets were taken away from their owners with the loss of land, leading to a reduction in agricultural production. Almost 300,000 homes and 700,000 small businesses were destroyed.

'Gukurahundi' followed a pattern that has occurred throughout human history. One has only to recall Hitler, Stalin, Mao Tse Tung and Pol Pot to realise the effect that one group of people have had on other groups, who suffered and died in their millions and in painful ways. These crimes against humanity were perpetrated by human 'monsters' as Simon Sebag Montefiore described in his book with the same name, detailing the mass cruelty inflicted on people. 'Gukurahundi' was followed by other 'moments of madness' in Zimbabwe which were designed to serve one purpose only – the grip of Robert Mugabe and ZANU on the country and to strangle, at birth if possible, any opposition to the single party rule envisioned by Mugabe and his supporters. In 2005, ZANU was nearly defeated in elections by the Movement for Democratic Change which had a large urban base. Operation Murambatsvina was the instrument for social engineering, used to neutralise or to attempt to eliminate the MDC. It was an example of violent, murderous gerrymandering. In a study done in Bulawayo, it was found that half the men who were affected by the operation died within 2 years. The United Nations called Operation Murambatsvina a crime against humanity. But that is all it was – hollow words which were of no comfort to those who suffered. No one was held to account.

Moven Mahachi (1948 – 2001) succeeded Enos Nkala as Defence Minister of Zimbabwe. He was close to Robert Mugabe but Nkala claimed in 2009 that Mahachi was assassinated on the orders of his friend Mugabe because Mahachi was opposed to the looting of diamonds in the Democratic Republic of Congo. This is a story in itself, but it is appropriate to recount here to understand the anarchy that prevailed at the heart of government in Zimbabwe, where the ordinary citizen was of little consequence.

Committee26 was an interesting yet powerful organisation if only for its membership and the ease of access to those who held the reins of power in the country. The Committee of 26 comprised persons of the Zezurus and Korekore tribes. Zimbabwe, like in most of Africa, is a mixture of people from different tribes. The dominant population is from the Shona group who inhabit mainly the eastern two -thirds of the country, which includes the capital, Harare. The Shona are made up of several groups - Karanga, Korekore, Zezuru, Manyika, Ndau and Rozwi. In the 19th century these various groups were amalgamated under the name of Shona. The Shona are the largest ethnic group in the country. About 20% of the population are Ndebele who live in the western parts of Zimbabwe.

Robert Mugabe was Zezuru and the heads of the various sectors of the defence forces of the country were Zezuru. The Chief Justice of Zimbabwe was a Zezuru as were many ambassadors who had been posted to foreign capitals. It is safe to say that all dominant positions and even the majority of the work force were Shona. In this sense the government and important administration and the judiciary in Zimbabwe resembled that in Rwanda under President Juvénal Habyarimana who was Hutu and all important posts were held by Hutus.

Enos Nkala said 'Moven was an outsider in an exclusive club – the Committee of 26 – comprising politicians of Zezurus and Korekore origin. This committee of looters have controlled the army, the police, the CIO and it appears that they went to war for self enrichment. To them Mahachi was an obstacle in their quest to amass wealth using the pretext of fighting a prolonged war to restore sovereignty in the DRC, just as they had done in Mozambique during the military campaign against Renamo. So he had to go'

Zimbabwe Defence Forces (ZDF) entered the war in the Democratic Republic of Congo (DRC) in August 1998. Almost half of the entire military of Zimbabwe was deployed in the mission in the DRC. Mugabe proclaimed that involvement in the DRC was necessary to support the 'democratically elected government' of the DRC. This followed the murder of the then President of the DRC, Laurent Kabila. Mugabe, no doubt, had other objectives too – one of which was to display his pan-African credentials to the world.

Robert Mugabe was interested in portraying himself and Zimbabwe as true Africans devoted to the cause of Africa. Some would say that he was side-lined in his prominence by Nelson Mandela who was at the time the dominant leader in Africa, if not in the whole world. Mandela had displayed a deep moral conscience to the world. He was almost a latter day Mahatma Gandhi. When he met with the widow of the late Hendrik Frensch Verwoerd (1901-1966), who was Prime Minister of South Africa from 1958 to 1961, it was a powerful symbol of forgiveness and a clear message to his black electorate that this was the beginning of forgiveness and co-existence, on the journey to a new South Africa. Verwoerd was considered the architect of apartheid. Following his release from captivity in Robben Island and his meeting with Betsie Verwoerd, Mandela sent a signal of reconciliation to his nation and to the world which had not hitherto witnessed such a magnanimous gesture. Mugabe was overshadowed not only by Mandela but also, as he perceived, President Yoweri Musoveni of Uganda. The comparison between Nelson Mandela and Robert Mugabe throw up stark differences despite their similarities as freedom fighters in the cause of black emancipation. Their respective countries, South Africa and Rhodesia, were governed by the minority white populations to the exclusion of blacks, from involvement in civil society. Mandela worked from the outset to heal wounds, encouraging reconciliation and unity not only between blacks and whites but also among blacks. Robert Mugabe preached reconciliation and unity at the outset of his ascent to becoming Prime Minister of Rhodesia which became Zimbabwe. But this did not last long, for he had a 'debt' to pay to those who engaged with him in the 'Bush War' and other attacks against the white regime of Prime Minister, Ian Smith. Unlike Mandela, Mugabe was ready to excuse away the excesses of blacks – especially those close to him. While preaching unity he practised separation not only between blacks and white but also between the Shona and Ndebele tribes.

Involvement in the war led to decline in Zimbabwe's economy. People in Zimbabwe suffered as a result of the military venture in to the DRC. Nelson Mandela pleaded against it and advised that the matter should be resolved by negotiation, rather than by war.

The other interest of Mugabe and the Zimbabwean military in the foray into the DRC was the quest for diamonds. It was estimated that since the start of the war in 1998, the DRC had lost $800 million per year to fraudsters, smugglers etc who illegally exported diamonds that were mined in the DRC. The DRC is in the top ten largest diamond producers in the world with 3,700,000 carats of diamonds being produced annually. Russia is the highest producer with 23,000,000 carats annually and Botswana is the second highest producer with 16,000,000 carats per year.

Zimbabwe was involved in the illegal production, looting and trade of diamonds. These diamonds are called 'blood diamonds'. What are blood diamonds or 'conflict diamonds'? The United Nations defines conflict diamonds as ' …..diamonds that originate from areas controlled by forces or factions opposed to legitimate and internationally recognized governments, and are used to fund military action in opposition to those governments, or in contravention of the decisions of the Security Council.' The diamonds are often produced by forced labour of men, women and children. They may be stolen during transport or shipment, by organised gangs using significant military hardware. These are diamonds mined in areas of conflict or war and traded with the sole purpose of financing war or to enrich warlords. They constitute a form a 'state capture' where the benefits of mining ventures are denied to the population of the country and are retained by a select few. Therefore diamonds mined in conflict areas like Sierra Leone, Angola, Ivory Coast, to name a few would come under this label.

To overcome the trade in 'blood diamonds' the DRC registered with the Kimberley Process (KP), also called the Kimberley Process Certification Scheme (KPCS), which registers legitimate diamond production, export and sale. KP, which was established in 2003, is a multilateral trade arrangement which aims to prevent 'conflict diamonds' from entering the market. Countries that sign up to KP have to implement safeguards on the production and shipment of diamonds and need to certify that exported diamonds are 'conflict free'. KP requires national legislation and transparency. It also obliges members to only trade with other countries and organisations which are included in the KP scheme. Simultaneously, public were warned to ensure that when they purchased diamonds, the product was the result of a legitimate process as recognised by the Kimberley Process and are certified as such.

Take the case of Charles Taylor, the ex- President of Liberia. He was tried for crimes against humanity during the war in Sierra Leone which started in 1991 and ended in 2002. He supported the Revolutionary United Front (RUF) which was a rebel group in Sierra Leone. Charles Taylor was accused of crimes against humanity by abducting children and adults, using women and young girls as sex slaves, rape and the mutilation and murder of civilians. Children and women were forced into labour or to become fighters in the liberation struggle. Foday Sankoh (1937 – 2003) was the head of the RUF, which used amputation and mass rape of women and children. He was indicted for crimes against humanity, but died before he could be sentenced.

Charles Taylor was rewarded with 'blood diamonds or 'conflict diamonds' by Sierra Leone. He gifted a blood diamond to the British model, Naomi Campbell, although she was not aware of the origin of the stone. Charles Taylor was indicted for crimes against humanity and serves his time in Her Majesty's Prison Frankland in County Durham, England. Charles Taylor was the first head of state to be sentenced for crimes against humanity since Karl Donitz at the Nuremberg trial. Donitz was briefly head of state in Germany after Adolf Hitler and immediately prior to Germany's surrender at the end of World War Two.

What is seldom appreciated is that at the time the Sierra Leone war commenced, another 'blood diamond' war had raged in Angola under the late Dr. Jonas Savimbi. It is estimated that rebels had laundered close to $10 billion in the illicit trade in diamonds over a decade.

The Final report of the Panel of Experts on the Illegal Exploitation of Natural Resources and Other Forms of Wealth of the Democratic Republic of the Congo, makes interesting reading. It acknowledges the role of the Zimbabwe Defence Forces (ZDF) in ensuring security for the government of the DRC. But under the guise of seeking payment for the military services rendered, senior officers of the ZDF 'enriched themselves from the country's mineral assets.' The ZDF did not stop there. It established business links with contracts, to continue Zimbabwe's economic interest in the DRC. For e.g. contracts were signed between the ZDF and the DRC before the former left the diamond centre in Mbuji Mayi, DRC in August 2002. To conceal its interest in the DRC, there was a proposal to set up a joint Zimbabwe- DRC company in Mauritius.

Zimbabwean and DRC politicians were able to control trade in the important minerals cobalt, copper, germanium and diamonds in the Government-controlled areas. The Panel was informed that in the three years preceding it's report about $ 5billion was diverted from the mining sector of the DRC to private companies, defrauding the DRC in the process. There was no compensation paid to the DRC.

in June 2002, the Panel heard of a secret joint diamond operation in Kalobo in the DRC, run by a company called Dube Associates. Colonel Tshinga Dube works for Zimbabwe Defence Industries. Zimbabwe Defence Industries had links with an illegal arms and diamond dealer.

A United Nations Report by a Panel of Experts on the Illegal Exploitation of Natural Resources and Other Forms of Wealth of the DRC in 2004, named the current President of Zimbabwe, Emerson Mnangagwa, as one of many officials, military personnel and corporate entities that looted diamonds and other mineral from war- torn DRC. The other important Zimbabweans were General Vitalis Musunga Gava Zvinavashe and Air Marshal Perence Shiri.

These are examples of massive and sustained 'state capture' of resources in African countries.

If all this happened in the DRC, one is left to ask what happens to gold mines in Zimbabwe. Zimbabwe is a small gold producing country with about 6000 gold deposits having been exploited in the country. Gold extracted in Zimbabwe can only be sold legally to the Reserve Bank of Zimbabwe and its approved and bank-owned partner, Fidelity Printers and Refiners (FPR). Sellers are paid 70% of the selling price in US dollars and the rest in Zimbabwean dollars. But because the latter fluctuates widely and has much less buying power it does not come as a surprise that there is an illicit trade in gold.

In the Gaika Mine in Kwekwe the paper, *Zimbabwe Today*, reported on 25th April 2019 that large scale looting of gold occurred at night. Police and security personnel who had been deployed there were reported to be part of the looting operation. The American economist, Steve Hanke, said that the situation in Gaika was an example of how property rights were being eroded by government officials and the ruling party, Zanu-PF.

On 6th October 2020, Henrietta Rushwaya was arrested at Robert Mugabe International Airport with six gold bars in her possession, with an estimated value of US $ 366,000. She was 56 years old at the time, and was the head of Zimbabwe Miners Federation and was at one time the President of the Zimbabwe Football Association. She was due to board a flight to Dubai.

Henrietta Rushwaya has a coloured history. In 2007 and 2008 she faced charges of theft of Football Association funds. In 2009 she was accused of football match-fixing in what was dubbed 'Asiagate'. She had organised a trip by the Zimbabwe national football team to Malaysia. It was found that matches had been fixed. Investigations revealed that she was the 'core central point' in the scam. Players, journalists and referees were involved in the deceit. In another match-fixing scandal, this time called 'Limpopogate' in 2016, it was found that she had been involved in match-fixing for the preceding six years. She was arrested in 2016 after it was alleged that she was involved in a match-fixing ring run from South Africa. She was dismissed form the Zimbabwe Football Association in October 2016 after being found guilty of the charges that she had been accused of.

In May 2021, Tashinga Nyasha Masinire who was Henrietta Rushwaya's driver was arrested in Oliver Tambo airport in South Africa with South African Rand 11 million worth of gold in his possession. The report *'Zimbabwe's disappearing gold: the case of Mazowe and Penhalonga'* describe these two cases as probably being 'a tip of an iceberg pointing to massive organized criminal activities in the sector.' Gold is smuggled to Dubai, China, India and other Asian countries.

Artisanal gold miners contribute to about 60% of gold produced in

Zimbabwe, with this group of miners producing 4-5 Kg of gold every month.. This activity is a source of income for, in excess of, one million Zimbabweans. And through this income they are able to support millions more dependants. Politicians and their associates try to seize control of as much of this gold production as possible. They do this by using middlemen called 'runners' who would source money to purchase gold and to pay the artisans directly. By such covert means, the rich and powerful remain hidden and distant from the dealings. One company, Betterbrands Mining Company, is owned by Pedzisai 'Scott' Sakupwanya, also known as Scott. He has connections to the President of Zimbabwe, Emerson Mnangagwa, and other high profile politicians. He sources millions of dollars from these persons and also from the Central Bank of Zimbabwe to help buy up gold. In the districts of Mutare and Mutasa in Zimbabwe, Zanu-PF is responsible for issuing licences for gold mining.

It is said that the control of artisanal mining by the ruling party has led to increase in gold smuggling. Additionally of course are the risks associated with mining - at least 200 deaths have occurred over a period of three years.

Looting of diamonds had been going on for many years in the mines at Chiadzwa. Local people and artisans who worked the mine had been protesting for an equally long period about the loss of revenues from mining in the region. With the continuing loss of funds to the treasury and therefore to the country at large, the finance minister in the unity government at the time, Tendai Biti, asked 'where the diamond money was going, as it was not finding its way to treasury'. He questioned Zanu PF cabinet ministers as diamond revenue was not entering the fiscal system in Zimbabwe in 2011 and 2012.; he implied that there was massive looting as a cause of the loss of income. It must be mentioned that Biti was from the Movement for Democratic Change (MDC) and was not a member of the majority Zanu-PF party.

In 2013, participants at a conference dealing with looting in Chiadzwa diamond mine expressed frustration and anger at what was happening and that they were being systematically disposed of their rights. War veterans claimed only a 20% share in diamond mining. They claimed that there had been no equitable wealth distribution since 1980 when the country overcame white minority rule. These are people who suffered, fought and died during the various battles waged by blacks against minority white rule of the late Prime Minister, Ian Smith. That they had been dealt unfairly after all their sacrifices must remain as a damming indictment of majority black rule. Chinese, who had been contracted to operate the mine had not involved locals. They had used Chinese nationals, depriving the locals who had the same skills. In an amazing statement from the director of finance and administration from the ministry of Mines and Mining Development, Olivia Mwamlowe, said 'we can see that people are concerned very much. It's very clear people want to be empowered…. We will consolidate these views…' There surely cannot be a better version of political waffle than this. 1980 was the landmark year for the oppressed blacks of the then Rhodesia. They saw and were promised a new dawn for themselves and their children where a brighter future was possible. The promised dawn never visited the vast majority of people in Zimbabwe. Zanu PF National Secretary for Administration, Didymus Mutasa, confirmed that high-ups in Zanu -PF party were involved in illegal diamond dealing, depriving the country of much needed foreign currency. He went on to say that President Mugabe was aware of what was happening and an investigation was under way!

In eastern Zimbabwe in the district of Mutare, the government took over control of diamond mines. Several thousand prospectors were attracted to the area. However, it is reported that the military tortured and killed many hundreds of the panners. How the Kimberley Process permitted diamonds from Mutare to be exported as legitimate was a matter of concern because of the documented human rights abuses.

Years later Biti claimed that between 2015 and 2019, Zimbabwe had lost public funds to the value of US$ 24 billion. Giving a virtual talk titled 'Unpacking the Pandemic of Corruption - Whither Zimbabwe' he went on to imply that the country had suffered a financial haemorrhage.

In 2020 Tendai Biti was arrested and produced before a magistrate in Harare for referring to a Russian woman as an 'idiot'. The story would be hilarious anywhere else but not in Zimbabwe. Biti was in court representing a client in relation to the Harare Airport Road scandal. Biti is the chairperson of the Parliamentary Public Accounts section and MP for Harare East. The case involved corruption in the construction of the road.

The Russian woman, Tatian Aleshin, was associated with businessmen linked to President of Zimbabwe, Emmerson Mnangagwa.

The US State Department protested about the case saying that democracy cannot survive when public servants are at risk when they expose corruption. The case took a further twist in July 2021 when Biti was summoned to appear in court despite having to self-isolate after coming in contact with a Covid – positive person. The prosecutor asked for an arrests warrant to be issued.

Another matter of concern is the extent of environmental pollution caused by illegal and legal activities. It was reported that the Chinese in Zimbabwe were not only looting gold but also other minerals. A report by Southern Africa Resource Watch (SARW), which is based in Johannesburg said that in 2013, Chinese workers were flouting environmental laws by allowing poison to leak into the Ngezi River. This is a threat to river life and to people who live and work downstream of the river. Chrome is illegally mined and washed on the banks of the river. They also work with little regard for employment laws. Workers do long hours, with limited pay and holidays. Protective clothing is not provided, with people working in their own clothes.

The 2021 report on Cartel Power Dynamics in Zimbabwe states that in the diamond sector alone billions of US dollars' worth of precious stone are not accounted for. The value of these is placed at US $ 15 billion. Domestic activity by cartels has resulted in billions of dollars being transferred from citizens to the private sector and to corrupt public sector officials. According to Transparency International, corruption involves the police, transport, education, local government etc. This is a loss of US$ 1 billion each year. It is estimated that about US$ 1.5 billion of gold leaves the country illegally each year, with most going to Dubai. In one instance it is reported that a single corrupt payment to a crony of Robert Mugabe led to a 23% devaluation of the Zimbabwe currency. This amounts to 23% theft from the public.

So what happened to Zimbabwe after 1980? How did the expected new dawn materialise. Has the average citizens of Zimbabwe, especially the blacks, benefitted from the change from UDI to democracy?

Robert Mugabe died in a hospital in Singapore on 6th September 2019, almost two years after he was ousted from power by Emmerson Dambudzo Mnangagwa. His public funeral was held in the National Sports Stadium in Harare. It was in many respects a sad occasion. Of course it was a day of immense sadness for his immediate family. But the sadness was also seen in the half empty stadium – a venue which could hold 60,000 persons. The long suffering people of Zimbabwe spoke on that day in silence by not attending the funeral of their liberator – the man who freed Rhodesia from white minority rule. It was supremely ironic that Mugabe sought treatment in Singapore and died there. In the early years of his rule, Zimbabwe had a good health system, that catered for all. He progressively destroyed the health service of the country and consigned many to unnecessary suffering and early deaths. Leaders who do not seek treatment in their own country speak volumes of their health system. Here was a man who promised much, yet delivered little. His only saving grace was that he improved the education system in the country as was befitting of a teacher by profession, which is what he was. But, even in the field of education, his achievements have in the end been futile. What happens to the many unemployed graduates who are left to roam the streets in desperation. Education is a means to a glorious end as much as it is a beginning. In Zimbabwe, for many young people it is a journey that promises much but ends in tears of disappointment. Those who can afford to do so, seek greener pastures abroad. The vast majority who are left behind in the country, constitute an unpardonable loss of human capital; something that no country could afford to be without.

Politics and the military are closely intertwined in the fabric of Zimbabwe. The involvement of the military goes far before 1980, when Rhodesia gained freedom form minority white rule and became Zimbabwe. Having been involved in the liberation battles in the previous decades, it is no surprise that the military would have considerable influence in the government of Zimbabwe and in close links with President Mugabe. However, one would have expected this relationship to have declined as Zimbabwe moved to a democracy, with accountability of the military to the government of the day. This did not happen; the military retained its stranglehold on the country and could not or would not, as in most democracies, be subjugated to the views and decisions of government. In 2008, General Constantino Chiwenga, who was commander of the armed forces, said that he would not salute a political leader of Zimbabwe who did not have credentials of the liberation wars. This was uttered a good 28 years after the country became Zimbabwe and reflected that the country was still not a fully functioning democracy with transparency and accountability as its guiding principles. A similar view was echoed prior to the Presidential elections in 2002 when the heads of the army, air force and the police said that they would expect any elected President to observe the objectives pursued during the liberation struggles. What were these objectives? Naturally, one would have expected there to be better democratic governance and equality for the majority black population. It was often claimed that the military was needed to stabilise the country and help improve the economy. But, as has been seen, the military contributed to the continued violence against blacks during the Mugabe Presidency. Besides, one would not expect the military to have the skills to manage the economy and help propel the country to prosperity – which it had during the times of President Ian Smith. There is an obvious and distinct difference between how South Africa managed its transition form the brutal apartheid regime to a democracy, without recourse to it's armed forces.

If one were to reconcile the foregoing with the words of Robert Mugabe in 2008, one discerns a clarity of intention – a clear and pervasive desire to maintain power, with a brutal elected dictatorship masquerading as democracy. This was a time when the MDC, under Morgan Tsvangirai, was progressively eroding the unbridled power of Mugabe. Tsvangirai was on the threshold of becoming Prime Minister of Zimbabwe. Mugabe said 'Zimbabwe is mine …..I will never, never, never surrender' in response to calls from some African leaders to relinquish control of the country. 2008 was also the year when the country was gripped by a cholera epidemic. Botswana, Kenya, Senegal, Zambia and Nigeria among others had called for Mugabe to step down. Jendayi Frazer who was US Assistant Secretary of State for African Affairs said that there was 'a complete collapse right now' in the country and that Mugabe needed to step down. These calls were made with the interest of Zimbabweans foremost. The economy had collapsed and the country was enduring an epidemic of cholera. The UN said that over 20,000 people were affected by the disease and 1,123 people had died at the time of reporting.

'a moment of madness'

Mugabe's response to all of this was obstinacy, to say the least. He threw down the gauntlet to his African neighbours saying 'I won't be intimidated. Even if I am threatened with beheading, I believe this and nothing will ever move me from it ..... Zimbabwe belongs to us, not the British'. He said that none of Zimbabwe's neighbours 'have the courage to order a military intervention....................What would they come and do militarily here? All that they would come and really pose is a threat to our stability'. He was able to articulate these views in the secure knowledge that his African counterparts were often themselves liberation fighters or revolutionaries and would not have the moral authority to do any thing about Zimbabwe, other than to call out from the side-lines. The President of Senegal, President Abdoulaye Wade, said that while he had supported Robert Mugabe in the past, he was now of the opinion that Mugabe was the cause of Zimbabwe's problems. This begs the inevitable question – why did it take so long for anyone in Africa to realise that the dire situation in Zimbabwe was solely due to Robert Mugabe? What was the African Union doing while Zimbabwe burned?

The response of Morgan Tsvangirai to Mugabe's invitation to be sworn in as Prime Minster was to remind the former of the continuing violence and intimidation and that 42 members of the MDC had been abducted.

It is instructive to compare the implications of the words 'never, never, never' uttered by Mugabe and the same words which were said by Nelson Mandela following his release from imprisonment, and in an entirely different context. Mandela was pleading for unity and a breakdown of racial barriers. On the contrary, Mugabe perpetuated not only differences between blacks and whites, whom he saw as colonialists, who made the majority black population dispossessed of their land. But he also divided blacks between 'us', the ruling minority and 'them', the proletariat. One speaker's words of unity were only words for another to sow the seeds of division.

The cholera epidemic which lasted from 2008 to 2009 led to 98,585 cases being reported and 4,287 deaths. The latter figure refers to the number of recorded deaths from cholera; the final death toll may have been much higher. An insight to why the epidemic occurred reflects on the state of the country at the time. Several factors conspired and coalesced at the time to precipitate the epidemic. The Zimbabwean currency had collapsed and inflation was 2,000,000% in July 2008. 'Jampanga', a slang word used to denote violence, was deployed in Zimbabwe during the take over of white-owned farms. The case of the Ron Smart's Lesbury farm in Rusape district in East Harare helps to illustrate the causes of collapse in the economy and the resulting hyperinflation. The Smart family had been farming in the region for about 80 years. The family had paid for, owned and farmed about 8000 hectares of land with the local Tandi people. His workers and he had a good relationship. In 2000, he agreed with the government to surrender ownership of 90 % of the land he owned, without compensation. He was left with 700 hectares, of which only 120 hectares were arable. However jampanga or 'direct action' had an adverse effect on his remaining holding of land. Bishop Trevor Manhanga, who was Presiding Bishop of the Pentecostal Assemblies of Zimbabwe and President of the Evangelical Fellowship of Zimbabwe and his associates arrived in 2016 and claimed part of Rob Smart's remaining land. With the help of his supporters and the aid of the local Police, Bishop Manhanga, damaged the household, which led to the Smart family leaving in fear. His family which included his grandparents, his son and daughter-in-law and their sons had to go into hiding. They dared not approach the farm for fear; they had witnessed the destruction of their home and its contents. The Smarts had built a local school which was attended by about 200 children; it is no surprise that the school closed. All the workers lost their livelihoods and their only incomes. They lost their means of support for their families and extended families. Like in Rwanda, one encountered yet again, the malign influence of the church.

The other contributory factors to the cholera epidemic were political and make sobering reading. There was a near complete collapse of public health. Poor water and sanitation that led to the epidemic were undoubtedly due to policies implemented and driven by politics. It is interesting to go back to the cholera epidemic of 1854 in London, when John Snow identified the 'Broad Street water pump' as the source of the epidemic. Since then it has been recognised that clean, safe water and proper sanitation are important in preventing the faeco-oral route in transmission of the germ causing cholera, Vibrio cholerae. Faeco-oral implies transmission from infected stools of one person to the mouth of another through food or poor public health, which in turn depends on a supply of clean, uncontaminated water. What do these basic facts in public health bear on the epidemic in Zimbabwe? In parliamentary elections in 2005, the MDC made strong gains against ZANU-PF, the party of Robert Mugabe. This was followed by a reversal of the 1976 Water Act by Zanu-PF. Water now came under the control of the Zimbabwe National Water Authority. This was also the time when the government deployed 'Operation Murambatsvina' or 'Drive Out Trash' in the Shona language. This led to 700,000 persons being displaced; it was no coincidence that the majority of these people had supported the opposition MDC. The effect of this change in control of water also led to two other consequences – the one was a loss of income to the local authorities in the areas which had lost control over water. These monies would have been used for maintaining critical infrastructure including the provision of safe water. The second was a positive financial gain to Zanu-PF who could use the monies gained for military spending at a time when it was short of funds. But the most malign affect of all was the government's control of another aspect of people lives; it had politicised food supplies during famine in the past; now it was doing the same with water.

Cholera epidemics had occurred in Zimbabwe in 1991 and 2002; nothing had changed. In effect the situation as regards public health had worsened. 'Operation Murambatsvina' affected the areas of Glenview, Chitungwiza, and Dzivarasekwa, which also happened to be the areas most affected by the epidemic. Doctors in Zimbabwe were told that the situation was 'under control'; Robert Mugabe initially declared that there was 'no cholera in Zimbabwe'; the head of the United Nations Office for the Coordination of Humanitarian Affairs in Zimbabwe, Georges Tadonki was dismissed.

What happened to food production during the time Robert Mugabe was President?. Rhodesia was considered the 'bread basket' of Africa. Was this a correct description of food production in the country prior to the time of Mugabe? What is, after all, a 'bread basket'? it is generally considered that a country should be able to produce enough staple food to meet the needs of its citizens. Over and above this requirement, a food commodity must be exported in significant quantities to be considered a 'bread basket' or 'food basket'. A review of information from the Food and Agriculture Organisation (FAO) of the United Nations for the year 1961 shows that Rhodesia produced far more maize than the rest of Africa from 1961 to 1981. This excess production continued until 1983 when it dropped off, only to return to levels in excess of previous levels in 1986/1987. From then on it continued to drop until 2013. Wheat production in Rhodesia was low until it began to pick up in 1977 and continued to remain at higher than African levels until 1984. From 1984 wheat production dropped below African levels and has stayed the same until 2013. Zimbabwe's maize production declined with the Land Reform Program of 2001.

In absolute numbers, the amount of maize produced was about 2 million tons per year in 2000. This dropped to about 500,000 tons in 2014; a 75% drop in production. This figure increased to 730,000 tons of maize in 2018. Wheat production was about 300,000 tons in 2001 – this dropped to 10,000 tons. There were reductions in production of coffee, milk and beef. All these significant reductions in food production led to the need for food imports which, in some years, increased seven fold compared to 2000.

The World Food Program stated that for 2020 Zimbabwe's population was 15.6 million with 63% living below the poverty line. Half the population or 7.7 million faced food security with 27% of children having stunted growth.

In 2020, in apparent recognition of the errors of the Mugabe administration, Zimbabwe's government entered into an agreement to compensate about 4000 white farmers at a cost of US dollars 3.5 billion. This money would be paid in tranches and is not for land lost, which does not attract compensation, but for infrastructure that was lost or destroyed. It was generally understood at the time of the announcement, that this was a move to try and improve the economy rather than a genuine act of contrition. However, as always, the devil was in the details. Zimbabwe at the time had an inflation rate of 200%, with scarcity of food and fuel and an unemployment rate running at 90% of the population. Healthcare workers for eg were pressing for an improvement in their salaries and the government was under immense economic pressure. It said that the compensation would be funded by 30 year bonds on international markets.

'a moment of madness'

What is the legacy of Mugabe and the fate of Zimbabwe since 1980? UDI and white minority rule of Ian Smith was abhorrent. But what was it replaced with? Yes, as has frequently been claimed, there is now, in Zimbabwe, freedom in the sense that there is a policy of one man and one vote. The black man has a right to vote and choose his government. But does that mean much when vast numbers of the population are suffering under the burden of food shortages, unemployment, very high fuel cost etc? One man, one vote or democracy of a kind is synonymous with hyperinflation. And what would one call their new rich masters – those who siphoned off money from gold and diamonds or who provided themselves with several farms and the profits from them? There is still now a stark dividing line – where formerly it was between white and black; now it is those in power who are rich and have access to the best society has to offer and the rest – almost 90% of the population – who have to eke out an existence as best they could. They are the people who dared to hope when the country became Zimbabwe.

After independence Robert Mugabe started with great promise. Unfortunately this honeymoon period was short lived. He reduced his country to penury. He replaced white oppression of blacks with black repression of a much more severe and violent form.

Cecil Rhodes gave his name to this green, verdant and potentially rich land. Rhodes is naturally hated here but what has the black man provided to his fellow beings? How do Zimbabweans abroad who clamour for statues of Rhodes and others to be taken down square their convictions with what is happening in their homeland? Does the man on the streets of Harare really care if a statue of Cecil Rhodes in England comes down or not?. He is hungry, wants a roof over his head and the ability to provide for his family. Is it too much to ask Zimbabweans to return to their homeland and bring the skills needed to build a better society for all their compatriots? That would be the finest example of reparation – if only it would happen. To paraphrase, 'Zimbabwe's green and pleasant land' needs them, needs the technocrats and other skills to build a vibrant democratic society.

The change of Presidency in Zimbabwe has, however, not changed the arrangements for constitutional governance in the country. Events in Zimbabwe have tarnished the reputation of the African Union (AU) which has been trying to deal with the epidemic of coups on the continent, where there have been 169 coups between 1950 and 2010. That a faction within a government can use its power to seize control of the military, which is then used to oust a sitting President, however unsavoury, is a persistent threat to constitutional governance in the continent. The AU has tried to confront this issue by reinforcing the principle of constitutional government and equally constitutional changes in its 'African Charter on Democracy, Elections and Governance'. However it appeared to turn a blind eye to the events in Zimbabwe despite its apparent dislike for the continuation of Mugabe or the accession of his wife to the Presidency.

STOMPEI, NKOSI, 'DR.BEETROOT'

The late South African novelist and philosopher, John Langalibalele Dube (1871 – 1946) founded the South African Native National Congress (SANNC) in Blomfontein in 1912. John Dube was educated in America having gone there with missionaries from his native South Africa. The purpose of the SANNC was to unite the various races in South Africa, blacks, whites and coloured, as a united nation with the same rights and freedoms for all. Its objective was to end the system of apartheid. Dube wanted all South Africans to unite; his was not a militant party. The SANNC eventually became the African National Congress or ANC as it is popularly known.

Dube emphasised the importance of black unity. He was influenced by Booker Taliaferro Washington (1856 – 1915). Washington was a teacher, orator and advisor to US Presidents. He emphasised the need for self-reliance. He taught skills to backs at the Tuskegee School that he founded. This is now Tuskegee University. Washington hoped that if blacks were active participants in society as diligent individuals, they would eventually be accepted as equals with whites.

The United Democratic Front (UDF) in South Africa was a group of political activists, teachers, students, clergy, civic leaders etc which was formed in 1983. Its initial purpose was to fight against the Tricameral Parliament of South Africa of 1984 which was established to include whites, Indians and coloured people of the country. Blacks were excluded from the Tricameral legislature. The aim of the UDF, as it was of the

SANNC, was to free the country from racism in all its forms. It had as its slogan 'UDF unites; Apartheid divides'. In this slogan alone one could envisage a single non- racial nation inclusive of all its people. The UDF was a non-violent organisation which embraced churches, student activists, trade unions and the like. In 1990 when the government of South Africa released the ANC and the Communist Party of South Africa from being banned, the UDF became irrelevant and it decided to close, which happened in August 1991 at its last meeting in Johannesburg.

It is said that the Mandela United Football Club (MUFC) was formed by the wife of the late Nelson Mandela, the late Winnie Mandela, in 1986. Its members were her bodyguards and who also served as her private security force, who were often violent towards other blacks. The phrase 'Football Club' is a misnomer for the Club was not involved in playing football or soccer. The group of thugs who were members of the club helped run a kangaroo court in Winnie Mandela's house where perceived traitors were violently dealt with. Punishment for traitors invariably took the form of severe beatings. But punishment did not always end there because houses were set on fire, grenades were thrown and various other vicious activities took place. It is reported that the Club carved the words ' Viva ANC' on the bodies of two teenagers.

To help stem the activities of the Football Club, some residents of Soweto organised and formed a 'Mandela Crisis Committee'. The Committee met with Winnie Mandela and urged her to curtail the violence perpetrated by the members of her Football Club. A Methodist Minister who was involved with the Committee had allowed some youth the stay with him. One of the youth had his throat cut with a pair of garden shears, by members of MUFC. The activities of the MUFC were so extreme that even the ANC, which at the time was in exile, condemned the Club. Nelson Mandela, who was in prison, called for the Club to be disbanded. Winnie Mandela resisted this advice from her husband. Even the ANC intervened to try to encourage her to disband the MUFC. After the end of apartheid, The Truth and Reconciliation Commission of South Africa (TRC) wrote that Winnie Mandela was 'politically accountable for the gross violations of human rights committed by the Mandela United Football Club'.

Winnie Mandela's predilection for violence is evident in a speech she gave on 13th April 1986 in Munsieville when she encouraged necklacing, where a person is burned alive with a rubber tyre filled with petrol placed around the neck and which is set alight. She went on to say 'we have no guns – we have only stones, boxes of matches and petrol,….together, hand-in-hand, with our boxes of matches and our necklaces we shall liberate this country.' It was a horrendous way to punish and a gruesome death for the victim. It was also called 'Kentuckying' or the victims were given 'Kentuckies' for the superficial resemblance of the dead victim to that on the menu of a Kentucky Fried Chicken diner.

The author Lynda Schuster wrote in *'A Burning Hunger: One Family's Struggle Against Apartheid'* that 'necklacing' was one of the 'worst excesses' during the years of the apartheid struggle. Many, even within the African National Congress (ANC), were appalled by what they had heard and seen. It was very seldom used against white people but was frequently used against blacks who were thought to be collaborating with the apartheid regime and against black policemen. The problem with the policy of necklacing was not only that it was an evil, vicious act but also that it left anyone and everyone in the black community vulnerable, traumatised and fearful. One had only to be suspected and summary justice would intervene. This was mob rule at its worst.

What is necklacing? Wrapped around the victim's neck and body would be motor vehicle tyres full of petrol. Usually the weight of the tyres would prevent the victim from running away. But for good measure their hands would be tied behind their backs, usually with barbed wire which inflicts the first pangs in the cascade of severe pain. The tyres would then be set alight. The victim would be engulfed in flames. Melting tyre produces boiling black tar which adheres to the skin, frying it. The whole act is gruesome as the helpless victim falls, writhing and screaming in pain. Silence finally descends to this barbaric spectacle when the victim is unconscious or more likely dead. The burning and roasting of human tissue continues. Such medieval brutality is as painful to describe as it is an unpardonable act of human evil.

Archbishop Desmond Tutu who was vehemently opposed to 'necklacing', once ran in to a crowd who were about to set a person alight. He covered the person with his arms and his body and protected him from certain death. He found the practice appalling and said 'If you do this kind

of thing, I will find it difficult to speak for the cause of liberation,..........
if the violence continues, I will pack my bags, collect my family and leave this beautiful country, that I love so passionately and so deeply.'

It was claimed that necklacing prevented people collaborating with the police. It is said that between 1984 and 1987, 672 people were burned alive, with half of them killed by 'necklacing'

Although anti-apartheid activists had been burning people alive for years, the first person to die by 'necklacing' was Tamsanga Kinikini, a politician, who was accused of corruption. The first 'necklacing' to be filmed was that of Maki Skosana, whose neighbours thought had been responsible for an explosion that led to the death of anti-apartheid activists. She was a 24 year old single mother to a 5 year old son who was grabbed while attending a funeral and burned alive while the cameras rolled. Her head was crushed with a rock and shards of glass inserted into her vagina.

Her case was heard by South Africa's Truth and Reconciliation Commission to which her sister, Evelina Puleng Moloko, gave evidence. Skosana was found innocent of the accusation of being a police informer and of being responsible for the death of the 'comrades' in the booby-trapped hand grenade incidents.' The Commission concluded that she was a pawn in a bigger struggle and a 'scapegoat'

The ANC President at the time, Oliver Tambo, appeared to condone it when he said "We don't like necklacing, but we understand its origins,' justifying it on the brutal oppression by the white South African government and the resulting provocation of blacks. But it was primarily used against blacks in such an indiscriminate and blanket fashion. It was an instrument of terror against blacks.

'Necklacing' was used in South Africa in 2008 against immigrants. In 2015 five teenage boys were 'necklaced' following a brawl in a bar and in 2018 two men were similarly killed after being suspected of theft. What is frightening is that 'necklacing' had become institutionalised and increasingly justified, as from this comment - 'It reduced crime.......people are scared because they know the community will rise against them' This is the worst from of citizen's justice – no investigation, no jury, no judge!

'Necklacing' is not unique to South Africa. It is known to have occurred in Haiti, Brazil and Sri Lanka among others.

Stompie and Nkosi were two black youth from South Africa. Both of them died young, but in different circumstances.

Let's start with Stompie. He was variously called Stompei Moketsi Sepei, Stompei Seipi and James Seipi. Let's refer to him as Stompie. He was born in 1974.

As a teenager Stompie Moeketsi Seipi (1974 -1989) was an activist in the UDF. He participated in street protests against apartheid from the age of 10 years. He was jailed for his activities and earned the reputation of being the youngest political prisoner; he spent his 12th birthday in jail without trial. When he was 13 years old he was expelled from school. Stompie also joined the Mandela United Football Club.

On 29th December 1988, the youngsters, Kenny Kgase 29 years, Pelo Mekgwe 20 years, Thabiso Mono 20 years and Stompei Moeketsi who was only 14 years old, were abducted from the church mission house of the Methodist church minister, Reverend Paul Verryn in Orlando East, when Verryn was away. Late on the night of January 7th 1989, Kenny Kgase, escaped from Winnie Mandela's house and arrived at the church, looking heavily bruised and pleading for protection. Stompei was murdered on 1st January 1989. Stompei was a leader for a band of about 1500 child activists aged between 8 years and 14 years.. When he died, Stompei who was accused of being a police informer, was only 14 years old. Stompei had a reputation as a child activist and as a leader. He was only 13 years old when he arrived in the church house. He had already been in police custody and it was feared that he had 'turned' ie. he had become police informer. All four of the youths were taken to a back room in Winnie Mandela's house where they were interrogated and beaten. They were accused of having had sex with the priest, Paul Verryn. Winnie Mandela used her fists to assault the youths. They were beaten so severely that Pelo said 'our eyes could not see for a week'. Stompei got a form of special 'treatment' called 'breakdown'. This is where the victim is thrown up in the air three times and allowed to drop on to the concrete floor. Perhaps his smaller size made Stompei an easy target for this vicious type of assault. While the bigger three boys were ordered to clean up and leave the house, attacks on Stompei continued. He confessed to having let out about four of his colleagues. This may have been done under duress and due to the viciousness of the assault he endured and which may have broken him. Whatever the reason for his confession, Stompei's fate was sealed at that moment. Dr. Abu-Bakr Asvat was invited to examine Stompei. His decision was that Stompei had brain injury. This decision by Dr. Asvat appeared to have sealed the fate of not only Stompei but also of the doctor. On the night of Sunday 1st January 1989 Stompei's throat was cut by Jerry Richardson, one of Winnie Mandela's bodyguards, and he was left to die in a field. His body was found near Winnie Mandela's home on 6th January 1989.

Katiza Cebekhulu who was at one time a member of the MUFC, was preparing to testify to the TRC that he had seen Winnie Mandela stab Stompei Moeketsi in the jacuzzi of her home in Soweto. However, on the eve of his appearance before the TRC he disappeared. He was whisked off to Zambia and was imprisoned by the then President of Zambia, Kenneth Kaunda, at the behest of the ANC. He was held in Lusaka Central Prison without charge. This is an interesting and worrying aspect of events. In his book, *'Katiza's Journey'*, Fred Bridgland describes the State Papers that the then President of Zambia, Frederick Chiluba had. These papers suggest that the person behind the kidnap of Cebekhulu was none other than Nelson Mandela himself. He had requested the then President of South Africa, Oliver Tambo, to request President Kenneth Kaunda of Zambia to accept Cebekhulu so that he was not available at the time for Winnie Mandela's trial. Kenneth Kaunda denied having had a conversation with President Oliver Tambo of South Africa, rather the message from South Africa was dealt with by officials of both Presidents. Kaunda maintains that he worked on trust, that the request had originated from Nelson Mandela. The British MP Emma Nicholson arranged for Cebekhulu to be released from prison and brought to the United Kingdom.

Fred Bridgland claimed that the ANC, who knew much about Winnie Mandela and her activities vis-à-vis her Football Club, was keen to conceal as much information so that planned reconciliation could proceed. It was a case of realpolitik which did not serve justice and left many to continue to suffer without closure, following the loss of their loved ones. In this sense, the Truth and Reconciliation Commission hardly lived up to its name; truth was concealed and reconciliation was prevented.

As Bridgland writes, Cebekhulu was jailed in a country where he had not committed any crime. He would have disappeared from the face of the world if it had not been for the inquiries of Emma Nicholson. She was in Zambia observing the general election at which Kenneth Kaunda and his party, the United Independence Party (UIIP) lost to Frederick Chiluba and his Movement for Multi-Party Democracy (MMD). When Chiluba became President of Zambia he invited Nicholson for discussion. This was her opportunity to inquire about Cebekhulu. Chiluba assured her that there were no political prisoners in Zambia but said he would check and get back to her. The same day Chiluba called Nicholson and invited her to a meeting saying 'I've found your man....You've got to come and listen to what he's got to say'. It is amazing, even to this day, that the President of South Africa, the whole judiciary in South Africa and many others conspired to pervert the judiciary, subvert the rule of law and thereby consign someone to die in a foreign prison with no offence having being committed and without due judicial process. In so doing they also attempted to deny closure to the victims of the MUFC generally and of Winnie Mandela in particular.

The TRC concluded that Winnie Mandela had 'initiated and participated in the assault' of the boys. She was found to have lied in claiming that Stompei had gone to Botswana. The Commission found that at best she had not acted pro-actively in preventing the death of Stompei. What is interesting was that during the hearings of the Commission, Archbishop Tutu literally begged of Winnie Mandela to apologise for the death of Stompei and for her role in it. Stompei's mother, Joyce Sepie, was left confused as she could not get straight answers to questions about her son's death. She said 'I do not care, because God knows the truth'.

Take the case of Finkie Msomi who was only 13 years old when she died. She died of burns in her aunt's house which was set on fire. It is written that Winnie Mandela watched the house burning from her car. Why did an innocent teenager like Finke have to die in such horrific circumstances? She was at her neighbour's house when it was firebombed by members of MUFC. It was described as a reign of terror by MUFC in Soweta at the time.

Winnie Mandela's bodyguard, Jerry Musivuzi Richardson, told the Truth and Reconciliation Commission (TRC) which was set up at the onset of black majority rule in South Africa, that Winnie Mandela had ordered the kidnap and murder of persons in the 1980's.

On 12th November 1988, Corlett 'Lolo' Sono who was 20 years old and his friend Siboniso Anthony Shabalala who was 19 years old, were abducted and killed. Sono's father said at the time that he saw his son in the company of Winnie Mandela and that he had been badly beaten. Winnie Mandela identified Sono as a spy and told Sono's mother that she was 'taking him away'. Both youth were stabbed before being killed. Their bodies were buried in a field close to Winnie Mandela's house. The journalist Fred Bridgland had covered African affairs for over thirty years. He found details of the events that led to the death of the two youth. It was reported that both had been at the home of the so called 'chief coach' of the MUFC, Jerry Vusi Richardson, on 9th November 1988. This was also the day when Richardson's home was raided by police, with the two boys present at the time. Their presence in Richardson's home at the time was sufficient evidence to label them as spies and they had to be disposed of. Jerry Richardson told the TRC that he and a colleague stabbed Sono and his friend Sibuniso Tshababala. However Winnie Madikizela-Mandela told the TRC that she did not know the two youths and that allegations of her involvement in the killings was 'rubbish'. Nicodemus Sono, father of Corlett Sono, told the TRC how Winnie Madikizela-Mandela had brought Cortlett to his home at gunpoint. When the father pleaded for his son to be released and left at home, she accused him of being a spy and that the 'the movement' would make the final decision about his son.

At the TRC, the mother of Sibonisa Shabalala, Nomsa Tshabalala, said that her son called her from Winnie Mandela's house before the call was cut off. The view of the TRC was that "'Madikizela-Mandela must accept responsibility for the disappearance of Lolo Sono and Sibusiso Tshabalala'.

At the TRC, Sono's stepmother pleaded with Winnie Mandela asking for his remains so that he may be given a decent burial.

The bodies of the two activists were exhumed in 2013. They had been buried in Avalon Cemetery in Soweto.

Piers Pigou, who was a senior investigator for the TRC, said that there was enough prima facie evidence to prosecute Winnie Madikizela-Mandela for the disappearances of Sono and Tsabalala. Pigou expressed concern why these disappearances had not been vigorously investigated.

The head of the TRC, Archbishop Desmond Tutu, begged Madikizela-Mandela for the truth, pleading with her, 'If you are able to bring yourself to say something went wrong, I beg you, I beg you, I beg you,……..You are a great person and you don't know how your greatness would be enhanced if you were to say: 'Sorry, things went wrong. Forgive me.' But she viewed the Commission with contempt and did not consider herself to be accountable for events during the momentous years of the struggles against apartheid.

It is estimated that about 21,000 people were killed during the apartheid struggles, some by the ruling white regime while others died at the hands of other black activists.

Many of those who died in the 1970's and 1980's during the struggle against the white minority regime in South Africa are buried in Avalon Cemetery, which is located in south west Soweto and has the graves of several hundreds of thousands of persons. It is a place to remember and honour those who died during the race struggles. Sadly, it is also the place where blacks who were killed by fellow blacks are also buried.

Dr.Abu Baker Asvat was a medical graduate from East Pakistan, which is now Bangladesh. He and his brother, Ebrahim, who was also a doctor, lived and worked in Soweto. He took over a Surgery at MacDonald's Farm in Soweto, which was commonly known as Chicken Farm. He and Ebrahim worked long hours, often into the night, to make the Surgery profitable. With a population of about 60 families at the beginning, they built the health service caring for people, working as counsellors and bringing the people food, blankets in winter etc. He also started a crèche and a soup kitchen for children. He would visit people in their homes if they could not come to his clinic. He did not decline to seen anyone if they could not pay.

When Winnie Mandela was confined to Brandfort in May 1977 by the South Africa security services, her physician was Dr.Yusuf Veriava. During one of Dr. Veriaya's trips to see Winnie Mandela he was accompanied by Dr. Asvat. Subsequently, Dr. Asvat saw her frequently and took over her medical care. Dr. Asvat became her physician and from all accounts had a good relationship with her.

Dr. Asvat was invited by Winnie Mandela to examine Stompei Moeketsi after he had been badly beaten up by members of the MUFC. On asking what happened to Stompei, he was told by Winnie Mandela that Stompei had fallen from a tree. He was in such a critical situation that Dr. Asvat advised that he be taken to hospital. This did not happen. Dr.Asvat was told by Winnie Mandela not to mention to anyone what he had seen and to maintain that he had not treated anyone. Asvat was so concerned that Stompei would die, that he discussed the matter with the Mandela Crisis Committee which comprised of Cyril Ramaphosa, who is the current President of South Africa. Nothing came of this meeting.

At that crucial moment, Dr. Asvat became a marked man. He had knowledge and he was therefore a risk to Winnie Mandela and to others in the MUFC. Thereafter, he had a premonition of his impending death. He would visit patient's in their homes in an agitated state, late in the day, wait a few minutes and depart. He once drove with a flat tyre because he was so afraid of stopping. He felt and knew that he was being followed. It was reported that, one day at prayer, he held his hands the wrong way; such was the sate of his agitated mind. Arsonists attempted to burn his house in 1986 and in 1988 men tried to attack him with knives, while on another occasion someone pointed a gun at him. On 27th January 1989 two men registered with his Practice and had an appointment to consult with Dr. Asvat in the afternoon. One shot him in his consultation room. He was 45 years old when he died. The link between Dr. Asvat's death and Winnie Mandela is one that has many theories. It is unlikely to be resolved. Some would maintain that she had a motive and a strong one at that, to eliminate Dr. Asvati, despite him being her personal physician and her friend. In accordance with his Muslim faith Dr.Asvat should have been buried the same day that he died. But the family agreed to a request for his body to be buried the next day in Avalon cemetery. Over 10,000 mourners attended his funeral. One mourner said 'The black community viewed Asvat as part of the black community. We buried him as an African'.

An old pensioner said 'The killers thought they were killing the doctor, but they did not know that they were really killing a people that is already down on its knees. His death has left us dead too.'

Following the murder of Dr. Asvat, police arrested Zakhele Mbatha and Thulani Dlamini on suspicion of murder. The reason for murder was alleged to be robbery, although none of Dr.Asvat's possessions or any of the contents of the Surgery had been stolen. The allegation gained credence that Dr.Asvat was killed because he had witnessed what happened to Stompei, especially the refusal by Winnie Mandela to take the boy to hospital. In November 1989 Mbatha and Dlamini were sentenced to death for murder. However, in September 1991 this sentence was set aside and the two were sentenced instead to life imprisonment for murder.

The TRC heard from both Mbatha and Dlamini that they were paid Rand 20000 by Winnie Mandela and that she provided them with a gun. Although Mbatha told the police that Mandela was responsible for the murder, this was discounted by the police. In October 1998, the TRC concluded that there was not enough evidence to link the death of Dr.Asvat to Winnie Mandela or to the MUFC.

In 2018, Mandla Mandela, who was an MP and the grandson of Nelson Mandela by his first wife Evelyn Mase, called for the murders of Stompei Moeketsi and Dr.Asvat to be re-examined and especially the role of Winnie Mandela in them.

With regards to these killings, only Bishop Desmond Tutu stands tall – morally towering and standing above all the other leaders of the ANC

The life and eventual death of Johnson Nkosi is in a different league. He too was a South African boy.

In 1976, the phrase 'Gay Bowel Syndrome' appeared in the medical and lay press. The phrase was introduced by the American physician, Henry L. Kazal and his colleagues to describe a series of sexually transmitted infections of the anus and the rectum that they had encountered in their specialist practice dealing with diseases of this region of the body, also called proctology. It was noted that most of the patients were homosexual. The causes of the infection in the rectum and anus were syphilis, gonorrhoea, herpes etc., which were thought to be transmitted through anal sex.

Some time in the early 1980's, Dr.Jim Curran was invited to peer review an article prior to publication in the *Morbidity and Mortality Weekly Report of the Centre for Disease Control* (CDC) in the USA. The paper described the cases of five gay men who had pneumonia in Los Angeles in the United States. They were all young and varied in ages between 29 and 36 years and had a rare form of pneumonia caused by a germ called *Pneumocystis carinii*. Infection with this germ is unusual in persons with normal immunity and who were not known to suffer from immunodeficiency.

Dr. Jim Curran was eventually made the head of the team in CDC which was set up to investigate the matter.

This was followed by instances of people with haemophilia who died, who had received blood transfusions or transfusions of blood products. This led the team to suspect that a virus was involved and was being transmitted between people.

The same *Morbidity and Mortality Report* of 1981 also reported 26 cases of patients with Kaposi's sarcoma in the preceding 30 months in the USA. This was diagnosed in homosexual (gay) persons who varied in age from 26 to 51 years with a mean of 39 years. This was a relatively large number of cases compared with the 50 cases of Kaposi's sarcoma in New York between 1970 and 1979. Kaposi's sarcoma is a rare type of cancer and arises in the skin. Dr. Curran wrote 'I realised that it was a virus that really separated us and a virus that none of us could have known about.'

The phrase' Gay Bowel Syndrome ' was soon considered derogatory and discriminatory of the homosexual population. In his book, *'Smearing the Queer: Medical Bias in the Health Care of Gay Men'* by Michael Scarce, which was published in 1999, the author described the bias against men which was inherent in the phrase. It conveyed the impression of gay persons as perverse 'and menace to society for all to behold'. He went on to describe the image given of gay men as 'physiological foreigners and aliens—tropical, animalistic, primitive, and unsanitary'. The discrimination and public attitudes at the time were widespread that some, for e.g., the Cracker Barrel chain of restaurants in the USA refused to employ gay men. Simply put, there was no Gay Bowel Syndrome. It was a catch-all phrase to describe anorectal conditions that could occur in anyone, but had a pre-ponderance in the homosexual population. It would take some years before the nature of acquired immune deficiency and its viral origins would be understood.

The years that followed the onset of AIDS (Acquired Immune Deficiency Syndrome) were a worrying and frightening time - alarming for many people, worrying for health care agencies and governments across the world. What was this strange illness? And how could it be conquered? There were many parallels with Covid, except that the latter was not sexually transmitted. And all the time it was spreading.

AIDS probably started in the 1970's and had been silently spreading, so that by the 1980's it had spread across the world, with infected persons in all five continents. The two predominant features were patients with pneumonia due to the germ Pneumocystis carinii and the unusual cancer presenting on the skin named Kaposi's sarcoma. In 1981 Pneumocystis carinii chest infection was found in intravenous drug users. By 1983 AIDS was found in females who had sexual intercourse with males who had AIDS. This showed that the virus could be transmitted from person to person by sexual contact; it is primarily a sexually transmitted disease.

In October 1985, the then famous Hollywood actor, Rock Hudson died of AIDS. He was homosexual and was one of the first major celebrities to die of the illness. On November 7, 1991, the legendary basketball player, Earvin 'Magic' Johnson declared publicly that he was positive for AIDS and that he was retiring from the game. He was one of the first sports personalities to publicly declare his infection. Johnson denied that he was either gay or bisexual. He attributed his acquiring AIDS to his life style and impressed upon the public that 'heterosexuals needed to know that they, too, were at risk'. The British singer Freddie Mercury of the Queen was diagnosed with AIDS in 1987; he died of the illness in 1991.

The first treatment for AIDS, Zidovudine, was licensed for use by the Federal Drugs Agency (FDA) of the USA in 1990. It had been developed in 1987 and had been used since then. Various drugs have been developed and are in use now in, what is known as, HAART or Highly Active Anti-Retroviral Therapy.

The Joint United Nations Program for HIV/AIDS (UNAID) was set up in 1993. UNAID declared in 2013 that deaths from AIDS had fallen by 30% from its peak in 2005. In 2002, AIDS was the main cause of death in sub-Saharan Africa. Between 2010 and 2018 there was sharp drop in new infections with AIDS in South Africa.

The continent of Africa was significantly affected by AIDS. It had the highest population of people with AIDS and other blood borne viral diseases like hepatitis.

It was against this backdrop of an evolving and spreading AIDS epidemic in South Africa that Nkosi Johnson was born on the 4th of February 1989. His mother was HIV positive and his birth name was Xolani Nkosi. Nkosi was born with AIDS. As his mother was too ill to look after him, Nkosi was adopted by a public relations officer in Johannesburg, Gail Johnson. His name was changed to Nkosi Johnson.

In 1997 when he was eight years old, a local school refused his admission on the grounds of his infection with AIDS. This event caused a huge backlash in South Africa about, of all matters, discrimination. Here was a population that had been systematically discriminated against for a long time under apartheid because of the colour of their skin, and now, there was an instance when a young child was being discriminated against because of his health. This event forced changes to anti-discrimination laws in South Africa, so that children would not be prevented from attending school because of their health.

Why did Nkosi Johnson have to suffer and not be able to get the treatment that he needed, the treatment that would have allowed him to live and possibly lead a normal or near-normal life? To live as long as possible was his cherished desire. He sometimes wished he was born white because what was happening to him did not happen to white boys.

The first case of AIDS occurred in South Africa in 1982. This was a homosexual man who contracted the illness while in California, USA. The first death from AIDS in the country occurred in 1985. By 1990 there were about 100,000 persons with AIDS in South Africa. In 1991 a new organisation, the National Advisory Group, Networking HIV & AIDS Community of Southern Africa (NACOSA) was established to help develop and set out a coordinated response to the emerging health crisis. This was the time of apartheid. In 1994 following elections, a national unity government was formed with Nelson Mandela as President. Dr.

Nkosazana Clarice Dlamini-Zuma became Minister of Health, under whose stewardship combatting AIDS/HIV became a leading health project for the government. In 1995, Cape Town hosted the 7th annual International Conference for People Living with HIV and AIDS.

In 2005 the Medical Research Council of South Africa said that the daily death toll in the country from HIV/AIDS was 600. South Africa had one of the highest number of people infected with the virus in 2005 - over 5 million. Despite these startling figures the government was slow to act in controlling spread of the infection and in providing access to effective treatment, which by then was emerging, for the virus infection. A National AIDS policy had been formulated in 1996.

The context of HIV/ AIDS in Africa and South Africa in particular is relevant here. In 2002 Alan Whiteside, Robert Mattes, Samantha Willan, and Ryann Manning wrote the *Afrobarometer* paper No: 21 titled *'Examining HIV/AIDS in Southern Africa through the eyes of ordinary South Africans'*. They described the significant difference in impact of HIV/AIDS compared to say, cholera. In the case of cholera, the illness progresses quickly and death occurs early. This has a devastating effect on families and communities, associated with a fear of the illness. This is in sharp contrast to HIV/AIDS. HIV silently spreads without causing much in the way of acute symptoms at the outset. Whiteside and colleagues described an almost 5-year lag period between the onset of HIV and the development of AIDS, with illness and death. This 5-year lag is a golden period for the virus and the infection to spread in the community. Hence the impact is felt much later. The authors continued in stating that even when AIDS deaths occur in large numbers, many people do not see it as a priority. Because there are other immediate needs for people that adversely affect them, if not immediately attended to. These are jobs, housing, crime, security etc. Whiteside and co-authors even concluded that people may be prioritising their immediate needs for food, shelter etc above the HIV/AIDS epidemic. HIV/AIDS was a 'largely invisible killer'.

Governments, however, look, as indeed they should, at the evolving picture of the HIV/AIDS epidemic and beyond the parochial needs and priorities of families and communities.

The South African National Aids Council (SANAC) was established in 2000. All the organisations dealing with the epidemic had as their guide the need to prevent, treat, educate, research etc within the framework of human rights and respect for human dignity. One of the first, and in retrospect significant, events in regards to AIDS in South Africa was the envisaged production of a musical called '*Sarafina II*' in 1995. This was billed as a means to increase AIDS awareness in the country and was the brainchild of the then Minister for Health, Dr. Nkosazana Dlamini-Zuma. The vice–President of South Africa at the time was Thabo Mbeki. Dr. D-Zuma said that the European Union (EU) would fund production of the musical, but the EU denied any knowledge of it. The EU had set aside the sum of South African Rand 48 million for AIDS awareness in South Africa. An EU representative said 'We have itemised budgets, listing every project and activity that the EU is supporting. An AIDS theatre project is not among them, nor was *Sarafina II* ever discussed with us as it would have had to be.' At a later inquiry Dr D-Zuma said that the plan proposed for *Sarafina II* 'was conveyed to the EU, but the EU responded – '*Sarafina II* was not included as such in the contract.... This contract requires agreement in advance, particularly on changes on budget allocations. Specific tendering and other procedures have also to be followed. In the case of *Sarafina II* no prior request was received by the (*European*) Commission.'

There was no clear bidding process to fund the project and when this became apparent Dr. D-Zuma suspended the bidding process. Dr.D-Zuma claimed that a mystery donor would fund *Sarafina II* for the cost of $ 4 million. However, she repeatedly refused to name the donor as would be required in any proper tendering process. This would have been especially so, if the government of South Africa claimed to be transparent in its dealings and in accountability to Parliament and therefore to the public. It became known that the donor had requested anonymity and to declare the donor's name publicly would have amounted to a breach of confidentiality. Eventually the government of South Africa had to bear the full cost of the play.

The debacle over *Sarafina II* exposed the conflicts in the government at the time. Loyalty appears to have carried a greater premium than the truth. Dr.D-Zuma was not held to account for failures in the project. Even Nelson Mandela attacked the media who were highlighting the matter and asked that Dr.D-Zuma be left alone to carry on with her work. He later claimed he was confident in the work of his Health Minister saying 'she has fully explained to me and I fully support her'. Mandela was followed by his vice-President, Mbeki, in affirming that there was no misuse of public funds for the musical.

The Director of the Centre of Policy Studies, Steve Friedman, said that 'The ANC (African National Council) has established a very clear pattern and the pattern is simple; you can be whatever you like as long as you are loyal. The minister of health may be responsible for *Sarafina* but she is loyal, so she will be defended. The problem is you can't deal with corruption this way.' Therefore blind loyalty and nepotism were masquerading as Parliamentary democracy; there was no transparency and no accountability. The inability to separate the ANC from government and Parliament exposed failure of leadership and the inability to transform from resistance and revolutionaries of apartheid years to properly elected government which is accountable to the electorate.

When *Sarafina II* was eventually produced, it was found that the play sent dangerous and confusing messages about HIV and AIDS. The New York Times reported in October 1996 that 'some of its dialogue dangerously inaccurate, its message unclear...'

However, later on Nelson Mandela admitted that the *Sarafina II* was poorly conceived and badly mismanaged. He went on to accept that it was a major mistake of his government.

Lest it is forgotten, HIV was spreading and people were dying of AIDS. The WHO declared in 1999 that AIDS was the biggest killer in Africa and the fourth largest cause of death worldwide. At the time there were estimated to be 33 million people worldwide who had the illness and 14 million had died across the world from when HIV/ AIDS first appeared. That there were an estimated 23 million people living with AIDS in 1996, gives one an impression of the rate of spread of the disease. Against this background questions had to be asked why South Africa was lagging in its approach to dealing with HIV /AIDS.

To try to appreciate what was happening in South Africa at the time in relation to HIV / AIDS one needs to recognise the changes in the country at the time. South Africa had emerged from the apartheid era and had its first black President, Nelson Mandela, inaugurated on 10th May 1994. A government of national unity was formed the next day with the majority of cabinet posts being held by members of the African National Council. Democracy based on one person one vote was introduced for the first time in the country. It was a period of euphoria with relief at the end of minority white domination.

Countries the world over were rushing headlong to find effective treatments for HIV/AIDS. In 1996, scientists at the University of Pretoria in South Africa announced that they had found a treatment for HIV / AIDS. The *Sunday Times of South Africa* wrote about the discovery that it 'arguably matches, or even surpasses, the first heart transplant performed by Professor Chris Barnard in 1967'. The research team comprised of Professor Dirk du Plessis, Dr. Carl Landauer, Olga and Zigi Visser from the medical faculty of H F Verwoerd Hospital in Pretoria. They arranged a meeting with the health minister at the time, Dr.D-Zuma, while reporting that 'unofficial clinical trials on informed, consenting patients' had apparently shown 'extremely encouraging results'. What was amazing was the claim that subsequently followed - that definite and conclusive proof of effectiveness of the drug would be available within three to six weeks. As any one familiar with medical research and pharmaceutical trials would know, this is a very, very short period indeed! There is no way that a safe, effective new drug could be brought to market in such a short time. The researchers were seeking government approval for their trial of the drug, as to them it was 'vital for South Africa to win the race towards the cure for AIDS'. This would ensure that the patent for the drug would remain South African and enhance the reputation of the country.

The Virodene saga shows how politics was closely intertwined in the management of HIV/ AIDS in the country. Salim Karim, a director of HIV in the Medical Research Council of South Africa told the *Washington Post* in 2000 that, 'The cabinet...believed the discovery would validate South Africa's black majority in much the same way that Christiaan Barnard's first successful heart transplant in 1968 affirmed apartheid South Africa to the world'. Blacks could demonstrate that they were equal to or better than whites.

Virodene is an industrial solvent and is toxic to the liver. News about Virodene reached the public when the government of South Africa announced in 1997 that a 'possible cure' for HIV/AIDS had been discovered. The drug's potential was realised in South Africa and medical trials were conducted in neighbouring Tanzania. It was reported that funding for the trial was obtained directly from the Presidency of South Africa. It was claimed that between 2000 and 2001, money was collected from the Union Buildings of the Presidency of South Africa. The article added that 'on numerous occasions, money was collected from 'the Presidency, in the Union Buildings in briefcases and always in US dollars, and always $100 bills'. The Union Buildings is the official seat of the government of South Africa and is located in Pretoria.

Commentators of the time were concerned with the rapid approval that was being sought for Virodene, which appears to have bypassed normal regulatory channels for medicines in South Africa. By far, a more important and relevant aspect was raised by those who observed what was happening at the time. Thabo Mbeki claimed and even lauded what was seen as an 'African solution' to the epidemic of HIV/ AIDS in South Africa. In April 1997 he welcomed the African Renaissance in saying – 'those who have eyes to see, let them see. The African Renaissance is upon us. As we peer through the looking glass darkly, this may not be obvious. But it is upon us.'

Virodene appeared to provide a means for side-stepping the pharmaceutical giants of the time who were producing anti-retroviral treatments for HIV/AIDs. The researchers claimed that following the use of Virodene, 'The results far exceed what we anticipated' and continued that the treatment was 'far superior and effective than any known treatment to date worldwide; It is effective at any stage of infection. (Terminal cases are and have been reversed); Patients have regained health and picked up as much as 10 kg within one month; Results are fast (within one to two weeks) of starting treatment.' It was claimed that Virodene use led to complete destruction of the AIDS virus rather than its suppression, which had hitherto been achieved. With such amazing results and accompanying claims of efficacy, it was natural for the government of South Africa, and indeed for any government at the time to support work on Virodene and to encourage its general use as a treatment for the scourge of HIV/AIDS, as the disease was then seen.

The buzz created by this wonder drug, as it was perceived, allowed politics to enter the fray and to be seduced to such an extent as to be seen to tamper with meaningful medical research and medicine development. Quarraisha Karim, the first director of South Africa's national AIDS program, said '... this drug would be the thing that offset the perception... of Africans as substandard and less than capable. All eyes were upon the ANC and the expectations were very high and they were really trying to find their feet but they didn't want to exercise caution. This was driven by the need to show the world: 'Yes, Africans can do this. We can do this. Virodene became our redemption'.

There was much political manoeuvring and push by the researchers to get Virodene approved for general use on patients with HIV/AIDS. However, the Medical Control Council (MCC) banned use of the drug because it was shown to contain a 'highly toxic industrial solvent which may cause irreversible fatal liver damage'. Safety and efficacy needed to be proven before patients could thereafter be exposed to Virodene. Eventually it was shown that the trials of Virodene had not followed correct protocols and had not had appropriate ethical approval. The extent of political support for the project can be gauged from the comment of one of the researchers – 'MCC approval will be obtained, but this will happen when it happens. Even if it takes the minister to replace the head of the MCC [who] is thought to be unreasonable. We have the President and cabinet support.' This appeared now to be setting a dangerous precedent where political support for a drug would be seen to trump properly conducted research after ethical scrutiny and with due regard to the efficacy and safety of the drug. The Minister of Health, Dr. D-Zuma was even prepared to overrule the MCC so that medicines that had yet to be approved or registered could be used on patients. The Chairman of the MCC, Dr. Peter Folb, was replaced by Dr. Helen Rees. However, the latter's appointment did not bring the expected relief for the researchers into Virodene. While she appeared to be less difficult to deal with, she still stood her ground on testing of the drug. The researchers and promoters of Virodene described Dr.Rees as being 'worse than Peter Folb.' It would appear that Dr. Rees was following due research process and in this respect was acting in the interest of patients, the ultimate recipients of treatment with Virodene.

It has ben written that the 'mission of the Mbeki-ites has been to restore 'African dignity, validate the black majority, and finally vanquish the 'demon of white racism.'

All the while people were continuing to die with HIV/AIDS due to denial originating from the highest political echelons in South Africa. One may also detect a hint of racism in the comments by politicians.

The late Dr. Manto Tshabalala-Msimang was an important figure in the HIV/AIDS story in South Africa. She was Minister for Health, for about nine years in the period after apartheid, in the South African government. There is no doubt she helped develop medical services in rural areas of the country and worked to reduce the cost of medicines. In this respect her contribution to health care in South Africa cannot be under-estimated. Prior to her work, many black South Africans could not access or were denied access to appropriate health care. But her policies in relation to HIV/AIDs were, to say the least, nothing short of disastrous.

She was a freedom fighter who was a friend and associate of the late President of South Africa, Thabo Mbeki. That she shared his views on HIV/AIDS is relevant as it may have contributed to her own doubts about the disease and its treatment.

Dr. Tshabalala-Msimang was said to have had a great mistrust of treatments that were advocated at that time for HIV/AIDS and especially a dislike for anti-retroviral drugs. These were the emerging treatments and remain to this day the mainstay of treatment of HIV/AIDS. Harvard University claimed that the policies of the South African government of the time had contributed to over 300,000 AIDS related deaths in the country. The Treatment Action Group (TAG) in South Africa was a thorn in her side and the two often seriously disagreed on how to deal with the enormous problems of HIV /AIDS. One has to be reminded that South Africa had the highest prevalence of the disease with approximately 6 million people affected. And this in a country with a population at the time of 50 million. TAG had to secure a court judgement to compel the ministry of health under

Dr. Tshabalala-Msimang to provide treatment for pregnant women with HIV/AIDS and to those in the advanced stages of the disease.

She was convinced of the limited value of anti-retroviral therapy and her lack of appreciation of their benefit in HIV / AIDS led her to say in 2005 'there are other things we can be assisted in doing to respond to HIV/AIDS in this country.' Her views gained much support and traction in traditional African culture which was sceptical of Western remedies. She recommended potato, beetroot, olives, garlic and lemon. These treatments earned her the names 'Dr. Beetroot' and 'Dr. Garlic'.

The 16th International Conference on AIDS was held in Toronto, Canada in August 2006 with the theme 'Time to Deliver'. It was noteworthy that the South African stand had a display of lemons and garlic. What this conveyed to the delegates at the Conference and to the world in general is, even now, difficult to comprehend. To Africans who are steeped in traditional cures this may have had a symbolic significance. To those who were grappling with managing and containing the AIDS epidemic it may have meant something entirely different. But that these items were on display at a time when the declared view of South Africa was of traditional remedies like diet, sat in contrast to the established medical view on how to deal with the epidemic. At the closing session of the same Conference, the United Nations special envoy on AIDS, Stephen Lewis, said that the government of South Africa was spreading theories about HIV /AIDS that are 'more worthy of a lunatic fringe than a concerned and compassionate state'. He claimed that 600-800 people were dying in South Africa each day. To enormous applause he said that the government had much to atone for 'and I am of the opinion they will never achieve redemption'. His harsh words 'I know what it is doing is wrong, immoral and indefensible' were met by protests from the African National Congress. Mark Wainberg, the co-chair of the Conference called what the Health Department in South Africa was claiming as 'scientific nonsense and it was unconscionable to use lemon juice as an HIV-prevention method'.

One has to place the view about diet held by Dr. Tshabalala-Msimang in some perspective. It was known that many of the patients with HIV/

AIDS were malnourished and underweight. Toxic anti-retroviral drugs could not be administered or be taken in full adult dose. These patients needed nutritional supplements at the outset. As their weights and nutritional status improved they were able to take the stated doses of anti-retroviral drugs.

In 2003, WHO and UNAID rolled out its ' 3 by 5' initiative. This was to ensure that three million people with HIV/AIDS in low and middle-income countries had anti-retroviral treatment by 2005. This was considered by some a human right. However this target did not take account of the available services and infrastructure in countries, to enable them to deliver the desired outcomes. It was described by some as 'laughable'. South Africa maintained that it would not be 'chasing numbers' but trying to improve the quality of health care.

However, the apparent emphasis on beetroot, garlic, lemons etc did not help the South African point of view regarding the need for adequate nutrition. The important aspect of nutrition did not appear to have been well articulated.

Some persons in South Africa called for Dr. Tshabalala-Msimang to be charged for genocide in relation to the numbers who died during her tenure as minister of health.

There was at the outset a significant denial in South Africa of the existence of HIV/AIDS. One is compelled to ask why this was so, as there was a compelling imperative to search for a cause of the illness. Most researchers pursued the accepted germ theory of disease, which has stood the test of time, for the benefit of humanity. However, there were dissenters. And notable among these was Peter Duesberg. He was professor of molecular and cell biology at the University of California, Berkeley, USA. He claimed that HIV was harmless and that AIDS was caused by long term use of anti-retroviral drugs and the use of recreational substances. Here was an astounding claim – that the treatment of AIDS was its cause!. This theory had no evidence to support it and was comprehensively discounted by the scientific community, which continued to pursue a viral cause for the disease.

Professor Peter Duesberg was invited to serve on an advisory committee set up in South Africa in 2000 by President Thabo Mbeki, to help with managing the evolving AIDS epidemic in the country. Duesberg's influence on the committee helped to shape the denial of AIDS by President Mbeke.

President Mbeke was accused of playing with words when he said that a 'virus cannot cause a syndrome .... AIDS is a syndrome, i.e. a collection of well-known diseases, with well-known causes. They are not, together, caused and cannot be caused by one virus! I said that HIV might be a contributory cause of immune deficiency'. In this claim he may be somewhat right. AIDS is an acquired deficiency in the immune system in comparison to congenital deficiencies of the immune system, where one is born with the problems of immunity. In AIDS one is born with a normal immune system that can fight off infections initially. But this ability to defend is severely impaired when one acquires immune deficiency. And the virus, HIV (human immunodeficiency virus) is the cause of impairment in efficiency of the immune system. In mother to baby transmission of the HIV virus that occurs in the womb, the latter is born with the virus and a normal immune system which is later compromised by the virus.

Anthony James Leon (Tony Leon) who is a South African politician and one time leader of the Opposition, appealed to President Mbeki to allow the use of AZT, also known as ZDV (zidovudine), as post-exposure prevention (prophylaxis) of AIDS in cases of rape. He spoke at a Parliamentary debate on the topic quoting a rape victim, Charlene Smith, who had written that if the drug was available '10,000 rape survivors in South Africa would have got the drug. Eighty percent of them would not have sero-converted and become HIV positive if raped by an HIV positive person.' Tony Leon accused President Mbeke of 'near obsession' with trying to find African solutions to African problems, even casting aside the known science of HIV / AIDS in favour of 'snake-oil cures and quackery.' To which Mbeki responded in words tinged with racism accusing Tony Leon 'the white politician' of showing his 'disdain and contempt for African solutions to the challenges that face the peoples of our Continent.'

The Treatment Action Campaign (TAC), which worked on behalf of HIV/AIDS victims, secured a ruling in 2002 in the Constitutional Court of South Africa compelling the state which included President Mbeke and the Minister of Health, Manto Tshabalala-Msimang, to provide anti-retroviral treatment to pregnant women. Had this treatment been provided, it would have limited or halted the vertical transmission of AIDS from mother to child as happened in the case of Nkosi Johnson. However, even after the court ruling, treatment was not made available. Significant progress was eventually made in this respect in 2008 after the retirement of Thabo Mbeki and Sbalala Msimang from office. It was known that 30% of women attending ante-natal clinics were infected with HIV.

Whatever one may choose to call the situation in South Africa at the time – denialism or delay – the effect on the AIDS population in the country was nothing short of cataclysmic. It was estimated that about 300,000 people died and 35,000 babies were born with HIV, who most likely would have avoided the infection had treatment in pregnancy been made available.

It was known that the life expectancy in South Africa dropped to 54 years in 2005. Tshabalala Msimang was replaced by Dr. Aaron Motsoaledi as Minister for Health. He introduced the drug Atripla, which is a combination of tenofovir, efavirenz and emticitabine for HIV/ AIDS. Treatment for the condition was now available. It was reported that life expectancy improved to 63 in 2015. It is a sad statistic that most adults who died in 2000 were in the age range of 20 – 40 years. This was because HIV/AIDS is a sexually transmitted disease which predominantly affect people in this age group.

Nathan Geffen who was a researcher at the Centre for Social Science Research, University of Cape Town was a vocal opponent of the AIDS policy in South Africa and had confirmed the improvement in survival from 2005 to 2013. He also helped dispel the notion that because the population of South Africa was increasing, there was no epidemic of HIV/ AIDS. He showed that, on the contrary, the rise in population was due to increase in births despite the increasing death rate from HIV / AIDS. He compared the deaths in South Africa in 1997 which was 316,505 to that in 2006 when it had risen to 613,040. This is an almost doubling of the number of deaths in the space of nine years. He then showed that death from tuberculosis rose from 22,071 in 1997 to 77,009 in 2006 and deaths from influenza and pneumonia rose from 11,518 in 1997 to

52,791 in 2006. Tuberculosis, influenza and pneumonia may be called opportunistic infections which affect those with reduced immunity, as happens in patients with HIV / AIDS. These numbers provide further evidence of the prevalence and spread of HIV in the country at the time. It is still difficult to understand the role of the government of South Africa when confronted with these statistics.

When all of these events were unfolding, where was Nkosi Johnson? Born in 1989, he died of AIDS on 1st June 2001, the longest surviving child born HIV positive in South Africa. And he lived and died during the turbulent time of debates in the country about HIV / AIDS and its treatment. His mother, as we read before, died of AIDS. The 13th International Conference on HIV / AIDS took place in Durban, South Africa from the 9th to the 14th of July 2000 and was attended by delegates from all round the world. As is common with such international gatherings, it was a place to discuss research and emerging treatments for the illness. It was, as is the practice, a place for cross-fertilisation of ideas by researchers from around the world. Unfortunately the continuing rancour between the medical community of South Africa and politicians continued on the fringes of the Conference. This did not pass un-noticed. This was noticed by Nelson Mandela too, 83 years old at the time, who was invited to speak at the closing of the Conference. He spoke about the importance of words and how one communicates with others especially on the subject of HIV /AIDS which was an extremely sensitive topic at the time. He paid equal tribute to the President of South Africa and to the medical community in the country. He appears to have pleaded for burying the hatchet and for the 'warring' parties in the debate about HIV/AIDS in South Africa to seek compromise saying 'that in all disputes a point is arrived at where no party, no matter how right or wrong it might have been at the start of that dispute, will any longer be totally in the right or totally in the wrong. Such a point, I believe, has been reached in this debate'. Nkosi Johnson also spoke at the Conference in an impassioned plea to his fellow beings - 'Care for us and accept us – we are all human beings. We are normal. We have hands. We have feet. We can walk, we can talk, we have needs just like everyone else – don't be afraid of us – we are all the same!.

Nkosi and his mother Gail founded a refuge for HIV positive mothers and children in Johannesburg, 'Nkosi's Haven'. The place offers residential care for about 140 people including children. Children are encouraged to attend school while mothers remain active and can participate in cooking, gardening etc. They may, depending on aptitude, become leaders in the haven. The objective is that mothers and children learn to lead normal lives with AIDS. The site provides classrooms, workshops an arts centre etc. The aim is to facilitate a wholesome life for the residents.

In 2005 Nkosi Johnson was posthumously awarded the International Children Peace Prize which was presented to Gail Johnson by the late Mikhail Gorbachev, who was the last President of the Soviet Union.

'WE ARE NOT YOUR BOYS'

Perhaps the most recent example of a large number of deaths of black people followed the violent events in Rwanda in 1994. And this was black on black violence driven by ethnicity and tribalism. The vast majority of those who were murdered, in what was to be designated a genocide, were Tutsis. This was a murder spree on an unprecedented scale which lasted 100 days.

Much has been written about the massacre in Rwanda and there was even a screen play 'Hotel Rwanda'. The story line was written by George and Keir Patterson and the film was directed by Terry George. The play is about a hotelier, Paul Rusesabagina and his wife Tatiana, who try to save the lives of about a thousand Tutsis in the Hôtel des Mille Collines. The story is about murder, bribery corruption and genocide. The film earned a gross revenue of about $34 million .

To understand why the bloody events of 1994 happened, one needs to go back to the history of Rwanda and its peoples. The origins of Rwanda may be traced back to the times of the Bachwezi people and the Bachwezi Empire. The Bachwezie founded the empire of Kitara which incorporated parts of modern Uganda, Tanzania, Kenya and the Congo. They were supposed to have spiritual powers and so were accorded the status of demigods. They introduced agriculture, especially coffee growing, and the ankole species of cattle. The Empire eventually disintegrated with, it is thought, the Bachwezi intermingling with the many tribes in the region. The vast majority, about 85% of the population, were Hutus who

'We Are Not Your Boys'

were mainly peasants. The Kings of Rwanda and the nobility were mainly from the minority Tuts©i tribe, although small segments of nobility were Hutus. This was probably the original grievance of the Hutus.

The kings were autocratic and dispensed favours and especially land on a system of patronage, largely to the Tutsis. The landlords in their turn demanded payments from Hutus to occupy the land. Herein lays the second cause of continuing animosity between the tribes.

In many respects the difference between Hutus and Tutsi are artificial. Tutsis came originally from Ethiopia while Hutus were from Chad. There were Hutu nobles. It is written that one could shed one's Hutu identity and assume 'Tutsiness' by accumulating wealth and power. Additionally the ruling Tutsi would label anyone from outside, for eg those they conquered as 'Hutus'. This had the effect of concentrating their influence in a small group, the Tutsi. As Johann Pottier wrote in 2002 'wealth, not race was the basis of the ethnic distinction between the Hutus and the Tutsis'. He described a tripartite administration of districts where a Hutu chief handled and managed land disputes, a Tutsi chief who managed cattle and an army chief who was appointed by the king. This arrangement seemed to bring about some degree of harmony and with it a kind of peace. However it was not to last, as the Belgians discontinued the arrangement in the 1920's. More importantly they supported and cultivated the Tutsi aristocracy at the expense of the majority Hutus. In 1959 violence erupted between the Tutsi ruling classes and the majority Hutus in the country. It had various names - the Rwandan Revolution or Hutu Revolution, Social Revolution or Wind of Destruction. It ended when the minority Belgian supported Tutsi rule was replaced by an independent republic which was dominated now by the majority Hutus. The revolution led to about 350,000 Tutsis fleeing over the border to Uganda where they were now refugees in a foreign land.

What happened in Rwanda was alarming to neighbouring Burundi where Hutu-Tutsi relations deteriorated and the government was keen to avoid a situation similar to Rwanda happening in Burundi. In 1972 the violence between the two major ethnic groups, Hutu and Tutsi, led to the death of about 100,000 persons or 3.5%of the population. Professor Rene Lemarchand wrote that this amount of death was the equivalent of England losing 3 million people or the USA losing 8 million in the space of a few weeks. In some places all Tutsis were killed by the Hutus using small weapons, machetes and spears. In some instances Tutsi were simply clubbed to death. However there was an accompanying organised Tutsi revolution which was equally gruesome. Lemarchand described the concept of 'prophylactic violence' by Tutsi against Hutus. The violence led to a large and sustained migration of Hutu refugees in the early 1970's to Tanzania, Zaire and Rwanda. The Tutsis embarked on a process of elimination of educated Hutus in Burundi. Lemarchand laments France's stance in relation to the events in Burundi, describing it as 'ignorance and opportunism' and its 'attachment to the presumed virtues of *francophonie*'. France sought to replace Belgium and so spread its own influence in Africa, to the detriment of individual countries and the continent. The French military played a crucial role in the Tutsi attack against Hutus. For e.g. it is written by Lemarchand that French helicopter pilots held their aircraft steady to allow Burundi soldiers to shoot and kill Hutus from the windows of the aircraft. They even pursued fleeing Hutus into Tanzania killing Tanzanians in the process. It is estimated that nearly 300,000 Hutus were murdered by the government of Burundi using the armed forces which were dominated by Tutsis. The US Ambassador to Burundi, Thomas Patrick Melady, called what was happening 'selective genocide' while the Belgian Prime Minister, Gaston Eyskens, referred to the events as 'veritable genocide'. One of the sad descriptions of the massacre of Hutus was their submission to their fate. They cooperated with their captors- because there was no alternative and / or because they benignly accepted their fate. The Organisation of African Unity (OAU) and the UN were noted to be ineffective in seeking to end the carnage. The US President at the time, Richard Nixon, was overtly distressed by the then Secretary of State who wrote to him - 'since the United States had few strategic interests in the country, it should limit its involvement in the affair'. Nixon wrote 'This is one of the most cynical, callous reactions of a great government to a terrible human tragedy I have ever seen. ...let's begin by calling back our Ambassador immediately for consultation. Under no circumstances will I appoint a new Ambassador to present credentials to these butchers.'

    Burundi became a democracy in 1993 and Melchior Ndadaye was its first Hutu President. But in a continuation of the circle of violence, Tutsi army officers murdered the President and other leaders. . Violence followed and Hutus proceeded to kill many thousands of Tutsis. Western countries, with the exception of France, ceased supply of arms and weapons to Burundi.

In his paper, *'An Ambassador's Reflections of a Bloodbath'*, Thomas Melady laments the descent to violence in many societies. He writes 'Where hate and fear have been around for a long time and become deeply rooted, people have frequently resorted to violence to solve social and political problems. Killing is justified because people see no other solution. When the use of violence is justified in societies troubled by long simmering communal hates, the horror of a bloodbath draws very near'. In a short but wide-ranging article he draws the net to cover the Armenians in Turkey, Walloons and Flemish in Belgium, the French community in Canada etc. He continues - 'In the final analysis every community must accept responsibility for assuring that violence will not become a way of life in resolving day-to-day problems.......I write with a feeling of great sadness, for I see no end to the business.... It would be a real tragedy if all the sadness in the foothills of Burundi is in vain.'

This was a painful, moral, powerful, prescient paper. The events in Rwanda were but a continuation of the ethnic mistrust and resulting hatred that was ingrained in the people and probably continue to this day.

While being refugees in Rwanda the Tutsis were plotting with the Rwandan Patriotic Front (RPF) the invasion of their homeland, Rwanda. This happened in October 1990 where they invaded more than 60 kilometres into Rwanda. However they were repelled by the Hutu government of Rwanda with the assistance of French forces. Defeated, the Tutsi invaders had to withdraw. Following this loss, the RPF continued with guerrilla attacks in Rwandan territory. Small, though some of these attacks were, they were sufficient to compel the then President of Rwanda, Juvénal Habyarimana, to enter into peace talks with the RPF. Talks took place in Arusha, Tanzania. With pressures from the Organisation of African Unity (OAU), the USA and Belgium, talks between the two warring parties commenced in July 1992. This was a complex arrangement also involving Uganda, Burundi, Zaire, Senegal and Tanzania. Apart from Senegal the other countries border Rwanda and have their own Hutu and Tutsi populations. It was described as one of the best deals arranged by and in Africa and it held out the only hope of peace, not only in Rwanda but also the region. President Ali Hasan Mwinyi of Tanzania acted as a moderator / facilitator of the conference while France, Germany, Belgium and the USA served as observers. A glance of the map of Africa would show Rwanda bordered by the countries who had a vested interest in negotiations. Each of these countries had their own tribal divisions and sympathies. They also had to contend in various ways with the flood of refugees from Rwanda and the risks of unrest in their own populations. After much soul searching, hand-wringing and discussion, both parties finally signed the Arusha Accords in August 1993.

These accords, were without doubt, the best solution for enduring peace in the country. Its plans were imaginative and conveyed a sense of purpose by promising constitutional changes and reform of the military so the that the regular Rwandan army and the military wing of the RPF would be integrated. It was planned in the accord that interim arrangements would last for up to twenty two months to allow for free elections.

But there was a major and history shows, the gravest stumbling block to implementation of the Arusha Accords. Put simply, it was this – would the signatories to the Accord abide by what they had agreed to? President Juvenal Habariyamana and his team did not want the Accord to work and did everything in their power to frustrate and obstruct it. As the human rights lawyer, Eric Gillett, wrote – 'the human rights workers, whether Rwandan or international, were not fooled. We did not think that someone capable of organising massacres would suddenly turn into a democrat. We kept telling the Belgian authorities'. Another interesting fact is what the vice-president of the RPF, Patrick Mazimhaka, related about Colonel Theoniste Bagasora. The latter was a Hutu and was the bridge between the Arusha discussions and the Hutu extremists. In his book, ' *A People Betrayed',* author L.R.Melver described how Bagasora had packed his bags and was leaving the discussions. When asked by Mazimhaka why he was leaving, Bagasora said he was returning to Rwanda to prepare for 'apocalypse deux', the second apocalypse. Bagasora wrote a report defining the Tutsi as the enemy. Anyone supporting the Tutsi, even a Hutu, or any one married to, associated or sympathising with a Tutsi fell into the category of enemy. This information was shared with the President and can be seen as the basis and plan for engaging in genocide against the Tutsi. The Tutsi were described as cockroaches (Inyenzi). To bring effect to their plan Bagasora set about creating a base for Hutu power within the army called Amasasu (Alliance des Militaires Agacés par les Séculaires Actes Sournois des Unaristes or the Alliance of Soldiers Annoyed by the Underhand Secular acts of the Unarists). It also meant Alliance of Soldiers Provoked by the Age-Old Deceitful Acts of Unarists (monarchists).On reflection now and with the benefit of hindsight one could see this as a sign of what was to come. It also says much about the extent of organisation of the Hutus for the genocide that was to follow. One may ask why France acted in the manner that it did? Francophone???

Habariyama came to power in 1973 after overthrowing the sitting President, Grégoire Kayibanda in a *coup d'état*. He then proceeded toestablish a totalitarian regime dominated by Hutus from the northern region of Rwanda where he hailed from. His party was the Mouvement républicain national pour la démocratie et le développement or National Republican Movement for Democracy and Development - MRND. He banned the Parmehutu party, which was the party of Hutus from the south of the country. All citizens of Rwanda whether Hutu, Tutsi or Twa had to be members of the MRND. Rwanda was therefore a dictatorial one-party state which worked to the detriment of the Tutsi who considered themselves superior, although being in a minority.

It is useful to note that while the Arusha negotiations were under way and in its aftermath, there prevailed an atmosphere of apartheid against the Tutsi in Rwanda. Tutsis continued to be indiscriminately killed – for the simple reason of being Tutsi or non- Hutu. These attacks were aided by those who supported the President and by elements in the military who helped distribute arms to civilians to facilitate the killings. There was no law or accountability during these years. Impunity was the order of the day.

Two militias were formed by the MRND and the CDR in 1992. The Coalition for the Defence of the Republic (CDR) was a group of extreme right wing Hutus who were opposed to rapprochement with the RPF and were critical of any approach in dealing with them. The *Interahamwe* ('Those Who Attack Together') and the *Impuzamugambi* ('Those Who Have the Same Goal') had the same objective, which was to preserve the power, authority and government of the Hutus and of President Habariyamana. These militias were vital in the coordination of attacks on the Tutsis and on anyone or group opposed to Hutu governance and dominance.

A human rights report at the time documented the extent of violence and killings, causing the Belgian ambassador to Rwanda to be recalled for discussions. To his eternal shame the French ambassador called what was happening rumours. France was culpable in many other aspects too. It helped the Rwanda army deal with the RPF invasion of the country. If it was a neutral party working to help implementation of the Arusha Accords, it would have sought a ceasefire and followed this with negotiations. Instead France chose confrontation and contributed to the catastrophe that unfolded.

The arms purchases by Rwanda in these years makes for interesting reading. Both sides in the conflict, the Rwandan armed forces and RPF purchased weapons to help prosecute war against each other and to commit various atrocities against each other. The Rwandan government purchased weapons from Egypt, South Africa, France and China. About $ 6 million of arms was purchased from Egypt with Credit Lyonnais, a French nationalised bank providing credit guarantees for the purchase. The weapons purchased included shoulder-fired rocket launchers, mortars, landmines, automatic rifles etc. According to the agreement between Rwanda and Egypt, Rwanda had to pay $1 million upfront and within six months of signing the contract. Another tranche of $1 million was to be paid by the delivery of 605 tons of Rwandan tea, in leu of money. The remaining had to be paid in instalments guaranteed by a 'first-rate, international bank approved by Egypt.' The Credit Lyonnais bank provided the necessary guarantee to Egypt. Similar munitions and of the same value of $6 million were purchased from South Africa. This purchase contravened a United Nations Security Council resolution which did not permit the purchase or importation of arms from South Africa. But this UN resolution was not mandatory. It was voluntary, allowing both Rwanda and South Africa to bypass the resolution. The relevant U.N. Security Council Resolution 558, adopted unanimously by the Security Council on December 13, 1984, 'Requests all States to refrain from importing arms, ammunition of all types and military vehicles produced in South Africa.' The contract for arms was signed by Conrad Kuhn, representative of Armscor, the national South African arms corporation, and Major Cyprien Kayumba, Rwandan Ministry of National Defense. For many years, even preceding the 1990's and the war, Rwanda had been purchasing weapons from France. In addition, France provided training and personnel to the Rwandan military.

There proceeded an arms war between the Rwandan forces and RPF. The Rwandan Minster of Defence stated 'the RPF had superior weapons. Whatever new equipment we acquired, they had it before us.' The country was flooded with weapons, helped by the Hutu administration arming the civilian population. It was said by one western diplomat 'two beers will get you one grenade.'

The role of Uganda is interesting because it apparently provided safe haven for Tutsi refugees from Rwanda. The RPF was based in southern Uganda and used Ugandan soil to train and arm itself. It used this base to launch into northern Rwanda. It was claimed that Uganda provided arms and ammunition to the RPF. The RPF is also reported to have stolen arms from Uganda. Rwandan refugees in Uganda are Banyarwanda who consist not only of Tutsis but also of some Hutus. They had a singular desire, to return to their homeland, Rwanda. They supported Yoweri Musevini when he was Defence Minister in Uganda. He then defected to form the National Resistance Army (NRA). Musevini overthrew President Milton Obote of Uganda in 1986; since then he has been in power. It was claimed by America's Central Intelligence Agency |(CIA) that Milton Obote's government was responsible for 100,000 deaths in Uganda. Several people of Rwandan origin, the Banyarwanda, joined the NRA of Musevini. Major General Fred Rwigyema was a senior NRA military commander and Major Paul Kagame was head of military intelligence for the NRA. Rwigyema was a Tutsi who was born in southern Rwanda. He and his family fled Rwanda and were refugees in Uganda. He was, by all accounts, a charismatic leader who led from the front. Both Rwigyema and Kagame, were loyal to Musevini. On 1st October 1990 the RPF attacked Rwanda with Rwigyema as head. However, Rewigyema was killed on the second day of the invasion and was soon replaced by Paul Kagame who had to return hurriedly from the USA, where he was at the time. There is much controversy as to how Fred Rwigyema was shot and killed. The historian Gérard Prunier stated that, from the evidence he has collected, Rwigyema was shot by one of his sub-commanders, Peter Bayingana. Prunier also maintains that Bayingana and one of his co-commanders,

Chris Bunyenyezi, were used by Paul Kagame to eliminate Rwigyema. This left Paul Kagame as the only candidate for leadership of the RPF.

The relationship between the NRA and the RPF had been close and long standing. Several of the leaders in both organisations were friends and school mates. They fought together and died for the causes they espoused. For e.g. the former army commander of Uganda, the late General Aronda Nyakairima who was also the Minister of Internal Affairs in Uganda, was the best man at the wedding in 1989 of President Paul Kagame of Rwanda.

However relations between the two countries deteriorated despite their close links and intertwined personal history. At one time, the border between Rwanda and Uganda was closed to cargo and human traffic. Musevini used to refer to the RPF and 'my children, my boys'. Only to be rebuffed by Kagame 'we're not your boys'. The RPF believes that Musevini used to them to do Musevini's 'dirty work'. As Brian B. Mukalazi, Director of Every Child Ministries in Uganda, wrote 'The problem with history is not that people fail to learn from its lessons, but that they learn the wrong ones. For both the NRA and RPF, their most prized asset is the rich intertwined history they share. If only they could seat – man-to-man – reflect and work out their differences, Uganda and Rwanda would both be winners.'

The undoubted architect of the violence in Rwanda was Colonel Theoneste Bagosora. The prosecutor at the International Criminal Tribunal for Rwanda (ICTR), Chile Eboe-Osuji, told the Tribunal that 'Bagosora was at the centre of the conspiracy to commit genocide,……..It was a conspiracy whose object was the whole or partial destruction of the Tutsi ethnic group from Rwanda.' Bagosora was referred to as 'Rwanda's Himmler' after the leader of the Nazi SS, Heinrich Himmler, who organised the transport of Jews to concentration camps where they were exterminated. Hence the reference by Bagosora to 'apocalypse deux', as he walked out of the Arusha meeting. A few years prior to 1994, Bagosora helped establish the Zero Network. This was a combined military and civilian death squad that was trained and prepared for the massacre of Tutsis.

The role of churches in the atrocities in Rwanda is a matter of great regret and one which churches did much to ignore over a period of years.

The church and politics in Rwanda were closely inter-linked. The church initially worked with the Belgian colonisers of the country. At the time the Tutsis were the favoured group and they in turn helped the church to enjoy access to government and to occupy important posts in it. But when the Tutsis began to find favour with communism, the tide of friendship between them and the church turned. Communism was seen by the church as an embodiment of evil. The church duly swung its association with the majority Hutus. Tutsis now became a hated minority. The church enjoyed greater power in Government with the Hutus and used its privileged positions in government to preach against the Tutsis. The Archbishop was an important member in government. The historian, Alison Forges, wrote that Archbishop Augustin Nshamihigo and his colleague, Bishop Jonathan Ruhumuliza, of the Anglican church acted as spokespersons for the government and attempted to explain what was happening in the country as the work of the RPF. The Catholic Archbishop Vincent Nsengiyumva was on the ruling Hutus party's central committee during the years it set in train its discriminatory policies and actions against the Tutsis, which formed the basis of the eventual genocide against the latter. And in a religious country like Rwanda, the word of the church carried great weight and was believed. In fact it was a crime to question the teachings and preaching of the church in Rwanda. This gave the church unrivalled power over the lives of the citizens. The church was used by Hutus to malign the Tutsis and to spread evil about them. Tutsis were viewed as the living embodiment of Satan. One can see the progressive indoctrination of the Hutus who began to dislike, no, to hate the Tutsis. Hutus were advised to kill Tutsis who were claimed to be enemies of God. God was on the side of Hutus. Catholic priests opened the doors of their churches to frightened fleeing Tutsis, only for them to be killed by marauding Hutus.

The story of Jonathan Ruhumuliza is interesting to say the least. At a press conference and in letters to foreign churches, he called the government of President Habariyamana 'peace loving'. In the first few weeks of the killings, in May 1994, Ruhumuliza wrote to Jose Chipena who was Secretary-General of the All Africa Council of Churches, blaming the killings on the Rwandan Patriotic Front, claiming that they were 'destroying everything, killing everybody they meet while the government is trying to bring peace in the country...... The (*cabinet*) ministers are doing their best to bring back peace to the country although they are facing many problems'. Jonathan Ruhumuliza was an ardent supporter of and an apologist for the Habariyamana regime.

He claimed that the government was working to stop the violence, ignoring that the killings were organised and supported by the government. Ruhumuliza, the Prime Minister of Rwanda, Jean Kamabanda and other cabinet ministers travelled the country apparently appealing with the people for peace. In reality they were encouraging violence and exhorting Hutus to kill Tutsis. Human Rights Watch wrote 'far from condemning the attempt to exterminate the Tutsi, Archbishop Augustin Nshamihigo and Bishop Jonathan Ruhumuliza of the Anglican church acted as spokesmen for the genocidal government at a press conference in Nairobi. Like many who tried to explain away the slaughter, they placed the blame for the genocide on the RPF because it had attacked Rwanda. Foreign journalists were so disgusted at this presentation that they left the conference'. He went on to blame the killings on rebels due to some minor anti-Tutsi hatred. In 1997 he moved to Canada and from 1998 to 2004 he was a Bishop in Cameroon. In 2015 he was appointed by the Bishop of Worcester in the UK, Peter Selby, as a priest in the village of Hampton Lovett, Worcestershire in England. There could not have been a bigger lie or smokescreen!

Jean Kambanda was the first head of government to plead guilty at the **International Criminal Tribunal for Rwanda,** to genocide and was sentenced to life imprisonment. The verdict against Kambanda also set a precedent against the legal principle of state immunity, which allowed state actors to be tried internationally.

Years later Peter Selby said that the church should consider referring the matter to outside authorities to scrutinise saying 'I think that over the whole child abuse thing, it's become clear that what the church has to do, and do immediately, is refer cases to the police. Because there's a recognition that the church, when it has presumed it was competent to deal with such things, clearly wasn't.'

Prior to appointment as priest, the Church of England (C of E) claimed that it had carried out checks and had not found evidence to support Ruhumuliza's complicity in genocide in Rwanda. The Church also claimed that the Archbishop of Rwanda at the time, Emmanuel Kolini, had recommended Ruhumuliza. It said the bishop had been commended to the C of E by archbishop Emmanuel Kolini.

However, Kolini claimed that he had warned the Church of England about Ruhumuliza and that he was not aware of any investigation about Ruhumuliza, that Lambeth Palace claimed it had done.

Jonathan Ruhumuliza's application for asylum in Britain was rejected by the then Home Secretary, Theresa May. But, this decision was overturned on appeal on the grounds that even if he was implicated in genocide, he had found redemption through religion!

Archbishop Kolini accused Ruhumuliza of collaborating with the Hutu government of the time and claimed that the Anglican Church in Rwanda was 'corrupt' with Ruhumuliza acting as an 'errand boy' of the racist Hutu government.

After the genocide, Jonathan Ruhumuliza became bishop of Kigali in Rwanda. This was not a position that other members of the clergy were prepared to accept and they called out for him to be asked to account for his actions. It was then that he offered an apology in saying 'I did not continue to energetically condemn either the tragedy which was in progress or the state communiqués which were broadcast on the radios during this time.' It would appear that his apology was not enough to quell the disquiet among the clergy of Rwanda who were more concerned of what he did in defending the government of President Habariyamana. These events may have prompted him to leave Rwanda.

Peter Selby was disappointed in Jonathan Ruhumuliza when he learnt from the latter that he had applied for asylum in the UK. Selby told Ruhumuliza 'That's a very weird thing for you to do because you've always said that you didn't have a problem with the government of Rwanda. Secondly, that if the government of Rwanda ever raised any issues about which they wished to charge you, you would immediately be prepared to return to Rwanda. He said that many times in conversations'.

Peter Selby and John Inge, who succeeded Selby as Bishop of Worcester said they 'were affronted by what we read.'

The Rwanda genocide survivors association, Ibuka, rightly criticised the Church of England for its lack of adequate scrutiny before allowing Ruhumuliza to serve as a priest. This case highlights how relatively easy it was for even a person like Ruhumuliza, who has a dark cloud hanging over him relating to his actions or omissions in Rwanda, to masquerade as an upright member of the community in England.

The Home Office in the UK refused the application of Ruhumuliza for asylum stating that he was implicated in crimes against humanity in Rwanda and that he was a 'genocide-denier'. Subsequently his application to remain in the UK was turned down three years later by Theresa May. But Ruhumuliza's appeal to the immigration tribunal was successful and he was given leave to remain in the UK. The basis of the tribunal's decision was that even if he was implicated in crimes against humanity, he had shown redemption and demonstrated this in his work in the church. This must be a most astounding decision which should make the legal profession hang its head in shame. Support the killing of as many of your countrymen, but, you shall be allowed to remain in the UK if you show sufficient contrition!. Here is a person who aided and abetted some of the most barbaric events and horrific crimes in the end of the last century and he is allowed to go free. Added to this, he is a member of the church, preaching peace, love and unity amongst all people – or so it seems. The only saving grace in this case was the dissenting voice of Lord Justice Singh sitting in the Appeal Court which upheld the tribunal's decision. Lord Singh, differing from the majority decision of the court said, that the tribunal should have considered that Ruhumuliza may have been responsible for crimes against humanity and that the tribunal should not have based its decision only on the fact that he had repented for whatever he did or did not do in Rwanda. The Tribunal should have considered that he may been 'directly involved in the killings at Shyogwe, including the requests for weapons and ensuring Tutsis were excluded from the protection of the parish'. How many more similar persons are walking the streets of the UK, one would never know.

In 2020, Ruhumuliza was appointed a priest in Manchester in the UK. The Church of England took the easy route in stating that 'the immigration tribunal and, subsequently, the Court of Appeal found in 2018 that Jonathan Ruhumuliza had the right to remain in the UK'. This was apparently sufficient for the Church of England despite the concerns expressed by the Archbishop of Rwanda, Emmanuel Kolini. Henceforth one needs to take the views of the church with suspicion, if this is not already occurring, especially following the various sexual abuse claims that it had and continues to sweep under the carpet. Is it too much to conclude that, in this instance, the church was an agent for evil?

The president of a group of genocide survivors in Rwanda, Jean Pierre Dusingizemungu, criticised the Church for not been inquisitive enough when confronted with the case of Ruhumuliza, especially in the light of events in Rwanda. He went on to say 'We do not see why Churches refuse to face history and reality,' This statement sums up the wilful blindness of churches in respect of many crises for eg sexual abuse. It is easier for churches to bury their heads in the sand hoping that issues would go away. But Churches fail to appreciate that these issues relate to real people who have had painful experiences and who carry their scars for life. They will always cry out for justice. Churches remain blind to victims and in so doing heap shame upon themselves.

Father Athanase Serombo was in charge of Nyange parish in western Rwanda. He gave shelter to about 2000 Tutsis. He followed this apparent act of kindness by ordering that the church be bulldozed. The International Criminal Tribunal for Rwanda found that about 12th April 1994 the church was surrounded by the Interahamwe and Hutu militiamen. When Tutsis resisted they were attacked. The Tribunal found that Father Serombo discussed with the driver of the bulldozer about demolishing the church and advised the latter about the weakest parts of the church. The roof of the church collapsed killing most who had sought refuge in it. Those who were still alive were killed by the militia. The ICTR found that Father Serombo aided and abetted the Interahamwe in their actions against the church and the Tutsi who were seeking refuge there. Following the war in Rwanda, Father Serombo escaped to Italy and worked in a parish in Florence, having been helped by the Church to escape Rwanda. The church knew that he was wanted but failed to surrender him to the tribunal. His name was changed to Father Anastasio Sumba Bura when he was in Florence. Father Serombo was a young man in his early thirties when he committed not only crimes against humanity but also evil that was against all that the church stood for. The chief prosecutor of the ICTR, Carla Ponti, accused the Vatican of obstructing the extradition of Father Serombo to face the charges against him. The Holy See claimed that Father Serombo was 'doing good works' in Italy. Eventually Father Serombo surrendered himself to the ICTR. He was sentenced to 15 years in prison and is serving his term in Benin.

There were many in the clergy who resisted the genocide and at great risk to themselves protected Tutsi. One notable example was Sister Felicitas Niyitegeka of Auxiliaires de l'Apostolat, a religious congregation. She was a Hutu, whose brother was Colonel Alphonse Nzungize of the Hutu army and worked in a nearby army camp. He pleaded with her to give up her work protecting Tutsis; she had helped many to cross to safety in neighbouring Zaire. She refused to abandon those who were in her care. She was taken by members of a Hutu militia to a nearby cemetery and shown Tutsi who had been killed, hoping that she would cease her work of protecting them. But, she was killed; shot and disposed of naked in an open grave. When her brother found her, he clothed her and arranged a proper burial for her.

Some of the methods of killing people were horrific to say the least. One example was where people were put into a hole dug in the ground for latrines. One report described how hot coals were put into the holes so that the prisoners burned to death. The Prime Minister of Rwanda at the time, was murdered together with her husband. Her vagina was stuffed with a beer can. Gruesome acts by the citizens of Rwanda were not confined to the Hutus. Equally evil were the actions of the Tutsis towards the Hutus.

During the genocide, tens of thousands of women and girls were raped, including one who was only two years old. Women were mutilated by cutting off their breasts, vaginas were pierced with spears, sticks or arrows. In her book, *'Leave None To Tell The Story'*, Alison Des Forges described one incident where an old Tutsi woman had her legs cut off and left to bleed to death. Tutsi women were forced to kill their children and to bury their dead husbands. Women sometimes had spears inserted through their vagina and forcibly advanced towards their heads. These acts were gruesome beyond imagination. The suffering endured is indescribable.

In 2017 the Catholic Church in Rwanda made a formal apology for its role in the genocide of 1994, in a statement signed by nine bishops. This was followed in 2017 by Pope Francis asking for forgiveness for the 'sins and failings of the church and its members' which he said had 'disfigured the face' of Catholicism. But, why did it take so long for the church to apologise? For over two decades it had information about the church and its personnel in Rwanda.

The Catholic and Anglican churches were not the only ones involved to varying degrees in the tragic events in Rwanda. Seventh-Day Adventists, Free Methodists, Baptists and Presbyterians were involved as well. The President of the Presbyterian Church of Rwanda, Michel Twagirayesu, who was at one time a vice-president of the World Council of Churches, is alleged to have been involved with the killers in Kirinda in Kibuye province, which was a predominantly Presbyterian area. Survivors reported that Bishop Aaron Ruhumuliza who was head of the Free Methodist Church in Gikondo, Kigali, helped the militia killings in his own church on 9th April 1994. This was by any standards as appalling as it was degrading. But, described as one of the worst bloodbaths of the massacre in 1994, was that by the President of the West Rwanda area of Seventh day Adventists, Elizaphan Nariratana who was in his 70's. He helped herd people in to his church and then called on the Hutu militiamen to murder them. He was aided in this gruesome process by his son, Dr. Gerard, aged 45 years. They surrounded the church with militiamen and arranged for the roof of the church to be removed to help with the massacre. There was no hiding place in the church. It was written that only a 1000 of the 50,000 Tutsis who lived in the vicinity of Elizaphan Ntakirutimana's church survived. Other pastors in the area wrote to Ntakirutimana – 'We wish to inform you that tomorrow we will be killed with our families', to which he replied 'There is nothing I can do for you. All you can do is prepare to die, for your time has come.' No attempt was made by him to help his people or to prevent the ensuing massacre. One of the judges at his trial said 'Pastor Ntakirutimana distanced himself from his Tutsi pastors and flock in their hour of need,' and referring to his son said 'As a medical doctor, he took lives instead of saving them.' Father and son also helped to turn the grounds of a hospital into a killing field. Ntakirutimana was sentenced to 10 years in prison and his son Gerard, to 25 years.

Christian nuns were not immune to killing in Rwanda. Nun Gertrude who was a Hutu was 'mother superior' of a Benedictine convent in Sova in Rwanda. She turned aways several thousand Tutsis who were fleeing murder and seeking shelter. Instead, she invited the Hutu militia to hack, stone and burn to death the Tutsis. Her sister, nun Marie, provided the

Ken Menon

Hutu militia with petrol to start a fire and burn to death 700 Tutsis who were hiding in a garage in the convent. Both were found guilty by a Belgian Court in 2001 of genocide. Gertrude was sentenced to 15 years in prison and Marie to 12 years. Following the court's verdict, Gertrude said 'I have nothing to add' but Marie retorted ' 'To say that I am guilty, as the jurors have said, is a lie'.

Clergy also died in the massacre that unfolded in Rwanda. The Vatican claimed that 3 bishops and about two hundred and fifty priests and nuns were killed during the genocide. This was acknowledged by the British journalist, Chris McGreal, while continuing that clergy were involved in the massacres of their own congregations. McGreal wrote ' The Vatican has sought to identify the church with the heroic priests. But ask Rwandans today which side the Catholic church as an institution was on during the genocide and many say it was allied with the killers'.

Rwanda must mark the lowest point of morality in the Church. Its encouragement to murder, murderous activities by clergy, the concealment of the accused and the reluctance to release these persons to be held to account make up a very serious charge sheet. In Rwanda, the Church surrendered its claim to morality. It can no more claim to speak for the downtrodden or the vulnerable without someone, somewhere asking what its own agenda is and what it stands to gain from its pronouncements and actions.

Churches – those sanctuaries of safety, peace and hope – became killing fields in Rwanda. For an overwhelmingly Christian country, the people of Rwanda would need a very long time to again trust in churches, if ever they do.

The Hutus largely killed with machetes. Close ones eyes and imagine thousands being literally cut down to death; no chopped to death. One gets a frightening glimpse of the gruesome spectacle. The number of deaths was, on average, 8000 people each and every day. This was equivalent to in excess of 25 fully laden aeroplanes crashing with the loss of all passengers in airports around the world daily for a hundred days. This is an absolutely horrible statistic; it was a much faster killing of human beings than the killing rate of Jews by the Nazis at the height of their power.

This is a mind-boggling, numbing statistic. But, and here is the crux of the matter, there was silence except for some reports in the press and on TV, in the initial stages.

This genocide showed yet again, if ever it was needed, the utter impotence of world institutions. Two of them in particular may be singled out. One, the United Nations, remained inert when its declared role is to identify and protect the vulnerable in the world. The other, the Churches, are there to provide succour to those in need. But it provided a veneer of protection and then proceeded to facilitate and participate in the killings. How could an apparently benevolent organisation like the church descend into this primeval violence?

The United Nations is known to be a sclerotic impotent organisation whose decisions are influenced by many who have vested interests, even if these interests include the wholesale slaughter of populations. But by its silence in this instance it stands accused as it did in Srebrenica, Yugoslavia in the 1990's, of being a party to genocide, by virtue of its impotence. The Catholic Church for its part has many unpardonable faults- it's stand on abortion, homosexuality, child abuse are but a few. Following disclosures of each of these, the Church has been reluctantly drawn to apologise and that too half-heartedly. But not for one moment could one have imagined it descending into murder.

What happened to the widow of President Habariyamana? Agathe Habyarimana, was the First Lady of Rwanda from 1973 to 1994. Following the President's assassination, Agathe was air lifted by the French from Rwanda and arrived in Paris. She was provided with a gift of French francs 230,000 by the French government. This money was from a fund which was set up by France for 'urgent assistance for Rwandan refugees'. She left France and at various times lived in Gabon and in Zaire. Because of the risk from the RPF, she entered France illegally, where she now resides. Rwanda's application for her extradition back to the country was denied by a French court. She is apparently still under investigation in France for her role in the genocide.

Who brought down the aeroplane carrying President Habariyamana and the President of Burundi, Cyprien Ntaryamira, remains an enigma. Many parties have been accused of the act- the Hutus, the RPF, the French,

Belgian, Americans etc. Each of these groups may have had a reason to assassinate President Habariyamana. The Hutus are suspected because they did not want to share power with the Tutsi and many of them were opposed to the Arusha Accords. The Tutsis had a powerful incentive to eliminate the President because they were denied power and were being persecuted. The same reason would apply in the case of the RPF. Alison Desforges laments the lack of a full investigation into the matter where many parties may have been responsible, including the President's party, or even the presidential guard.

Paul Kagame's army chief at one time had claimed that the RPF was responsible for downing the aeroplane. Faustin Kayumba Nyamwasa made this claim on the basis of what he was told by Paul Kagame, that the RPF had carried out the attack on the aeroplane. Apparently the missiles had been smuggled into Kigali airport with firewood. Nyamwasa lives in South Africa, having sought asylum there.

Felicien Kabuga was at one time one of the richest men in Rwanda. His wealth partly came from his large tea and coffee holdings. It was alleged that he helped to set up and finance the Interahamwe and that he used the radio station, Radio-Television Libre des Mille Collines, to broadcast messages of hatred and to incite Hutus to kill Tutsis. The strategy of the radio station was to attract the young. To do this it played music all day long interspersed with messages of hatred. It radicalised young Hutus who would then go on to do much of the killing of Tutsis. Kabuga was close to President Habariyamana and to the seat of power in Rwanda – one of his daughters married Habaryamana' eldest son. Another daughter married Augustin Ngirabatware, who as planning minister in Rwanda and who was responsible for the genocide. Ngirabatware was sentenced to 30 years in prison. Kabuga had been on the run after the genocide in Rwanda but was eventually captured in Paris in May 2020 from where he was transferred to the Hague to face justice for his part in the genocide. He was 87 years old at the time; he had been on the run and in hiding for over 20 years since the genocide.

Kabuga was described by some as a 'diabolical genius' and was also called ' Mr. Machete'. A report in London Sunday Times newspaper in February 1994 detailed how the tool manufacturer, Chillington, sold more machetes to Rwanda in one month than it did in an entire year. While being a commonly used agricultural implement in Rwanda, Zaire etc it was also an effective tool, in the killing fields that Rwanda descended into during the 100 days of genocide. The method adopted was to use a machete to attempt to kill 50 people in a day and to render immobile another 50 persons by severing their Achilles tendons. They would be left to die where they fell or the murderers would re-visit sometime later to finish executions. Such a scheme of killings could only have originated in the mind of an evil genius like Felicien Kabuga. The Achilles tendon is the main tendon behind the ankle whereby the calf muscles are attached to the back of the heel bone. Contraction of the muscle allows a human to remain upright. Lose the power of the tendon to transmit weight to the heel and the person is rendered immobile; a veritable paralysis of both limbs. In Greek mythology Achilles was the son of Thetis a goddess and Peleus. To render him invincible Thetis dipped the infant Achilles in the mythical river Styx which was supposed to make him invincible. Except of course that her fingers which encircled the infant's Achilles tendons prevented the waters of the river from touching that part of his body which was thereafter vulnerable. Achilles eventually died when an arrow pierced his tendons.

It is known than between January 1993 and March 1994, Rwanda imported 581 tons of machetes - each machete weighed about 600Gms. This is an astronomical 1 million machetes having being imported in a single year!

In his paper of 2011, *'Risking Irrelevance: The Threat of Impunity to the African Union'*, James Nyawo states that the African Union, must act in concert to bring t o justice those who are charged with war crimes, crimes against humanity and genocide against African people. He cites the problems faced by the International Criminal Tribunal for Rwanda in attempting to bring to justice nine fugitives who are responsible for the genocide. Most genocide fugitives were reported to be living and often working and running businesses in African countries, especially in Zimbabwe and Kenya. Nyawo acknowledges the solidarity between many African leaders who had fought against colonialism and white dominance and have a natural kinship, having endured much in their respective struggles for liberation. But he makes the point that the continent risks irrelevance if it continues with impunity and the protection of fugitives from justice.

The case of Protais Mpiranya is an example He was a Rwandan soldier who rose to the position of Commander of the Presidential Guard Battalion. Following the death of President Habyarimana, he is alleged to have lead the Presidential Guard, which eventually killed the Prime Minister of Rwanda, Agathe Uwilingiyimana and ten Belgian peacekeepers who were protecting her. He was reported to be in Zimbabwe. He was Hutu and is a high profile fugitive wanted by the ICTR. Zimbabwe said in 2012 that they were looking for Mpiranya. The ICTR has offered a reward for his capture. Mengistu Haile Mariam, dictator of Ethiopia, also found refuge in Zimbabwe, which refused to surrender him.

France, Belgium, Egypt, China, the World Bank, IMF all bear responsibility to for the events that befell Rwanda. They individually and / or collectively did not exercise sufficient scrutiny about the funds and aid they provided. But the greatest responsibility must fall, as indeed it has, on the shoulders of the French. France chose to remain blind to the atrocities taking place and also chose to deny their existence. It actively contributed to the loss of life by arming and protecting the President and his associates. More importantly, France manned checkpoints for the Rwandan Army and by some descriptions actively participated in the war. For e.g. In 1992 the commander of French forces in Rwanda, Lieutenant Colonel Chollet, assumed the role of Chief of Staff of the Rwandan Army. France was deeply involved in the activities of the Interahamwe. A former member of the Interahamwe who was the son of a Rwandan diplomat said 'We had two French military who helped train the Interahamwe. A lot of other Interahamwe were sent for training in Egypt. The French military taught us how to catch people and tie them. It was at the Affichier Central base in the centre of Kigali. It's where people were tortured. That's where the French military office was... The French also went with us Interahamwe to Mount Kigali, where they gave us training with guns. We didn't know how to use the arms which had been brought from France, so the French military were obliged to show us.'

However not everyone in the French political establishment of the time agreed with the direction of French foreign policy vis-à-vis Rwanda. France under the late President Mitterrand exerted as much pressure as it could to encourage Hamabariymana to introduce multiparty democracy in Rwanda and to include the minority Tutsis and the southern Hutus. Hutu opponents including women and children were murdered by the governing Hutu elite. This is interesting because Habariyamana let down both the Tutsis and Hutus. His government consisted largely of friends and family of the President, and in that sense he let down his own tribe too, especially the Hutus from the South. The case of the late Prime Minister, Agathe Uwilingiyimana, is an example. A moderate Hutu, she was the first Prime Minister under a power sharing agreement. As Minister for Education she abolished quotas and introduced admission on merit for which she earned the dislike of other Hutus. She was raped and shot dead together with her husband on 9th April 1994. On the other hand Mitterand viewed the alarming developments in Rwanda as a threat to French influence in Africa and its policy of Francophonie on the continent. He said that Rwanda was 'at the edge of the English-speaking front. Uganda cannot just do as it pleases. We must tell President Museveni (of Uganda) - it's not normal that the Tutsi minority wants to impose its rule over the Hutu majority'. In this mindset one may see the French need to preserve the Francophonie even at the expense of a tribal war, which is what it turned out to be. While continuing to support Rwanda with arms and personnel, France was at the same time conscious of the risk to French lives. It was known that the UK, USA and Belgium did not support or like Habariyamana. The latter considered France and Mitterand as his greatest international ally and military supporter. France for its part saw the situation on the ground as 'disastrous: it provides an avenue to the RPF, which, with Ugandan military support, Belgian sympathy for the Tutsis, an excellent system of propaganda emphasizing the wretched abuses committed by extremist Hutus, and the benevolent complicity of the Anglo-Saxon world, has been steadily scoring points on the military and political map.' With the ever deteriorating situation, France sought the help of the United Nations and so attempted to make the Rwandan problem an international issue. In the paper *The Rwandan Crisis seen through the eyes of France* edited by Arnaud Siad and translated by Christina Graubert, President Mitterand ' did not want to squander too much French blood and treasure on a former Belgian — not French — colony.' Mitterand and France were 'fiddling' while Rwanda 'was burning'.

France gave asylum to many of the people involved in genocide in Rwanda. Rouen in Normandy is known as the 'European capital of genocidaires'. Among those living here are persons who were close to the late President Habariyamana. These include his daughter, Marie-Merci Habyarimana, and widow Agathe Kanziga. The group also includes a catholic priest, Father Wenceslas Munyeshyaka and Sosthene Munyemana, who is nicknamed 'the butcher of Tumba'. Munyema was a gynaecologist who lived and worked in Butare, a region known for a degree of peaceful co-existence between Hutus and Tutsis. But in inflammatory speeches, Munyemana encouraged hatred and eventual violence and killing by Hutus of Tutsis.

On February 23, 1993, the Federation of French Abroad sent a letter to then President Francois Mitterrand in which they criticised France's role in supporting the Habyarimana regime. Their damning words point to the silent approval or disinterest of Mitterand — 'Rwanda is more than ever on fire and drowning in blood... General Habyarimana's militias are massacring the Tutsi population with impunity... the French military intervention in Rwanda has neither succeeded in avoiding massacres nor in restoring peace in the region.'. Importantly, and here is the critical statement — 'Worse, it now appears that the presence of French military in that country is providing international protection as cover to allow General Habyarimana to order more atrocities.' In the face of these criticisms it is hard to understand the position of France and especially of President Mitterand in apparently being blind to the continuing and massive loss of life.

Later that same month, head of French diaspora in Burundi, Gérard Fuchs declared 'I question the decision to send more French troops to Rwanda, given that human rights violations by general Habyarimana's regime show no sign of stopping,'

The French Minister of Defence at the time, Pierre Joxe, wrote to Mitterand suggesting that Habyarimana is 'largely responsible' for the violence and murders in Rwanda due to his 'political intransigence.' And he advised that France withdraw its troops from the country to facilitate a political solution to the crisis. He recommended pressuring Habyarimana to soften his position by threatening to withdraw French troops and to negotiate a political solution in the country.

The historian Vincent Duclert said 'French policy in Rwanda contributed to the setting up of a genocidal process without the French authorities even understanding it, without them wanting it.' He goes on to state that there was, in the French establishment of the time 'a willingness to ignore the many warnings that came from the heart of the State, where several protagonists had expressed their opposition to a system – opaque – of unconditional support for an undemocratic regime, held by extremists who promoted a racist policy of persecuting the Tutsis. This blindness consisted of deliberately ignoring all these warnings in order to maintain the Habyarimana regime at all costs, using methods that we have shown to be irregular.'

Duclert refers to a political, intellectual and institutional bankruptcy in the French establishment of the time.

On the twentieth anniversary of the genocide, in 2014, the President of Rwanda, Paul Kagame accused France and Belgium of having had a 'direct role' in the events that happened in 1994. He was even more forthright with France, accusing it of direct involvement in the genocide. The Foreign Minster of France at the time, Alain Juppe' said Kagame's comments were a 'falsification of history'. However, he later admitted that there were errors of judgement and that 'the French authorities above all lacked the understanding which would have enabled them to act without delay against the massacres.' He went on to add 'We did not measure that we were abandoning hundreds of thousands of Tutsi promised to death. .... We did not imagine that our forces would have been able, provided they had the support of Belgian paratroopers, Italian commandos, American marines, all associated with the blue helmets, to oppose the killers, to protect the victims. This act of international cowardice as he describes it, cannot exonerate France from its own responsibilities.

Rwanda cut off diplomatic relations with France in November 2006.

Following the publication of the Duclert report, Bernard Kouchner, who served as minister under Presidents Mitterand and Nicholas Sarkozy said that François Mitterrand and 'the people of the Élysée did not want to see anything'. He made several explosive claims, the main one of which was that when he warned Mitterand of what was happening in Rwanda, the latter said 'you are exaggerating'. He went on to claim that the French were battling for influence with Western competitors and that Paul Kagame was a 'servant of the Americans'.

The current in cumbent of the Élysée Palace, President Emmanuel Macron, visiting Rwanda in 2021 admitted that France bears 'overwhelming responsibility for the events in country in 1994. This admission fell far short of an apology for France's involvement and contribution to the atrocities. He added that 'no suspected genocide perpetrator will be able to avoid justice'. However, Buteanine Munyeshuli, a Rwandan researcher working with survivors of the atrocities said ' it is not what is said at the memorial, but which actions -- judicial, legislatives -- will be taken. I want it to become impossible for officials to minimize France's involvement in the genocide.'

Rwanda has provided France an opportunity to re-appraise its relationship with the continent of Africa, where it has too often associated with and helped keep in power brutal dictators. France stands accused of being reluctant to facilitate transition to democracy. Time alone will pass judgement on France.

In an apparent rejection of Francophone and a metaphorical slap in the face to France, Rwanda joined the British Commonwealth of Nations.

The UK harbours about five fugitives from justice, related to genocide in Rwanda. Attempts to extradite them to face justice in Rwanda have been frustrated by the courts, fearing that they would not get a fair trial. Other countries with similar or even better systems of justice like Canada, USA and Sweden have returned persons to Rwanda to face Justice. Is the system of justice in the UK so superior and / or are the courts much farer than those in other countries? If Sweden, Canada and the USA consider that persons can get a fair trial in Rwanda what is the obstacle that the UK courts see? How did Vincent Bajinya, who changed his name to Vincent Brown, even get citizenship of the UK? He is a medical doctor who acted against all ethics of the medical profession. He organised road blocks where Tutsi were trapped and murdered with machetes provided by him. This was the first time that an English court had blocked an extradition request from a foreign government on the basis that doing so would be at variance with Article 6 of the European Convention on Human Rights, which safeguards the right to a fair trial. This is even though the European Court of Human Rights determined in 2011 that Rwandan authorities had provided sufficient guarantees regarding the right to a fair trial.

The UK judiciary had yet again demonstrated that it does not act in the interest of justice in general or in the interest of the people of the UK. Until genocidaires are extradited to the countries where they committed heinous crimes, the UK government and the judiciary would have a stain on their consciences.

ICONOCLASM, WOKEISM

To try and understand the philosophy of iconoclasm one needs to ask why monuments are pulled down. History is replete with stories of monuments being erected and years or centuries later being torn down, only to have other monuments to other persons or ideas erected. And so the cycle goes on of erection, destruction, further erection ad infinitum throughout history..

To appreciate why monuments are pulled down a good starting point would be a realization, if that were completely possible, of why they were erected in the first place. Separated by time and interpreted by successive writers, the reason or reasons for erection may be many according to whom one reads or consults.

The philosophy of iconoclasm is probably no different to why books are burned or manuscripts, works of art etc. are cast aside but replaced by others. This is either a destruction of history or its reinterpretation or a hybrid of the two.

It is not impossible to conclude that erection of a monument reflects the time when it came into existence. A monument represents people and their values of the time. Additionally it reflects a dominant view of the time. Not everyone at the time would be in support of a monument. Opponents may eventually remain silent, accepting the eventuality. Or in the fullness of time their voices would crystallise into themes which carry through the years and even centuries. These voices may find a cause much later, even centuries later, as we see in what is happening now with the toppling of statues by black people. As Keith Lowe wrote in his book, *'Prisoners of History'*, 'monuments reflect our values and every society deceives itself that its values are eternal'. But there were others who did not share those values at the time. They have gained a voice now, so powerful and conveyed with conviction and vigor that society succumbs to its persuasions; hence monuments fall.

Iconoclasm is not only the destruction of history but also its creation. As one chapter in human history is erased, another one, at another time in history is being opened. This too, with the progress of time, is likely to be wiped out.

What are the values that are so pervasive at the time while simultaneously being powerful as to drive others to cooperate in creating a monument? Take for example the Washington Monument in Washington DC, USA. It is an obelisk commemorating the first President of the USA, George Washington (1732- 1799) who was in office from 1789 to 1797. He was one-time commander in chief of the Continental Army that fought in the American Revolutionary War and he was a Founding Father. The Monument was at one time the tallest structure in the world until it was dwarfed by the Eiffel Tower in Paris, which was completed in 1889. The single dominant value of the time that underscored the construction of the Washington Monument was the need to be free from Great Britain, the perceived coloniser. Washington believed that no-one had a right to tax an individual, save the representatives of their own choosing. Washington believed that the Parliament of Great Britain 'hath no more right to put their hands into my pocket without my consent, than I have to put my hands into yours for money'. In the *Rights of Man,* Thomas Paine wrote 'no man in his sober senses will compare the character of any of the kings of Europe with that of George Washington'. Implicit in this statement was that Washington was a 'Patriot King' of such stature that even monarchs of Europe could not reach. On the death of George Washington, Henry Lee wrote of him ' first in war, first in peace, first in the hearts of his countrymen'. Despite enormous and overwhelming public sympathy and support, there were others who were royalists and pro-British, who opposed Washington. However time has shown that Washington was right and he is now considered the 'Father of the Nation'.

The enduring legacy of George Washington is also seen in the massive sculpture carved into Mount Rushmore in South Dakota. The four faces are of Washington, Thomas Jefferson, Theodore Roosevelt and Abraham Lincoln. Designed by sculptor, Gutzon Borgium, it was created between 1927 and 1941, with each head being 60 feet tall. This National Memorial represents the USA at 'birth, growth, development and preservation'.

Then again look at the gruesome monuments erected by Timur in Asia and Europe. He had many versions of his name like Amir Timur and the nickname Tamerlane. He was born in 1336 in Modern day Uzbekhistan; he was a devout Muslim calling himself the 'Sword of Islam'. Descended from Turcs and Mongols he was by all descriptions a violent man who tried to recreate the empire of Genghis Khan. Following the death of Genghis Khan his empire disintegrated due to factionalism. In setting out to create a vast Timurid Empire, Timur killed several million people. It is estimated that 17 million people or 5% of the world population at the time died at the hands of Timur. He would strike fear in his opponents and also serve a warning to others by creating towers made of human skulls of those whom he vanquished. It is not likely that his armies dissected the dead and collected skulls. What more likely happened was that bodies were dismembered and heads were piled up high. Environmental heat and progressive decay left the dried out skulls as a reminder to others. In these monuments there was no universal values that were represented. Rather they were designed by one person with the sole purpose of subjugation and dominance by striking fear.

In April 2002, a 40 foot (12 metres) statue of the late President Saddam Hussain of Iraq was erected in Firdos Square in Baghdad. It commemorated the 65th birthday of the President. Firdos means paradise and the square is a public space in central Baghdad, the capital of Iraq. Following Iraq's misguided invasion of Kuwait in August 1990 and the subsequent first Gulf War in January 1991, Iraq was defeated. The statute of Saddam Hussein was toppled in April 2003, to much Iraqi jubilation.

The monuments of Timur and Saddam Hussein were created by single persons to further their personal interests. In the case of Timur it was to instil fear and serve as a warning to his enemies not to rise up against him. However in the case of Saddam Hussein it was to show his people who he was and that he and he alone was in charge and that all authority resided in him. It was also a monument erected to a person who was alive. Such monuments are not common and also not likely to last any significant duration. In the case of Saddam Hussein one could see the extent of reverence to him. This was obviously not genuine; people were forced to almost venerate him or face dire consequences. The joy that accompanied the fall of Saddam's monument is a measure of the dislike that ordinary Iraqis had of him.

It is appropriate to look at the Mamayev Kurgan monument in Volgograd, formerly Stalingrad in Russia. Meaning 'the Motherland calls', the monument was for a time the largest sculpture in the world. It still is the largest sculpture of a woman. Mamayev commemorates Russian victory over the Axis powers in World War 2. This was one of the deadliest battles in history with 500,000 dead. Marshall of the Soviet Union <u>Vasily Chuikov</u>, is buried at Mamayev Kurgan. He led the Soviet army against the German army and is the only Marshall of the Soviet Union who is not buried in Moscow. Mamayev Kurgan is a near- sacred place for Russians. They commemorate their existential victory against the German and Axis forces. The context of the Mamayev Kurgan memorial is relevant today.

Both the Washington memorial and the Mamayev Kurgan monument are likely to last a long time. It is difficult to envisage them being pulled down or destroyed in any way, barring a national cataclysm. Both monuments, in their own respective ways represent the survival of the two nations.

In this respect Washington and Mamayev differ markedly from mere human monuments. The former have deep seated national values which underpin their relevance to their respective citizens. Take away these monuments and the existential history of the two countries history is erased.

Religious iconoclasm is based on the concept of destroying a religion's culture either because it does not fit with one's views or because it is perceived as being offensive or sacrilegious. The destruction by the Taliban of the Buddhas of Bamiyan in Afghanistan in 2001 is a case in point. Various descriptions of why these statues were destroyed have emerged. A view is that the Taliban saw the statues as idolatry. Another view is that the order to destroy then was given in a fit of rage when foreigners agreed to pay for their restoration. When they were asked for money to feed children in Afghanistan, apparently this was refused. The choice of preserving the statues instead of helping suffering children may have been too much to bear, for some in the Taliban.

Similar iconoclasm occurred with monuments in Palmyra in Syria. Palmyra which is known as the 'Venice of the Sands' was an ancient city constructed between the 1st and third centuries AD. It was a trade hub like ancient Venice was, with desert sand as the sea and camels as the means of transport, instead of boats. Palmyra had imposing columns, a theatre, the temple of Bel or Baal etc. Palmyra was attacked and parts of it including the temple of Bel destroyed by ISIS (Islamic State of Iraq and Syria) after 2011. The eminent historian and care-taker of Palmyra, Khaled al-Asaad, refused to divulge to ISIS militants where some of the important treasures at Palmyra were to be found. He was beheaded and his mutilated body was hung from one of the columns. All this was done in Palmyra because of idolatry which, in the view of ISIS, had no place in human society.

In their paper of 2017, 'Iconoclasm and strategic thought: Islamic State and cultural heritage in Iraq and Syria', Matthew Clapperton and colleagues describe three factors that need to be present in the strategy of iconoclasm - '... the degradation and delegitimization of the existing societal fabric, the removal of all reference to the previous society, and an attempt to reconstruct society in keeping with a new ideological vision.' These facets are as relevant as they are important in the iconoclasm of modern times. What may be occurring is an attempt to erase history or to re-write it in the moulds of the movements, concepts and personalities of the day.

Cultural property does not belong to any one group of persons or to one society; they are collectively owned by mankind. The United Nations Security Council unanimously adopted Resolution 2347 in 2017, which dealt with protecting cultural property. This was the culmination of a long journey that began in Brussels, Belgium on 27th July 1874. The Brussels Declaration of 1874 stated that in times of war, 'all seizure or destruction of, or wilful damage to historic monuments, works of art and science should be made the subject of legal proceedings by the competent authorities.'

The Hague Convention for the Protection of Cultural Property in the Event of Armed Conflict and its two Protocols (1954 and 1999) contain two crucial words – 'safeguard' and 'respect'. It declared that – 'Damage to cultural property belonging to any people whatsoever' is internationally recognized as 'damage to the cultural heritage of all mankind'.

These legal instruments have allowed the successful prosecution of individuals responsible for cultural vandalism For e.g. UNESCO in association with the UN International Criminal Tribunal for the former Yugoslavia successfully prosecuted in 2004 the Yugoslav naval officer, Miodrag Jokić, to seven years of imprisonment. Under Jokić's command mortars had been fired in October 1991, damaging the old town of Dubrovnik which was listed as a World Heritage site. This was the first prosecution of its kind.

In 2016, the Malian jihadist Ahmad Al Faqi was found guilty by the International Criminal Court of destroying ten religious sites in Timbuktu. Timbuktu was then under the control of the group, Ansar Dine, who were suspected to have had links with al Qaeda. Al Faqi was sentenced to nine years' imprisonment. This judgement was again a first, as destruction of cultural heritage was now considered a war crime.

About fifty countries adopted a resolution which prohibited trade in cultural artefacts from Syria and Iraq.

In her paper of 2019, *'The History of Iconoclasm'*, Ellen Sharman describes iconoclasm as a 'visceral response' to human rage. She raised the important point of humanity reflecting on the need for visibility in art. The same would apply to the visibility of monuments. Take away visibility and history is either subdued or takes an entirely different meaning. The important question of how things came to be, are submerged by the needs of the moment; the need to tear down. Relevant to our time is her statement that 'During the French Revolution, iconoclasm became associated with blind acts of uneducated vandalism, likened to cultural ignorance'. Are we witnessing, in the current epidemic of iconoclasm, an ignorance or rather a failure to acknowledge the truth. Which brings one to the crucial aspect of context, Context would help the vandal to reflect and then if needs be to pull down, if still persuaded to do so. It also brings into focus the concept of respect for the person, especially the humanitarian aspect, even if one denigrates for e.g., the person's association with slavery.

What is the link between cultural vandalism and the pulling down of statues that the world, especially in the West, has witnessed in recent years?

It is not as if the statues being pulled down now are cultural sites or that they have a special status accorded to them by the United Nations or any such body. The words used to describe various episodes of cultural vandalism are relevant to what is happening today. Words such as ownership, respect, safeguard and context. Many who orchestrate the destruction of statues today may not find much sympathy for the word 'respect'. One is not asking that one should respect a slave trader or someone who has had a peripheral association with it. There is a case to respect what that person stood for at the time of the events and especially the philanthropy that the person has bequeathed to society. This philanthropy does not benefit only a single group, for if it had been, it would be discriminatory. Rather people of all races, religions, beliefs etc benefit from the philanthropy of these persons. Take the Rhodes Trust and Rhodes Scholarships for example. They are open to persons who have ' truth, courage, devotion to duty, sympathy for and protection of the weak, kindliness, unselfishness and fellowship...... and moral force of character and instincts to lead and to take an interest in one's fellow beings'. In its statement, *'The Bold Dream: Transcending the Impossible'*, the Rhodes Trust states 'When different people come together in a shared spirit, exciting new things begin'.

And so it came to be that the American, Alain LeRoy Locke was the first black Rhodes scholar, in 1907. That was only 3 years after the first white American Rhodes scholar was elected in 1904. Locke said - 'For me, as for others, Oxford was a college education over again, though naturally a 'deluxe' version....... I temporarily abandoned formal education for the pursuit of culture......one had every facility for becoming really cosmopolitan — it was a rare experience in the company of many foreign students to pay Englishmen the very high tribute of not even attempting to be like them, but to be more one's self, because of their example.' In these words one recognises a remarkable person who had transcended culture and broken down barriers. His words almost pays gratitude to Rhodes for the wonderful opportunity he had. He wanted to show what the 'New *Black*' was like.

In an interesting twist to the story it was realised in 2014 that Alain LeRoy Locke had not been buried, having died on 9th June 1954 at the age of 68 years. On learning of this, the Rhodes Trust carried the following statement on its website -'In 2007, the Association of American Rhodes Scholars conceived and planned a symposium in conjunction with Howard

University on the centenary of the election of Alain Leroy Locke as a Rhodes Scholar from Pennsylvania. ... An unexpected outcome of the research was in learning that Locke's cremated remains were still in the custody of the University.

From this discovery arose the commitment to arrange for a proper interment for this eminent American scholar. 'With the financial support from African-American Rhodes Scholars, we have purchased a burial plot at Congressional Cemetery, Washington, D.C. and commissioned a memorial headstone to honor our distinguished predecessor.' The interment occurred on 13th September 2014.

In the words of the late Reggae singer, Bob Marley- 'lets get together and feel alright', Rhodes scholars got together and did what was right, irrespective of colour etc. Here again lies the need to respect Rhodes for what he gave to Oxford and to generations of Rhodes scholars.

There is also a need to safeguard these monuments, if not in their current location, then in some other place where the public may learn about the acts and works of these persons. Not all their work could have been bad, for they have given much to this nation from which many benefit. When Rhodes scholars return to their countries, they take with them not only learning but also an enlightenment which, if channelled appropriately, would benefit millions more people at home. This is a real transfer of benefits and in some ways is a reparation, if that is needed, by home countries. These statues may not belong to mankind but they belong to the nation. Then again one could claim that they do indeed belong to mankind - if only to convey the abhorrence of domination, whether slavery, political or other forms of domination. Take all these together and one soon sees the importance of context. Take away a statue and its context and one has denied succeeding generations of the opportunity to learn about and to understand slavery and human domination. Here one sees a path through the fog of arguments and counter-arguments on statues and give life and meaning to the words of the late Nelson Mandela, President of South Africa, at his inauguration in 1994 – *'Never, never and never again... (must we)... experience the oppression of one by another'*

Sir Robert Geffrye also written as Geffrey (1613-1703) was a merchant associated with the East India company and the Royal Africa Company, and he was a slave trader. He owned a slave ship, the China Merchant, and was involved in forced labour and slavery. He was a member of the Worshipful Society of Ironmongers and became Lord Mayor of London. He constructed fourteen alms-houses in Hoxton in the London Borough of Hackney for use by poor persons in the local community. He was born in Landrake in Cornwall. He left money to the poor in Landrake and also to St.Erney's Church in Cornwall. There is also the Sir Robert Geffrye school in Cornwall which describes itself as a Primary Academy with a Christian ethos. Reading the school's website one notes that it recognises that each child is unique and that the school works to encourage and provide the opportunity 'to fulfil their potential academically, socially and morally. We are proud of our children and always offer support and celebrate achievements'. It goes on to state that ' each child is a highly valued individual, each with his or her own unique characteristics and abilities. With each one we seek to celebrate the achievement of his or her full potential…. We hope that our children will develop self-confidence and self-esteem, linked with respect for others and for the environment'

That Sir Robert Geffrey was involved in the slave trade is not in doubt and is not being contested by anyone. But the context in which the slave trade took place, over 400 years ago, is not being considered in any discussion of the person. His association with slavery, at a time, when it was considered 'normal' business practice is not given due consideration. If it is given consideration it is with the morality of modern times and not with that which obtained 400 years ago. Who is to say that the views of the moralists of today would not be discarded in the years and centuries to come? That Sir Robert also contributed to the community In Hackney is also not in doubt. And above all the school that bears his name is a shining example of what it seeks to achieve with children. To help children achieve their full potential as this school says is something to be treasured and emulated. And of course children in the school need to be told about the life and activities of the person who gave his name to their school and place it in the context of the times. Children would evaluate and understand if information is provided in a non- partisan and non-judgemental manner. They would decide and individually or collectively pass judgement on the matter of slavery and on Sir Geffrey.

A statue of Sir Robert is in the Museum of the Home in Kingsland

Road, London. It was formerly called the Geffrey Museum. Following protest by the Black Lives Matter (BLM) movement, the Museum duly consulted on the matter and decided to retain the statue as it is. It is imperative that the statute and what is written about Sir Robert is placed in context. Visitors to the Museum can then inform themselves about slavery, when it happened, Sir Robert's role in the slave trade and about his philanthropy. Public can formulate their own views on the matter and if they choose to cast judgement through the prism of 2021 morality and ethics on events that occurred 400 years or more ago. The context of slavery needs to be discussed because at the time there were no Human Rights laws or even a concept of what a persons' rights were.

Some of the persons who protested about the statue are worthy of note. Olawatoyin Agbetu is a British citizen of Nigerian origin who is a social rights activist. He gained notoriety on 27th March 2007 when he slipped pass security personnel to confront the Queen who was attending a church service being held in Westminster Abbey to celebrate the 200th anniversary of Great Britain's Abolition of the Salve Trade act 1807. Standing about ten feet away from the Queen, he shouted at her 'You should be ashamed. We should not be here. This is an insult to us. I want all the Christians who are Africans to walk out of here with me!' This, at a time and on a day when the abolition of slavery was being celebrated.

At a time when the country was striving to contain the Covid-19 pandemic, it is unfortunate that Agbetu claimed that 'a magical vaccine is round the corner form the Viagra specialists. There is a lot of nonsense out there and it is coming from No: 10'. This is a 'profit over people government that wants to privatise speed over safety and effectiveness is ethically unsound'. Such anti-vaccine rhetoric from someone who has not reckoned with the facts and with the scientific research behind the clinical trials and eventual production of the vaccine, is troubling. This is especially so when we know that the Black community are at greater risk of infection with the coronavirus and of death from it.

The BLM petitioned for the removal of an obelisk to Sir Thomas Picton (1758-1815) in Carmarthen, South Wales. That Sir Thomas was not the most agreeable of persons is not without much doubt. Wellington wrote - 'I found him a rough foul-mouthed devil as ever lived, but he always behaved extremely well; no man could do better in different services

I assigned to him'. He had the rank of lieutenant- general and was by all accounts a brave soldier. He was the most senior officer to die in the Battle of Waterloo.

In 1797 Thomas Picton became Governor of Trinidad. He was accused of the execution of slaves. He was charged with detention and cruelty towards those on the island who practiced a form of spiritual healing called obeah. Obeah was, at the time, practised by African slaves in the West Indies. Picton adopted a policy of '*let them hate so long as they fear*' in his dealings with sections of the Trinidad population. William Fullarton who was a senior commissioner appointed by Britain to govern the island, brought charges against Picton about his treatment of the local population. The Privy Council dealt with the majority of the charges against Picton. He was charged with cruelty to slaves and execution without following due process. The case eventually fizzled out as there was a conflict as to whether Spanish or English law applied on the island. Trinidad was a Spanish colony. Picton died at the Battle of Waterloo when a musket ball penetrated his temple. He went to battle in civilian clothes and wearing a top-hat. His body was brought back to England and a monument was erected in his memory in St Paul's Cathedral. The obelisk was erected in Carmarthen in 1823 from subscriptions, to which the King also contributed the sum of one hundred guineas.

The historian Alessandro Barbero wrote that Picton was 'respected for his courage and feared for his irascible temperament'.

The interesting feature of the petition to remove the statue of Sir Thomas Picton is that of 18646 signatures only 3897 were from persons in the UK. The rest were from abroad. However, in a local Council survey on the matter more than two-thirds of respondents supported the view that the Council do nothing about removal of the obelisk and that it remain in place.

Sir John Cass (1661-1718) became a member of the court of assistants, Board of Directors in modern parlance, of the Royal Africa Company which traded on the west African coast in gold, silver, ivory and slaves. There is no evidence that he was actively and personally involved in owning or trading slaves. He worked for the Royal African Company which traded in slaves in the 1600's and owned shares in the company.

Sit John Cass was a philanthropist. He founded a school for fifty boys and forty girls in the churchyard of St.Botolph's in Aldgate. Following the George Floyd protests, the school changed its name from Sir John Cass Redcoat School to Stepney All Saints School.

The Sir John Cass Foundation is one of the largest charities dedicated to the education of children and young persons. This is its mission. Again, following the George Floyd protests the Foundation decided to change its name in acknowledgement of the link between the name of Sir John and slavery. The foundation stated 'It is important to us that our new name reflects our beliefs and charitable work, and will remain relevant through the next 300 years. We therefore ask for your patience in the coming weeks while Trustees, partners, and stakeholders, consult on the name and then undertake the legal applications to officially change our name as a charity.'

In April 2021, the Cass Business School was renamed the Bayes Business School after Thomas Bayes who was a theologian and statistician. He is buried close to the campus. The absence of context denies those who have benefitted from his philanthropy, to understand the person of Sir John Cass. Generations have gained from his largesse and to deny recognition of this is to deny an important lesson in history. Future students may not have reason to ask who Sir John Cass was and therefore may not have occasion to learn, among other matters, another chapter in the history of slavery. Slavery, paradoxically, brought beneficence to many.

However it is regrettable that it is not clear if the name of Sir John would be retained by the Foundation but placed in context. This is an important aspect of any name change. One cannot under-estimate the impact of the history of slavery on society but it is also vital not to under-estimate the enormous contribution of philanthropists like Sir John to education and emancipation in the locality and generally. To ignore the latter would be a tragedy and deprive young persons of a balance of information from which they can make their own judgements. In the continuing discussion on statues, street names etc there cannot be a single unchallenged narrative. Nor should one ignore the contribution of philanthropists to society. One may compare what happened then with the current migrant crises that are almost a daily occurrence. How could a few who are in pursuit of profit endanger the lives of other vulnerable persons? How could a few slave seekers and owners in Africa have trapped their own countrymen and traded them for profit? It will always remain paramount that society informs and educates children and young persons and not corral them into the folly of a misguided and not uncommonly erroneous view of slavery. Context! Context! Context!

'Context' is often a loosely used word. But it is the essential ingredient that brings to life any meaningful discussion. Context may be defined as 'the circumstances that form the setting for an event, statement, or idea, and in terms of which it can be fully understood'. An event or a statement is set against a background which one needs to appreciate to place it in its appropriate environment. One may then be able to understand the event or what is being said. Context nourishes an event or object or a statement. Devoid of context, an event becomes featureless. It is deprived of vibrancy and life. Context, by setting an event within the fabric of society, its morality, the imperatives that operated at the time etc., allows one to understand matters better; it permits an intellectual evaluation and aids decision making.

The greatest wisdom gained from looking back is to illuminate current thinking and to provide guidance for the future. The Chinese artist Ai WeiWei (1957-) said ' I think public statues are like a seal, or some mark on history. We have to respect our memory, but learn from our mistakes. Removing statues is something to me like talking about a man having a facelift as he gets older; you know, you think you want to make changes but they are not necessarily for the better. The debate is interesting, but not logical. If you follow [its argument], most buildings would be destroyed because they all come from that colonial time.'

On 23rd August 1939, Russia and Germany signed the Molotov-Ribbentrop Pact. It was thus called because the signatories were the German Foreign Minister Joachim von Ribbentrop and his Soviet counterpart, Vyacheslav Molotov. Its official name was the Treaty of Non-Aggression between Germany and the Union of Soviet Socialist Republics. The Pact allowed Germany and Russia to invade Poland and to partition it. It also allowed Russia to invade and take over large parts of the Baltic- Lithuania, Estonia, Latvia, Finland etc. While on the surface the Pact appeared to work comfortably, there were tension developing between the two countries. This was especially so in September 1940 when Germany invaded Romania, interested, in part, in its oils fields. After November 1940 Hitler was planning for the invasion of Russia. The Molotov-Ribbentrop ceased to exist on 22 June 1941 when Germany invaded the Soviet Union in <u>Operation Barbarossa</u>, after the name of the Holy Roman Emperor, Frederick Barbarossa and German King Frederick 1 (1122-1190).

Fast forward to February 2022 and one can begin to appreciate one of the reasons for the Ukrainian War. Reassurances from NATO or the European Union of non-malevolence towards Russia are insufficient to assuage the concerns of the latter. It has history to remind itself of how a non – aggression pact was violated. Russia's security is a genuine concern to its leaders. The threat of a functioning liberal democracy on its western border, associated with the inevitable militarisation of Ukraine that would follow on it becoming a member of NATO, was probably too much to bear thinking of in a country that had suffered a lot in World War Two. Russia was not likely to accept reassurances with any degree of seriousness. It sought guarantees of its own security.

Then again listen to the words of President Vladimir Putin of Russia reading his views on recreating the land of Peter the Great. In June 2022 President Putin talked to young scientists and entrepreneurs in Russia about the greatness of Peter and about the Northern Wars. These were a series of wars between 1555 and 1721, These included the Russian-Polish war of 1654-1667 and the Russio-Swedish Wars of 1554-1557 and 1590-1595. The Great Northern War between 1700 and 1721 between Sweden and Russia led to Russia becoming a dominant power in Europe. Putin said of Peter 'You might think he was fighting with Sweden, seizing their lands…..but he seized nothing; he reclaimed it!'. 'It seems it has fallen to us, too, to reclaim and strengthen'. Putin argued that Slavs had lived in the regions for many centuries. He went on to say that the land that is now St. Petersburg was not recognised by neighbours as part of Russia at the time but that it is now an integral and recognised part of Russia.

President Putin blamed Lenin (Vladimir Ilyich Ulyanov), who founded the Soviet Union, for creating Ukraine out of historical Russian territory.

Although not complete in any way, the foregoing descriptions provide some context and insight into the Russian rationale for the Ukraine war.

This background information taken together with others provides one with a more wholesome view of what is happening in Ukraine than a bland description of a war between two nations. The propaganda battle that is present in any war colours and distorts the reality and an appreciation of the basis of the conflict. However, the more strands of context that come into the information envelope of an event, the better it become for an observer to make an increasingly informed opinion of it. Of course that opinion is open to change and re-interpretation, when additional information is discovered. And that is how it should be; it remains open for the individual to come to a settled view as it remains for the person to be free to change that view.

The relevance to iconoclasm is that those who clamour to tear down monuments need to provide as much information and context so that history remains alive and not submerged by the fashions of the day.

Take the case of the petition to remove the statue of Sir Robert Peel, which is located in Piccadilly Gardens In Manchester. Sir Robert Peel was a former Prime Minister who founded the Metropolitan Police in the 1820's when he was Home Secretary. Police were called Bobbies after Robert of Sir Robert Peel, Bob being a common nickname for those with the name Robert. Protesters had targeted the wrong Robert Peel. It was his father, with the same name, who had opposed the abolition of slavery. When the organisers realised that they had made a mistake, they were not deterred. Instead they still wanted the statue taken down. This time the reason was that 'we should not celebrate colonisers'.......'with the legitimacy of current policing in question, the history of policing, its origins in colonialism and its role in suppressing dissent deserves greater scrutiny........Peel's statue belongs in a museum, as part of an exhibition for others to learn about the history of British colonialism.'

One may discern in this statement that the BLM is not only about slavery and emancipation of blacks, but that there is a wider agenda which include colonialism and the abolition of capitalism. Colonialism was far from perfect but also had its virtues and benefits to the countries that were colonised. The recent protests in Hong King for example are partly a clamour to maintain the status quo.

The business minster in the UK, Nadhim Zahawi said ' My opinion is any slave trader should not have a statue. But I wouldn't be breaking the law to take statues down, it should be done through our democratic process. This country is a democracy, a proud democracy and it should be up to local people to decide what they want to do with that statue and any other statue. If the majority of people decide that we want the statues down, then they should be taken down.'

This takes one to the matter of due process which Zahawi was talking about rather than anarchy. The Mayor of London, Sadiq Khan implied the same when he said ' I don't condone at all any attacks on our police, any disorder or criminal damages.'

Contrary to what the 'Topple the Racists' website says that statues 'pay tribute to slave traders and racists', they are there for a different reason. They serve to remind public of what the person had done, bad and good. Again, there is no doubt that slavery is unacceptable and evil by the standards of today. But these persons were also philanthropist's who contributed to society. Their contributions benefited and continue to benefit generations of people. An interesting and worrying ethical issue arises here. Philanthropy could not have occurred without the profits of slavery which helped to make the companies run by the persons profitable, especially in the sugar industry of the Caribbean. Is it therefore ethical to accept the philanthropy from ill gotten gains? Does society have to stop with tearing down statues? Or should this be extrapolated to dismantle the entire edifice of slavery including the benefits that have accrued to generations from schools, education, houses etc. Seen in this light, statutes are not objects of 'adoration'. They mark staging posts in history. Society needs to learn about events gone by and resolve not to repeat them or turn a blind eye when they occur now. It is only by remembering that one would keep the issue of slavery alive. As the philosopher George Santyana said 'those who cannot remember the past are condemned to repeat it'. The rise of modern slavery illustrates, if it were needed, Santyana's warning to society. And what better and sadder example of the fickleness of human memory than the events currently unfolding in Ukraine. Addressing the German Parliament, the Bundestag, on 17th March 2022, Ukrainian President Volodymyr Zelensky said ' I address all of you who heard politicians say every year 'never again' ... 'but I can see these words are worth nothing.

Now, our whole nation is being exterminated in Europe, why?'….'I address the older people among you who have survived the Second World War, who were rescued during the occupation, who survived Babyn Yar, where President Steinmeier visited last year for the 80th anniversary of the tragedy, and where Russian missiles struck,'….'It was there that families were killed. Again, 80 years later.'

In July 1995, more than 7500 Muslim and boys were killed in a genocidal act in Srebrenica in the Bosnian War during the break up of Yugoslavia.

These are events in Europe after the words 'never again' were said. Hollow words indeed to the victims.

Contextualised statues are a powerful and recurring reminder of the evils of slavery. They cease to be objects of veneration or even gratitude. They remain as lessons to humanity.

The Save our Statues campaign group is right in emphasising the need to retain statues. The history of the nation is at stake here and is at risk from those whose only wish is to pull them down. The harm that this would cause is lost – in years to come children would not have the benefit of statues to emphasise the evil of slavery but also to understand the benefit it brought to society. This is not the justify slavery but to allow people to make an informed decision about the matter. BLM has metamorphosed from a movement which was genuinely committed to increasing awareness of black lives to a political movement which is likely to alienate many who are sympathetic to its message and the inequality endured by black people.

To take down statues and to leave a void or to replace them with others which have little relevance would be anathema to the majority of the public and to right thinking blacks themselves.

The logical extension of the current wave of iconoclasm is that all statues, historic monuments, roads buildings etc would be removed or renamed. The effect of this is to wipe out significant aspects of the history of the UK. What is relevant is that history, good and bad, be taught so that the listeners or readers may formulate their views on matters. Additionally, and this is the most important and relevant aspect of the issue, history needs to be placed in and critically analysed in context.

The reader of history should, by inference, dispense with the use of the 'retrospectoscope'. The greatest wisdom gained from looking back is to illuminate current thinking and to provide guidance for the future. Iconoclasm denies future generations of this important contribution from history. Society needs history to remind humanity of where it was then and where it is going tomorrow.

The removal of a statue of the late Nelson Mandela, for example, may appear logical to some. Greta Thunberg may have monuments, objects and other sites in her name. But one has to ask why? It is fashionable among some to celebrate her apparent commitment to climate change. But her enthusiasm for climate change belies the rate at which change can be effected? What about the cost to millions of people in the developing world? Many in the developed countries of the west my not be aware that the only source of fuel for millions of people in the developing world is wood – used for cooking, heating etc. But burning wood produces significant amounts of carbon dioxide which makes its way into the atmosphere. The natural decomposition of or burning wood is not a carbon-neutral process, if the source of the wood is not managed. Destruction of forests without replantation releases more carbon dioxide, without the ability of trees to re-absorb it. Burning wood also releases soot, carbon monoxide and methane. Carbon dioxide concentrations are now double pre-industrial levels and the amounts of methane have trebled. Many countries, India and China in particular, are still polluting the planet. They cannot suddenly stop what they are doing as they race to catch up with agreed international targets. A monument would have little significance to billions of people across the world as would pulling down monuments related to slavery have little impact on the average person in Africa. Would future generations look back at a monument of Greta Thunberg as inappropriate and worthy of being pulled down? Or would one ask that they be viewed as stepping stones in history which inform and educate. Approach them, as indeed all monuments, with a critical mind and with a thought for the context in which they came into existence. One would then, in all likelihood, end up being better informed.

When all monuments have been pulled down, roads and schools etc renamed, what would black parents say to their children and grandchildren about slavery? Would they not be met with disbelief at what is being said and incredulity at what happened centuries before? Soon slavery would disappear into the forgotten chasms of history and consigned to an aberration.

Katharine Birbalsingh is the undoubted villain of the liberal left in the United Kingdom. A teacher by profession, she maintains that it is vital to move away from the simple cliches of racism and look at matters with an open mind. What is an open mind one may ask? It is the ability to seen all sides of an issue, analyse and criticise them, accept some viewpoints while rejecting others with the primary aim of formulating a personal view. In this journey one may seek additional information, if only to reject it. This is as it should be in the process of critical evaluation. The road may have been long, it may have been painful, but one has reached a destination which is the view one holds. It may not be final as further information may alter and fashion the held view. The process is a fluid one which changes as it is continues to be coloured by events, information and experience. It all started with an open mind and the road is long, winding and un-ending.

Birbalsingh said that the education system in UK is broken and 'it keeps poor children poor'. In that statement she has thrown down the gauntlet not only to educationalists but also to those who subscribe to BLM and to those who think the world is racist. This was particularly incandescent material from some one who is of Indo-Guyanese origin. She went on to say - 'black children under-achieve because of what the well meaning liberal does to them'. The latter group always try to understand but does not try to fix the problem. She maintains that black children are not being taught about Britishness and the need to feel British. She advised parents to take children's claims of racism 'with a pinch of salt' when they are disciplined at school. An apparently strict disciplinarian, she has banned mobiles phones from the classroom. She is critical of BLM as it does not encourage children to be responsible, encourages racism and 'to focus on identity politics or victimhood'. In this respect she is opposed to teaching children about white privilege or unconscious bias. These, she believes, do not contribute to understanding but help to exacerbate segregation.

Following her comments on education at the Conservative Party conference of 2010 she was asked not to attend the school in where she was teaching at the time. This was to give the governors of the school the opportunity to 'discuss her position'. One may read into this statement many things but one may conclude that her views did not go down well. She left the school as she was being asked to comply with conditions that she found unacceptable.

Described as 'the strictest school in Britain', The Michaela Community School in Wembley, London opened in 2014 with Kathleen Birbalsingh as headmistress. Run with military precision, discipline is instilled from the first day. New children who join at 11 year have a 'boot camp' in their first week where they learn how the school is run and also learn to comply. There is a black line that runs down the middle of the corridors where children walk on either side as they move from class to class silently. Bullying is eradicated. The slightest infraction is punishable, for eg 'ten seconds to take out your book and turn to page 32'. A large clock is located in each class room which helps to ensure time-keeping and therefore discipline. Ex-servicemen who visited the school commented that the school reminded them of the British Army. Lunch is a combined effort of students- who are assigned to lay the plates, serve each other, clear plates etc. Discussion at lunch, where a teacher also joins in at each table, is around what was done during the morning. There is no room for small talk . Children love their school and are quite proud of it. The emphasis in the school on instilling knowledge is frowned on by some educationalist who think that children are denied the opportunity to be spontaneous in their thought and comments. The first group of students sat their A-level examinations in 2021; 82% were offered places at Russell Group universities. There is no better accolade; it confirms how discipline, hard work and responsibility lead to achievement. Success has instilled not only a sense of pride in the children but also likely to lead to greater aspiration.

The then Minster for Women and Equalities, Liz Truss, said 'by expecting high standards and not indulging the soft bigotry of low expectations she is producing amazing results at Michaela School and giving children the best chance in life.' These must surely be the answers and antidotes to racism, exclusion, social isolation and under-achievement in life. They are the stuff of dreams for any parent.

Birbalsingh makes the valid point that if there is racism, and there undoubtedly is, it has to act as the spur to propel oneself to do better, aim higher and achieve as well as or better than others. She talks about British culture and described Rudyard Kipling's 'If' as a 'beautiful poem'. She would be 'absolutely thrilled' if one of her pupils were to offer 'a repudiation of Kipling'. Now, would one rather not read Kipling because of a misguided impression of racism? On the contrary would one read it, appreciate it if one is so disposed or provide a critical appraisal of it? It is interesting to note that the UK journalist, Melanie Phillips, made the same point by saying that there was 'something wrong with teaching'. She claimed that parents, some disillusioned teachers and even educational psychologists were of the view that children were not taught to read. Reading is viewed by some as a form of oppression. The statement of Melanie Phillips predates anything Kathleen Birbalsingh stated - that children were not only from under-privileged backgrounds but they were made to stay that way by the actions of the liberal left. How could something so awful happen? And in its place one has the concept of victimhood. Parents who are able and willing, communicate with their children and encourage them to be focussed on their education and other useful childhood pursuits.. The so – called underprivileged children who are often from single parent families often have no recourse to home support and their only education is what they get from school. School is also the place where discipline is enforced and boundaries learnt. Hence Birbalsingh's plea to parents to treat a child's accusation of racism 'with a pinch of salt'. The creeping culture of life without a man at home is damaging to the psychological and social development of children. Such children are likely to grow up aggressive and have low self-esteem while performing poorly at school. The environment that Birbalsingh provides is a substitute to the absence of these at home- discipline, boundaries and personal responsibility. The alternatives is, as one sees in society, people being consigned to being under-privileged through generations.

One returns inevitably to the issue of racism, victimhood and the current wave of iconoclasm in society. It is simply so easy to pull down statues, rename buildings, roads etc and feel good about them. But have they changed anything? What society is witnessing is the 'wokeism of snowflakes'. Melanie Phillips, wrote in 2020 that 'even coronavirus can't kill our grievance culture'. Wokeism is intolerance of speech and of thought by another name. It seeks to establish the superiority of one view and to abolish counterarguments. In this sense it is a tyranny. The words of C.S.Lewis are timely here – ' Of all tyrannies, a tyranny sincerely exercised for the good of its victims may be the most oppressive. It would be better to live under robber barons than under omnipotent moral busybodies. … those who torment us for our own good, will torment us without end for they do so with the approval of their own conscience. They may be more likely to go to Heaven, yet at the same time likelier to make a Hell of earth. This very kindness stings with intolerable insult. To be "cured" against one's will and cured of states which we may not regard as disease is to be put on a level of those who have not yet reached the age of reason or those who never will; to be classed with infants, imbeciles, and domestic animals.' By for eg subtracting context from iconoclasm, 'illusions' are created which focus on being under-class, perpetuate an alternative racism and in doing so being oppressive. As the philosopher Friedrich Nietzsche said 'whoever fights monsters should see to it that in the process he does not become a monster.' The singular view propounded by BLM and which seeks to tear down monuments, is to banish understanding and debate and to replace it with its view. Until of course that view is also changed by a superseding view in later years. Why not allow children and adults to engage in healthy debate? Those who propose and propagate a single view on a subject are fearful of debate and of being proven wrong. They hate nothing more than an alternate view for their very existence would then be challenged. But isn't inquiry and debate the route to knowledge, understanding and enlightenment?

An effect of pulling down monuments is to air-brush from history the part played by Africans themselves in the slave trade. They were active participants. And like any business or trade, they sought to expand their business and to maximise profits. This was the trend at the time. Neither the seller nor the buyer thought any more of the human-financial transaction. Society looks with today's eye at events which occurred hundreds of years ago. Awareness of slavery and it abhorrence was not evident at the time. Eventually it did and Britain played its part in trying to limit the trade. The legacy of slavery continues in Africa to this day.

Tracing events backwards one could ask BLM if they would proceed to take down all statues of royalty because of their historic links with slavery.

Extrapolate back far enough and one would reach the point where there would not be any statues or monuments to British history. And what about statues and monuments in Africa? Does the ordinary person in Africa care about monuments or even about slavery.

A pertinent alternative course would be to retain all statues in their original form and associate them with statements about their past. This would go a long way to show the person in true light- both as having been associated with slavery and also as a philanthropist who worked for the benefit of society, for people of all colours. These would be constant reminders of the ugliness of slavery and a lesson for people, especially young persons whose ideas and practice on human relationships would be better fashioned. Take statues and icons away and one is left with not only a structural and historical void but also with a lost opportunity to understand human progress.

As Rod Liddle wrote in the UK Sunday Times newspaper 'every country did what it could get away with, according to the morals and expediencies of the time'. This is an important statement for what we are witnessing now is a review of events of the past with the moral microscope of today.

Are those who seek to tear down statues, doing so out of a personal sense of victimhood? Or are they seeking to come to terms with a historical sense of injustice to their ancestors? If it is the former, one would wish to understand the nature of their victimhood. How has an ancestor who was a slave directly impacted on their station in life today? How has it hindered them? With passage of the centuries since the abolition of slavery it is nigh impossible to establish a direct link between ancestral slavery and adverse current impact. However they may still bear a deep seated sense of victimhood. How would iconoclasm ameliorate this feeling of victimhood in a person? The psychologist Daniel J Phillips PhD wrote ' when we protect people from encountering stimuli that might trigger them to re-experience their trauma, we may in fact be inhibiting their healing, protecting them from the process by which people resolve the wounds of trauma'. Another psychologist, David J. Ley wrote 'we must encourage people in a way that supports their ability to move forward in their lives …… and a belief in supporting their resiliency'.

When the reason for iconoclasm is the injustice visited on their ancestors by slavery, people are rightly highlighting the deprivation and pain inflicted on ancestors and therefore on their class of people and on their culture. Slavery has had the effect of stunting the development and progression in the world of their ancestors and therefor of their kin. Here again, iconoclasm is unlikely to relieve the distress felt apart from the visceral satisfaction of seeing statues being removed even though some of the iconoclasts may be benefitting or have benefitted from the philanthropy of the purported slave trader. That statues are being pulled down when there has been no or very peripheral attachment to slavery, points in this direction. So, are there other causes at play here?

It is of great concern when someone of the stature of the Archbishop of Canterbury, Justin Welby, joins the iconoclasm bandwagon. He said that statues in Canterbury Cathedral would be looked at 'very carefully' to help decide if they should be retained. He went on to say that that some statues would have to come down but the decision was not his to make. He then proceeded to add confusion by saying that monuments would be placed 'in context'. Some statues would come down, some would have changes to their names and others placed in context. This is a recipe for disagreement and indecision. It may lead to an unsatisfactory decision. It is better to place statues, as always, in context. To claim that some church statues needs to be taken down as their presence would offend some persons is to fail to recognise that such action would affect the sensibilities of a great majority of the church-goers. Statues in churches are potent symbols to many believers. Their feelings are trampled over in an insatiable appetite to remove icons. Would one also remove or close churches because there was slavery in early Christian teachings? Scripture is ambiguous about slavery, simultaneously condoning the practice while also condemning it.

But isn't the church joining the bandwagon and moving with current fashion. It has many other urgent matters on its agenda, which it had chosen to disregard. Why for eg would it protect killers from Rwanda in its midst which is a much greater concern? Why is the church recalcitrant in its acknowledgement of sexual abuse by the clergy?

Take the example of St.James the Moor slayer in Spain. Known in Spanish as *Santiago Matamoros*, it is either a sculpture or a painting of

James who was son of Zebedee. James is a legend in Spanish Christian belief. A statue of St. James is found in the Santiago de Compostela Cathedral. It is one of the holiest places in Spanish Catholicism. There was a clamour for it to be relocated from its public site in the cathedral and for it to be placed in a museum. This furore was following the train bombings in Madrid on 11th March 2004. Ten bombs had been placed in four trains in Madrid's Atocha railway station during rush hour traffic. As result 191 people died and more than 2000 people were injured. The Prime Minister of Spain at the time, Jose Maria Aznar, initially and erroneously attributed the attacks to Basque separatists. It was the worst terrorist attack in Europe since the downing of Pam Am flight 103 over Lockerbie in Scotland on 21st December 1988. All 243 passengers and 16 crew members of the flight died. Also killed were 11 residents of Lockerbie. Eventually, after a judicial inquiry, an al-Qaeda terrorist cell was held responsible for the attack. It was said that Prime Minister Azna lost the next general election due to his handling of the affair.

According to legend James appeared riding a white horse with a white banner to help the Christian army of King Ramiro 1 of the Asturias (modern Spain) to defeat the Moors in the battle of Clavijo in 844.

In 711 AD a Moor attack occurred from North Africa into Spain. Large numbers of Christians were taken captive, towns were destroyed and robbed and the attack continued eastwards over the Pyrenees into France. Local governors were ordered to pay a tribute of 100 virgins every year. The Battle of Clavijo was an attempt to reverse the attack of 711 and restore the Christina faith in Spain..

Removal of the statue of St.James was intended to respect local Muslims and help in understanding and reconciliation after the attacks. Church authorities of the time said that the decision to move the statue was not related to the tragic events of 11th March 2004. It had been planned previously because it was felt that the violence depicted in the statues and the painting of James did not fit the teachings of Christ.

The cathedral of Santiago de Compostela is the third holiest site in Christendom after Jerusalem and Rome. The decision to remove the statue caused considerable outrage among Catholics and it was reported as 'political correctness gone mad' while others described the proposed removal as an act of 'intolerable heresy'. These two phrases are relevant in the iconoclasms of today.

A place like the cathedral of Santiago de Compostela is of great religious significance to a segment of the population. Its contents and icons have a meaning that relates to them and in this case their faith and the story of Spain.. It is also a historical site for people of all faiths and none. The cathedral is a world heritage site.

One may look at two other sites that are of religious importance but are also of immense historical value. The Sikh Golden Temple at Amritsar, India. It is the holiest site in Sikhism. It was twice attacked by the Afghan ruler Ahmad Shah Durrani, in 1757 and 1762. In the attack of 1752 Ahmad Sha Durani polluted the temple's pool by pouring waste and the entrails of slaughtered cows in to it. Karbala in Iraq is a place of holiness for Shi'ite Muslims. The shrine in Karbala has lasted from time immemorial but was destroyed in 850 by the Abbasid Caliph Al-Mutawakkil. It was rebuilt in 979. These sites are of immense significance to millions of worshippers and believers. It is neither an easy task nor acceptable to erase history.

The Liverpool Guild of Students chose to change the name of a hall of accommodation, Gladstone Hall, named after William Gladstone, following a vote of 4000 students. The hall of residence building was renamed after Dorothy Kuya. The reason for the change in the view of the Guild was that it did not wish to have a name that was associated with slavery.

Who were Dorothy Kuya and William Gladstone? The former was a Liverpudlian who was born in 1932. Her father was from Sierra Leone and mother was a white British woman also from Liverpool. The surname 'Kuya' is that of her step-father whom her mother remarried after her father left home. Dorothy grew up in Liverpool and was exposed to much racism; Liverpool of the time was an exclusively white part of England. She joined the Communist Party of Great Britain as a teenager. She trained as a teacher and as a nurse. She was a teacher in London before she moved back to Liverpool. During her life Dorothy Kuya campaigned tirelessly against racism. When in London she was Head of Race Equality for Haringey Council, working with the Labour MP for Haringey of the time, the late Bernie Grant. She campaigned for the creation of a slavery museum in Liverpool in 2007and worked to increase public awareness of slavery. These are noble credentials that would appear to justify naming a hall of residence after her.

William Ewart Gladstone (1809 – 1898) was a Liberal politician and Prime Minister from 1868 to 1894. He was Prime Minister on four occasions, making a total of 12 years in that position. It is worth looking at the political contribution of Gladstone. He was a liberal who was convinced of the need for independence in Ireland. He introduced The Government of Ireland Bill in the House of Commons in April 1886.His speech at the time lasted three hours and twenty five minutes and it is written that the House was 'spellbound'. His Chancellor of Exchequer, on learning of the proposal, thought Gladstone a 'criminal lunatic'

Gladstone was a towering figure at the time. In foreign policy, he was against the Opium War with China and was an ardent supported of Italian freedom. He once said 'Here is my first principle of foreign policy: good government at home.' In 1851 he visited Naples and was appalled by conditions in Neapolitan prisons, where people were held for speaking in support of freedom. The Italian patriot, Giuseppe Garibaldi said that Gladstone had 'sounded the first trumpet call of Italian liberty.'

William Galdstone entered Parliament at the young age of 23 years. He stressed the importance of liberty which was to him a guiding moral principle. Such was his stature that the historian J.L. Hammond wrote that 'It is safe to say that for one portrait of anybody else in working-class houses, there were ten of Gladstone.' He found common cause with the ordinary man. On one occasion travelling with his wife and daughter by train, thousands of people braved bitterly cold weather to see and hear him.

One of his famous quotes 'There should be a sympathy with freedom, a desire to give it scope, founded not upon visionary ideas, but upon the long experience of many generations within the shores of this happy isle, that in freedom you lay the firmest foundations both of loyalty and order.' And ' the sanctity of life in the hill villages of Afghanistan, among the winter snows, is as inviolable in the eye of Almighty God, as can be your own.'

Gladstone's father, Sir John, was one of the largest slave owners. The young William opposed the immediate abolition of slavery and said in 1832 that emancipation should come at the end of moral emancipation by education and inculcating in the slave 'honest and industrious habits.' Then, he said 'with the utmost speed that prudence will permit, we shall arrive at that exceedingly desired consummation, the utter extinction of slavery'. Robert Lowe, 1st Viscount Sherbrooke, (1811 1892) who was to become Chancellor of the Exchequer thought that Gladstone 'had proposed a well-considered and carefully prepared scheme' of 'gradual emancipation'.

As a 23 year old in his address to Newark electors, William Gladstone said he supported 'measures for the moral advancement and further legal protection of our fellow-subjects in slavery' He continued 'My principle is, let emancipation go hand in hand with fitness to enjoy freedom; and let fitness be promoted and accelerated by all possible means, which the Legislature can devise. Such has ever been, such is and such please God shall be my language.' Gladstone concluded by claiming that factory children in England grew up 'in a state of almost as great ignorance and deadness of heart as the slaves of the West Indies'. He maintained that 'the material conditions of the Irish and some of the English poor were worse than those of the slaves.'

Context is jettisoned here in renaming Gladstone Hall. William Gladstone's only sin is one of association. Here was a person who stood for individual freedom but who is adversely judged by the young of today. Gladstone does not fit the narrative of those who sought to rename the Hall. That Dortohy Kuya sought to increase awareness of slavery is commendable. But the freedom of the individual that Gladstone sought is what gives those in modern times the ability to make the decisions that they do.

Gladstone died at age of 88 and he was buried in Westminster Abbey. It was estimated that 250,000 people came to pay their respects when his coffin lay in Westminster Hall.

In June 2021, some academics of Oxford University called for their colleagues to withhold teaching to students at Oriel College, Oxford. This campaign was spearheaded by Professor Kate Tunstall who is not from Oriel College but from Worcester College.. The reason behind the move was the decision of Oriel College to retain the statue of Cecil Rhodes. It is an unfortunate call, to say the least, because the academics had themselves profited from education and were now being asked to deny their students of the opportunity to learn. It was, as one Oxford teacher said, 'despicable and mean- minded'. Despicable because it is trying to deny students, some of whom are from disadvantaged and poor backgrounds, the opportunity for achievement in life. Mean-minded because it is a demonstration of selfishness without consideration for their students. Considerable sums of money had been paid by parents and carers of students; some may be from poor countries. As the Universities Minister of the time, Michelle Donelan, said 'universities have a duty to maintain access to good quality tuition as a priority – especially given the disruption the pandemic has caused students'. Hence a double whammy for students.

Worcester College was taken by surprise by the actions of Professor Tunstall and stated on its website ' actions taken and views expressed by Professor Kate Tunstall in a petition concerning a teaching boycott in Oriel College were made in a personal capacity. Worcester College was not consulted in advance and remains focussed on its primary purpose of educating students and protecting their welfare'. With the apparent interference by Professor Tunstall in another College, a source wrote 'the prevailing attitude is that one College shouldn't be intervening in how another College runs. There is a level of respect amongst the senior heads of Colleges and they wouldn't call out other heads'. These words demonstrate the extent to which Professor Tunstall has broken unwritten rules of decency and civil conduct between Colleges.

It was therefore right and proper for Lord Wharton, chair of the Office for Students, to ask the academics who threatened to boycott teaching their students to 'leave their personal political views at home'. He went on to say the threat was 'baffling and inexcusable' and would set a 'deeply concerning precedent'. Continuing he said ' This is an abuse of their privileged status and is at the expense of students. .... I wonder how many working people would threaten to effectively work to rule to change the building or logo of their employer'. Apart from reneging on their duty of care to students, the 150 or so academics involved in the action are also in breach of their terms of employment. The University may chose to act against them as indeed the students would be liable to compensation. Having been deprived of continued face-to-face teaching and having had to engage in e-learning due to the pandemic, to burden students further with a teaching boycott must raise questions as to why students need to pay for a system of education that does not serve their needs.

The academics issued a joint statement - 'Faced with Oriel's stubborn attachment to a statue that glorifies colonialism and the wealth it produced for the College, we feel we have no choice but to withdraw all discretionary work and goodwill collaborations.' To claim that Oriel College is stubbornly attached to the statue of Cecil Rhodes is to display a remarkably shallow understanding of the importance of context in slavery. The statue is a significant reminder of the philanthropy of Rhodes. This is implicit in the statement from the protesting academics. The statue is a reminder of both aspects of the life of Cecil Rhodes – his involvement in the slave trade and his contributions to education and society. These need to be appreciated and taught to present and future generations. Take away the statue and what is left is a submerged story which is not likely to be told or appreciated as would the presence of the statue, with a legend explaining the man and his work. It may be worth remembering that benefactors of that era did not seek to use slavery for providing later generations with the benefits of their ill-gotten gains. Nothing could be further from the truth. Slavery is not the simple story of the immoral white man capturing the innocent black man into slavery. Slavery is more nuanced than that and always pleads for an impartial explanation of people and events.

Marc Glendenning of the Institute of Economic Affairs said that students 'were being collectively and irrationally punished for a matter and a decision over which they are not in any way responsible'. And one graduate of Worcester College said that Professor Tunstall had no business interfering the affairs of another college when she needs to look after her own College. What do these academics think?. Many of them have benefitted from a free University education. Remember, tuition fees only came recently. Some of them may have had to paid high fees as overseas students. Current students who may be from poor backgrounds pay several thousand of pounds each year for their educations. It is often money that their parents can hardly afford and which goes towards paying the very academics and teachers who are refusing to teach. This is nothing short of the mass punishment of innocent students for the political views of teachers.

If teachers at Oxford and other Universities are genuinely interested in increasing knowledge and awareness of Britain's imperial record, they would be advised to do so by using appropriate examples placed in context of the times at which events happened.

The composer Richard Wagner (1813 – 1883) was antisemitic and nationalist. He believed in 'superior' and 'inferior' races and was opposed to miscegenation. But he was one of the greatest musicians that ever lived. Many statues of him are to be found around the world but especially in Germany. Would one seek to tear down his statue in the Tier Garten in Berlin? Or worse still, would one choose not to attend performances of his music? People appreciate the musical genius that he was although they may have grave reservations of his antisemitic views. The extent of antisemitism in Germany during World War 2 was so profound that for a long time the holocaust was denied within and unknown outside of Germany. The German people at the time were either immoral in accepting antisemitism or they chose to turn a blind eye to what they heard and knew to be happening. At the time of slavery, the practice was not viewed as immoral. It had been happening for centuries, long before the arrival of the first Portuguese in West Africa. There was also, at that time, no concept of human rights. Slavery was part of the cultural fabric in Africa at the time.

It is interesting to read extracts of a transcript of the conversation in 1988 about Wagner, between Edward Saïd, Professor of Comparative Literature and English at Columbia University and the world famous musician Daniel Barenboim. Edward Saïd asked the question –'Given the history of association between Wagner and National Socialism – and the horrendous results of that association, perhaps, in the Holocaust – there is a massive weight there that one has to deal with somehow, in looking at the work. You're a Jew, and I don't need to add that I'm a Palestinian, so it's an interesting…' To which Barenboim replies 'We are both Semitic. So he was against both of us!'. Barenboim continued - ' Well, I think it's obvious that Wagner's anti-Semitic views and writings are monstrous. There is no way around that. And I must say that if I, in a naïvely sentimental way, try to think which of the great composers of the past I would love to spend twenty-four hours with, if I could, Wagner doesn't come to mind. I'd love to follow Mozart around for twenty-four hours; I'm sure it would be very entertaining, amusing, edifying, but Wagner…' When asked by Said as to whether Barenboim would invite Wagner to dinner, the reply was in the affirmative for educational purposes and study but not for enjoyment, saying - 'Wagner, the person, is absolutely appalling, despicable, and, in a way, very difficult to put together with the music he wrote, which so often has exactly the opposite kind of feelings. It is noble, generous, etc. But now we are entering into the whole discussion of whether it is moral or not and this becomes too involved in a discussion. But suffice it to say for now that Wagner's anti-Semitism was monstrous. That he used a lot of, at the time, common terminology for what could be described as salon anti-Semitism, and that he had all sorts of rationalizations about it, does not make it any less monstrous. He also used some abominable phrases which can be, at best, interpreted as being said in the heat of the moment – that Jews should be burned, etc. Whether he meant these things figuratively or not can be discussed. The fact remains that he was a monstrous anti-Semite. How we would look at the monstrous anti-Semitism without the Nazis, I don't know. One thing I do know is that they, the Nazis, used, misused, and abused Wagner's ideas or thoughts – I think this has to be said – beyond what he might have had in mind. Anti-Semitism was not invented by Adolf Hitler and it was certainly not invented by Richard Wagner. It existed for generations and generations and centuries before. The difference between National Socialism and the earlier forms of anti-Semitism is that the Nazis were the first, to my knowledge, to evolve a systematic plan to exterminate the Jews, the whole people. And I don't think, although Wagner's anti-Semitism is monstrous, that he can be made responsible for that'. Barenboim also made the comment that in Wagner's operas there was not a single Jewish character and not a single anti-Semitic remark.

'I think that Wagner's anti-Semitism is one thing, and the things that we have been forced to associate with his music are another'.

Why am I telling you this? Because I think this shows very clearly that one has to distinguish between Wagner's anti-Semitism, which is monstrous and despicable and worse than the sort of normal, shall we say, accepted-unacceptable level of anti-Semitism, and the use the Nazis made of it. I have met people who absolutely cannot listen to Wagner. A lady who came to see me in Tel Aviv when the whole Wagner debate was taking place said, 'How can you want to play that? I saw my family taken to the gas chambers to the sound of the *Meistersinger* overture. Why should I listen to that?' Simple answer: there is no reason why she should listen to it. I don't think that Wagner should be forced on anybody, and the fact that he has inspired such extreme feelings, both pro and con, since his death, doesn't mean to say that we don't have some civic obligations. Therefore, my suggestion at the time was that the orchestra, which was willing to play – and they were the musicians or rather the descendants of the musicians who had voted in 1938 to boycott, in other words they were redoing the vote and closing the circle – should not play it in a subscription concert where anybody who has been a loyal subscriber to the Israel Philharmonic for so many years would be forced to listen to something that they didn't want to listen to. But if somebody does not make these associations, especially since these associations do not stem from Wagner himself, he should be able to hear it. Therefore, my suggestion was that it should be played in a non-subscription concert of the Israel Philharmonic where anybody who didn't want to hear it didn't have to do, and anybody who wanted to go had to go and buy a ticket for that specific concert. And the fact that this was not allowed to happen is a reflection of a kind of political abuse and of all sorts of ideas that again have nothing to do with Wagner's music. And this is really the chapter of Wagner and Judaism.'

In a subsequent talk Barenboim said 'I find it all the more important to do away with certain misunderstandings and false claims about Wagner precisely because perceptions of him are often so confused and controversial. Today we also want to devote ourselves to the extra-musical sides of Wagner's personality, and among these are of course his notorious and unacceptable anti-Semitic statements.

Anti-Semitism was not a new development in nineteenth-century Germany. It was only in 1669 that it become legal for Jews to move somewhat freely in Berlin and the surrounding area, and even then only rich Jews were allowed to take up residence there. Jews who were only passing through Berlin had to enter the city through the Rosenthaler Gate or Rosenthaler Tor, which was otherwise used only for livestock. The philosopher Moses Medelssohn for example could enter Berlin only through this gate which he did at the age of 14 in 1743, and had to pay the same tax a farmer or merchant would have paid for his livestock or wares. In contrast to the Huguenots, it was forbidden for Jews to own land, to trade in wool, wood, tobacco, leather, or wine, or to pursue a profession.

There were taxes for every imaginable occasion in the lives of Jews: for traveling, marriages and births, among others.'

In 1850 Wagner published an essay *'Das Judenthum in der Musik'* or *'Judaism in Music'*. This was nothing unusual as antisemitism was an accepted part of Europe at the time with Jews being blamed for all the problems of the time - economical, political, cultural etc. Vienna was the epicentre of European antisemitism. However Wagner had several Jewish friends; his favourite conductor was <u>Hermann Levi</u> and the pianists <u>Carl Tausig</u> and <u>Joseph Rubinstein</u>. He described his association with Samuel Lehrs, in Paris in 1840 as 'one of the most beautiful friendships of my life'. Later in his life, Wagner made a comment to his wife Cosima – 'If I were to write again about the Jews, I should say I have nothing against them, It is just that they descended on us Germans too soon, we were not yet ready enough to absorb them.' This did not prevent him considering Jews as the 'born enemy of humanity and everything noble in it'.

Barenboim compared the words of Wagner with those of Theodor Herzl, the founder of modern Zionism. Herzl said in 1893 that to 'cure the evil' Jews would have to 'rid themselves of the peculiarities for which they are rightly reproached. The 'Jewboys have to to be baptized' to help them in life. He appealed to Jews to go underground among the people – 'Untertauchen im Volk!'. Interestingly, Wagner also spoke of the 'Untergang' or the sinkings – 'consider that only one thing can be the deliverance from the curse that weighs on you: the deliverance of Ahasver, — sinking! (der Untergang)' Both Herzl and Wagner supported the emigration of German Jews.

That Jews were sent to the gas chambers during the holocaust to the accompaniment of some Wagner music does not prevent his music being played and enjoyed by many millions. Barenboim recalls his performance in Berlin in 2001 of Wagner's Prelude and the Love and Death of Tristan. He suggested to the audience that those who wanted to leave could do so; only 30 people who did not want to hear Wagner, left the hall.

Barenboim said 'The entire Wagner debate in Israel is linked to the fact that steps toward a Jewish Israeli identity have not been taken; all concerned continue to cling to past associations which were absolutely understandable and justified at the time.' In so doing Barenboim believes that 'we are giving Hitler the last word' .

The words of Daniel Barnboim have relevance and resonance to the iconoclasms of today. Society is clinging to 'past associations' regarding slavery and not recognising the here and now. Not acknowledging the music of Wagner is akin to ignoring the philanthropy of Rhodes, Cass, Colson etc. while clinging to their 'past associations' with slavery. Destroying the work of Richard Wagner would be easy, if it was possible. There have not been mass protests regarding the work of Wagner or calls for his works to be banned, his statues pulled down etc. His work continues to be enjoyed to great acclaim. Why is that so when the holocaust, which was a mass industrialised slaughter of millions of human beings by choice, is acknowledged as one of the worst atrocities the world has witnessed. Adolf Eichmann who played a pivotal role in the murder of Jews said 'If I have to go, I will go to the grave with a smile, for the knowledge of having five million Jews on my conscience gives me a feeling of great satisfaction'. Despite the sheer banality of the killings and the extent of it, the words of Daniel Barenboim illustrate three inter-related aspects – the holocaust was pure evil executed by choice and devoid of any morality other than the unadulterated hatred of Jews, Wagner was in many ways associated with the holocaust while producing exquisite music and finally the ability of people today to exercise freedom in their choice of listening to Wagner or to avoid his music. All three facets are retained without ever diluting the horrors of the holocaust. That magnanimous accommodation described and practised by Barenboim is a lesson to those who espouse the iconoclasm of today. All those who clamour for monuments to be pulled down, whether they be students, teachers, workers etc, have the freedom given to them to be there or to leave. They were not compelled to be there. By their actions they betray an intolerance which is the negation of learning and teaching. A university is an abridgment of the universe where students and others from around the world gather to learn, exchange ideas and to broaden their intellectual horizons. The statement for eg 'Rhodes Must Fall' is an expression of herd mentality generated by those who are entrusted with encouraging debate and understanding. They are the opposite of what Daniel Barenbloim says and does.

William Hesketh Lever (1851–1925) was a businessman and entrepreneur who manufactured Sunlight Soap. Production of soap needed palm oil, which Lever sourced from Britain's West African colonies. When he needed increasing amounts of the oil that could not be met from West Africa, Lever turned to the Belgian government to obtain the product from the Belgian Congo. He purchased 750,000 hectares or 1,900,000 acres of land under his company in the Congo called Huileries du Congo Belge (HCB). The site where the palm oil was processed was named Leverville in the Province of Leopoldville. William Lever was a friend of King Leopold of Belgium and the Congo. The working conditions in the Congo were nothing short of exploitation and constituted forced labour which was the system operated by Belgium at the time. It appears that the Belgian authorities were 'grateful to have a partnership with an enlightened entrepreneur to help salvage their battered reputation'. The author Jules Marchal wrote 'Travail forcé pour l'huile de palme de Lord Leverhulme' which was translated by Martin Thom 'Lord Leverhulme's Ghosts: Colonial Exploitation in the Congo'. Marchal maintained that, 'Leverhulme set up a private kingdom reliant on the horrific Belgian system of forced labour, a program that reduced the population of Congo by half and accounted for more deaths than the Nazi holocaust'.

Lever who became Lord Lever, the 1st Viscount Leverhulme in 1922, was the benefactor of the school of tropical medicine in Liverpool University. The Leverhulme Trust provides funding for education and research.

Many teachers and professors have benefitted from grants provided by persons like Rhodes who lived and worked in the colonial era. Protestors engaged in the 'Rhodes Must Fall' campaign may not be aware that two of the teachers supporting the boycott of teaching, Dr Dan Hodgkinson and Dr Zoe Cormack, are beneficiaries of the Leverhulme Early Career Fellows. Others who have benefitted from the Leverhulme Trust are Dr Julia Viebach, a lecturer in African studies and Dr Agnieszka Kościańska. Professor Wale Adebanwi is the Rhodes Professor of Race Relations. The latter post is funded by the Rhodesian Selection Trust. Funding for research by Kathrin Bachleitner is provided by the IKEA Foundation. The IKEA company had admitted using East German political prisoners as forced labour during the Cold War.

In these few instances that are known, one realises the double standards applied by some university teachers. While having befitted themselves in their education and in their careers, they seek to deny the same to their students.

Jacob Rees- Mogg, MP and a Minster at the time in the UK government said 'We must not allow this wokeness to happen'. It is more than wokeness; the actions of the university teachers is a deliberate step designed to deprive students of their education. The government said - 'Students rightly expect to get a good deal for their investment in higher education and we would expect universities to take appropriate action should any student be seriously affected by these actions which could include compensation. We fully believe in protecting academic freedom but universities have a duty to maintain access to good-quality tuition as a priority especially given the disruption the pandemic has caused students already.'

Some would say that the protesting teachers who had benefitted from colonialism and imperialism were 'biting the hand that feeds them'.

Professor Nigel Biggar who is regius professor of moral and pastoral theology at Christ Church College, wrote in 2017 about the affair of the Rhodes statue at Oriel College as 'authoritarian' and that it 'displays the ugly intolerance of its supporters'. A defender of free speech, Biggar maintains that it is important not to feel guilty of Britain's colonial past saying '…..it involves being able to speak freely and do research on things colonial and the British Empire in a manner that may conclude that the British Empire and colonialism were not all bad.' Biggar draws attention to the century long battle by the Royal Navy to suppress the Atlantic slave trade which was a force for good. He places this in comparison to the Jallianwala Bagh massacre or Amritsar massacre in India on 13th April 1919. People had gathered in the area to protest peacefully about the arrest of the leaders of the pro- independence movement of India, Dr. Satya Pal and Dr.Saifuddin Kitchlew. Brigadier-General R. E. H. Dyersurrounded the protesters with his Gurkha British Indian Army unit and Sindh regiment to shoot at the protestors who had only one exit from the site, which had been blocked. The numbers who died were estimated to be 400 and over 1200 were injured. Brigadier Dyer withdrew his troops leaving the dying and wounded where they lay. He was made an honorary Sikh by the elders of the Golden Temple and he was excused from growing a beard. He was also praised by the governor of the Punjab, Sir Michael O'Dwyer. In the

Iconoclasm, Wokeism

House of Commons, Winston Churchill condemned what he called 'an extraordinary event, a monstrous event, an event which stands in singular and sinister isolation'. While Brigadier Dyer died in 1927 in England, Sir Michael O'Dwyer was assassinated in London in 1940 by Udham Singh, a Sikh revolutionary who had been injured in the massacre in Amritsar. Mahatma Gandhi called Udham's act 'senseless'. He was hanged for the murder of O'Dwyer. As a result of the massacre, the first Asian Nobel laureate, Rabindranath Tagore of India, renounced his knighthood.

In describing these events, Biggar shows that the British Empire was 'morally mixed, just like that of any nation state'. When one encounters the phrase, 'Amritsar massacre' it is not immediately apparent that there is much more that meets the eye than a superficial reading of the topic. In a similar vein, African slavery or more specifically, west African slavery, was more than the single description of slaves being transported to the west.

One has only to look at the history of recent years in Hong Kong to appreciate that British imperialism and colonialism brought great benefit to the colony. One witnesses the clamour of its citizens for the values etc that are increasingly being lost.

The Save our Statues campaign group is right in emphasising the need to retain statues. The history of the nation is at stake here and is at risk from those whose only wish is to pull them down. The harm that this would cause is indescribable – in years to come children would not have the benefit of statues to emphasise the evil of slavery but also to understand the benefit it brought to society. This is not the justify slavery but to allow people to make an informed decision about the matter. BLM has metamorphosed from a movement which was genuinely committed to increasing awareness of black lives, to a political movement which is likely to alienate many who are sympathetic to its message and the inequality endured by black people.

Iconoclasm and BLM are closely interrelated and intertwined with wokeness and wokeism. But what are these terms? It is said that wokeism is related to Marxism from which it probably originated. Its basis is the eradication od racism and social injustice. Noble as these objectives are and most if not all people would subscribe to them, the project of wokeness has transformed to a situation of disagreement with and protest against those that have an alternative opinion to what one or one's group hold or think should be the correct one. It progresses to the stage where there is an attempt to silence those with alternative views, wokeism. A world of wokeness would be good, as injustice and equality would have been subdued or eliminated. But this is a social utopia which is hardly likely to be attained. As Michael Karson, professor at the University of Denver, wrote 'hate requires the obliteration of context'. And this is the crux of the issue in iconoclasm – there is only one storyline - that of the group who are woke. There is no room for context or rational debate. Hence those who campaigned against the writings of Nigel Biggar claimed that they were racist and 'whitewashed' the British Empire. He was labelled a bigot. This was their view and apparently they were not open to a critical analysis of what was written. It did not fit in with their firmly held views on the matter.

The extent to which wokeism has intruded on current thinking is seen from the views expressed about Her Majesty the Queen and Winston Churchill. Magdalen College in Oxford University proposed the removal of a portrait of the Queen. The matter was put to the vote by graduate students of the Middle Common Room (MCR). The vote involved only 12 of the 250 members of the MCR. In any other situation such an unrepresentative vote would be considered null and void. But the President of the College, Dinah Rose QC did not move to ignore or overturn the result. Magdalen is a college like all universities and other centres of higher learning should be, that prides itself on debate, freedom of expression and the airing and tolerance of diverse views. In 1687, Fellows of the College rebelled against the imposition of a President, by King James II. The King demanded that the Fellows be expelled. This led to national outrage against the King who at the time was quite unpopular. Compare these event with the pettiness and mediocrity of the debate that must have preceded the decision to remove the portrait of the current Queen. The decision to remove the portrait of the Queen was labelled as 'offensive and obnoxiously ignorant' by Lord Patten the Chancellor of Oxford University.

The professor of black studies at Birmingham City University, Kehinde Andrews, has called the Queen the 'number one symbol of white supremacy in the entire world'. His comments are laughable if not for the amazing degree of ignorance they display. For e.g. he said of the Royal Family – 'A born to rule elite of this really white family. The head of the Commonwealth which is actually the empire.' Most readers, even those opposed to Royalty, would agree that the Queen could hardly be called a white supremacist. And as for ruling the UK, it appears to have been missed that the country is a democracy with a Parliament and the Queen as head of state. She is a figurehead who represents the country. How can one call the Commonwealth an empire when countries in the Commonwealth are independent nations who choose to be in it? At the time fo this writing the current Commonwealth Heads of Government Conference was taking place in Kigali, the capital of Rwanda. Rwanda chose to join the Commonwealth in 2009. Two other west African nations, Gabon and Togo, joined the Commonwealth on 25th June 2022. These are two countries with little or no historic ties to Britain. The President of Rwanda, Paul Kagame was the host of the Conference. The Togo political scientist Mohamed Madi Djabakate, said that joining the Commonwealth was a good step as he blamed the economic problems of his country on French policies. Other Francophone countries have also joined the Commonwealth. Mozambique which was a Portuguese colony joined in 1995. All of these are voluntary associations of independent nations who chose to join in what is not a 'Commonwealth Empire'. Countries are also free to leave, as Zimbabwe did in 2003 when it withdrew its membership.

None of this implies that the Commonwealth is a perfect organisation. Far from it; it is a group of independent nations with varying aspirations and relationships with the Queen and Commonwealth. As regards slavery, Prince Charles who was attending the Conference in Kigali said that talking about colonial history 'was a conversation whose time has come' and that it was up to the individual nations of the Commonwealth to decide whether the Queen should be their head of state ' calmly and without rancour'. His words show the Commonwealth as it is and that it is not; it is not an empire as had been suggested. He continued to say 'I cannot describe the depths of my personal sorrow at the suffering of so many, as I continue to deepen my understanding of slavery's enduring impact………. if we are to forge a common future that benefits all our citizens, we too must find new ways to acknowledge our past'. However not all the countries in the Commonwealth share the same ideals of democracy, transparency, accountability etc. For e.g. Yoweri Museveni has been President of Uganda since 1986 without any recent peaceful transfer of power. The desire to 'acknowledge our past' must be a genuinely wholesome process that involves all aspects of slavery as it affected Africa.

Kehinde Andrews also claimed that the British Empire was worse than the Nazis and that the Second World War would have ended even if Sir Winston Churchill was not there,- 'I'm pretty sure that if Churchill wasn't in the war it would have ended the same way'. In February 2021, the Conservative MP, Andrew Bridgen, said 'Well if he holds those views why is he living off the public purse?' Yet another example of 'biting the hand that feeds one'.

A not dissimilar view on Winston Churchill is held by Dr Shashi Tharoor in his book *'Inglorious Empire'*. Tharoor believes that Churchill must be remembered alongside the worst dictators of the time and is only 'fit to stand in the company of the likes of Hitler, Mao and Stalin'. He holds Churchill responsible for the Bengal famine of 1943. This view is not supported by the facts or by other historians. The main cause of the famine was the fall of Burma, when the invading Japanese cut off supply routes and starved imports into India. In the first half of 1943 when the famine was on, India exported 70,000 tons of rice for war supplies, which could have ameliorated part of the famine.

There is no evidence in support of the claims of Shashi Tharoor.

The Queen was the single most important unifying figure in the country and probably across the whole world. She has welcomed and associated with persons from all countries and cultures, even with dictators like Nicolae Ceaușescu of Romania. At Commonwealth conferences she associated with all the heads of Commonwealth countries without exception. In her commitment to the Commonwealth, the Queen had demonstrated an inclusivity rarely seen elsewhere in the world.

Thomas Guy (1644- 1724) was a bookseller in Lombard Street, London. He helped to build three new wards in St. Thomas' Hospital, London. But he soon discovered that the hospital was becoming overcrowded. Guy proceeded to build a new hospital close to St.Thomas', the Guy's Hospital of today.

Thomas Guy was a Member of Parliament who held shares in the South Sea Company which helped to transport slaves to the West Indies.. He sold these shares before the company collapsed in 1724 and invested the proceeds in the British East India Company. Both companies were owned by the British Government.

Thomas Guy's tomb is in the chapel of the Guy's Hospital. The statue of Thomas Guy has been in the hospital since its erection in 1734 and is a tribute to Guy who built his hospital to treat 'incurables'. In a public consultation, more than 75% of the population opposed a call to move his statue.

While Kieron Boyle, the chief executive of Guys and St. Thomas' NHS Foundation Trust is right in saying that the Trust has a duty to listen to its ethnic minority patients, this does not in any way mean that it has to supinely accede to their requests. The philanthropy of Thomas Guy and Sir Robert Clayton, whose statue is at St. Thomas' Hospital, has helped the patients from London and across the country for many centuries and will continue to do so for many more years to come.

The UK Culture Secretary of the time, Oliver Dowden MP, asked that the statue of Thomas Guy be retained where it is, saying that 'this looks like bad, misplaced priorities from these institutions. Instead of pandering to wokery, they should be focussed on their important day jobs. Confident nations retain and explain, they don't hide their history away'. The last words are important – history should not be hidden or air-brushed. As a great nation, Britain has the maturity to accept it's past in an era which was different to that of today. Retain, contextualise and explain must be the order of the day. Those who are against context have chosen to close their minds to discussion and debate. They are content to live and think within the straight-jackets of their thoughts and what they have heard. They are not open to alternate views and have been brain-washed into accepting the one view of matters; anything else is obviously false, intimidating and therefore unacceptable. One now sees the emergence of 'snowflakes' who are easily pained by alternative views and by the invitation to discussion and to open their minds. With each additional bit of selective information they sink deeper in their prison. They are the opposite of those living in Platos' 'Allegory of the Cave'. Unlike the prisoners in Platos' cave, an intellectual snowflake has voluntarily surrendered reasoning and does not want to see the light. They have put themselves in a prison of their making. Gilded a prison it may appear to them, but to the rational thinker it is unbearable and screams for escape. A multi-pronged evidence–based narrative must be the antidote to the single view of wokeism. Escape is difficult if one is surrounded by like-minded persons who reinforce a singular view. As George Orwell said- 'If liberty means anything at all, it means the right to tell people what they do not want to hear.' But one increasingly sees the resort to cancelling speakers and lectures – the 'cancel culture'. In wokeism one is witnessing a malign form a slavery – stubborn adherence to one view to the exclusion of all others. Orwell implied that the world was inexorably moving not towards anarchy but the reimposition od slavery. He may have meant the slavery of thought and speech. Again as Orwell said - 'He is a slave with a semblance of liberty which is worse than the most cruel slavery'. Those who subscribe to wokeism are slaves of a kind and have chosen to be so. Wokeism is almost a perpetual state of white guilt and worship at the altar of non- white victim hood. Many people are prepared to do so and to dislike their intrinsic whiteness. Much as one would try to bring equality and extinguish racism, wokeism strives to bring it back. A course at Duke University in the USA teaches that there are certain characteristics of white supremacy. These are striving to be perfect in what one does, accepting the written word, objectivity etc. The course taught that it is important to eliminate these characteristics. One is now back to the lack of evidence and context. Progress is unlikely if this trend is not reversed. If not for evidence and objectivity we would still be inhabiting a world where people considered the earth to be flat. Nor would the central position of the sun as postulated by Copernicus have made the light of day. Human progress depends on objectivity, questioning of what is here and now and revising what is known, taking into account emerging facts. Wokeism is the opposite of this; only one view counts; 'my truth'.

The British Library's chief librarian reportedly described racism as a 'creation of white people' in a video message to staff. Liz Jolly is said to have made the comments as she urged staff to support the library's 'anti-racism action plan' in the wake of the Black Lives Matter movement. This comment drew criticism as columnist Rita Panahi commented 'How can the British Library chief be so pig ignorant? Racism is a creation of white people? Say that in Asia or the Middle East and they'll laugh at you.' 'Can no black, Asian, or any other race or colour be racist!'

As part of the changes, the busts of Sir Robert Cotton, Sir Joseph Banks, The Right Honourable Thomas Grenville and Sir Hans Sloane which are located in the Front Hall of the library will have their legends changed to provide a 'wider historical context'. This is now a more balanced approach to statues, which sets the scene for visitors who now have an opportunity to for their opinions on the statues. And it must be said that all statues and monuments should have a balanced legend relating to them- not only monuments of white persons. Dispense with slavery as the dominant theme and provide information for the reader to decide.

Trevor Phillips (1953-) who was one time head of the Commission for Racial Equality) and chairman of the Runnymede Trust on racial equality in the UK, wrote - ' the march of workeism is an all pervasive new oppression'. He claims that woke appears to represent the excluded in society but remain blind to the talent available in coloured people. While claiming the need for justice they are opposed to those who hold an alternative view to their own. He describes wokeism as a fashion that serves to perpetuate victimhood.

On 3rd March 2021, 33-year-old Sarah Everard was kidnapped in South London, England and murdered by a serving police officer in the London's Metropolitan Police. Following this tragic event there was a vigil in Clapham Common close to where Sarah was murdered. It was organised by the campaign group 'Members of Reclaim These Streets' and was held on Clapham Common on 13th March 2021. Following friction between the Police and members of the public at the vigil, the journalist, Matthew Syed, wrote that 'one should walk a mile in someone's shoes before passing judgment'. He wrote about the relevance of a 'root cause analysis' or RCA before coming to any conclusions on a controversial matter. And the issues of slavery is one of those issues that need not only a RCA but also the need to place matters in context. Anything less that this would be virtue signaling which does not bring closure to those who are pained, for whatever reason, from the issues of slavery. And here one needs to consider not only the slaves and their descendants but also those who worked in the slave trade; it was an international business. Think for a moment about the 44000 slave owners in Britain and also of all those who worked in the trade, however peripheral or marginal their roles may have been. There were those who worked in the manufacture and fitting of the ships, suppliers to the ships, sailors etc. They were all involved in the trade. And how many descendants, not only of slaves and slave owners but also of those who were involved in the trade there are in Britain today. Of course the great culpability fo those in Africa who caught and enslaved their fellow Africans should remain prominent in any discussion on slavery.

In August 1518, Spain transported slaves from Africa to America on the authority of King Charles 1. However this was not the origin of African slavery which had been going on for much longer. In 1441 the Portuguese brought the first slaves from West Africa to Portugal. It is written that one horse would help in the purchase of about 30 slaves from traders in Africa, slave traders, who were willing to sell their own people. Portuguese explorers continued down the west coast of Africa until they encountered the east African slave trade conducted by Muslims in the eastern ports of the continent. In 1555 a London merchant named John Lok brought some Africans from modern day Ghana to England. The purpose was to teach them English and use them in Africa to break the monopoly that the Portuguese had on trade in Africa.

In 1562-9 John Hawkins became the first Englishman to have transported slaves from Sierra Leone to Hispaniola and St Domingue, which are now the Dominican Republic and Haiti. the slaves were traded for sugar, ginger and pearls.

Inaya Folarin Iman (1996-) is a British journalist whose interests are in culture and race. She is also politically active, being in support of Brexit. Opposed to 'taking the knee' which she describes as a culture war, she believes that the death of George Floyd in the USA is used as a means to promote an ideological agenda which would harm race relations in the UK. She maintains, as indeed many do, that there is no comparison between the USA in UK following the murder of George Floyd. Policing is different in the USA to that in the UK. She also views the Black Lives Matter movements as an 'opportunistic pretext for an outpouring of self-righteous rage'. She said that what matters is our common humanity and not the colour of our skin, and appealed All Black Lives Matter 185 to people to accept diversity and to reject racial identity politics. She is an active member of the Free Speech union (FSU) which is working tirelessly to counter the cancel culture that is pervading society.

The risks inherent in iconoclasm associated with replacement of pulled down statues with those of black persons, however honourable and deserving they may be, are only too apparent. Extrapolated, such a progressing scenario would destroy or at least submerge the history of the UK and supplant it with a black history. This would not be acceptable to the majority of Britons of whichever skin colour. Society would be bordering on a 'black apartheid'.

REPARATIONS

An elementary meaning of the word 'reparation' is to repay or to make amends or to compensate. This basic understanding assumes that wrong occurred in terms of the laws and customs of the time when the events or omissions occurred. A right act today may be considered a wrongful act tomorrow, if the law changes. This is especially so when the separation of time extends to years or as in the case of slavery, to centuries. Laws, customs, statutes progress from the time of the alleged wrong. It is reasonable to assume that a wrong was done at the time of its occurrence. Take the example the life of the late Alan Mathison Turing (1912 – 1954). A brilliant mathematician and computer scientist, Turing was convicted in 1952 in the UK of homosexuality. That was the law at the time. Today there is no law outlawing homosexuality, same sex marriages etc. Here is an example of a wrongful act of yesterday which is not considered in the same light today, and restitution followed.

Reparations may be made to individuals, a group of people or a state. It is relatively easy to understand the concept of reparation to a state following war. Germany made reparations to several countries following World Wars One and Two. In the Treaty of Versailles, following World War One, Germany was branded the aggressor that had caused devastation to the other countries. It was made to pay reparations. Hard as these conditions were for Germany, they were subsequently watered down. They caused much resentment in Germany. In 1936, in violation of the Treaty, Adolf Hitler militarized Germany, which brought no response from the other countries. This may have spurred Hitler on to further aggression in Europe. The reparations amounted to 132 billion gold marks (US$33 billion).

When payments were not forthcoming from Germany, France occupied the Ruhr in 1923. This led to the arrangement of a new payment plan by Germany. The payment of reparations was a humiliation to German people. According to the London Schedule of Payments, the sum of 132 billion gold marks was a compromise between a higher amount demanded by the French and the lower amount claimed by the British and 'represented an assessment of the lowest amount that 'public opinion ... would tolerate'. Sally Marks wrote in *'the Myth of Reparation'* that German leaders clearly 'recognized the political implications of the reparations issue and, from beginning to end, devoted their inexhaustible energies to avoiding or reducing payments.' She goes on to imply that the resentment caused led to greater suffering for all 'demonstrating the futility of imposing large payments on nations which are either destitute or resentful and sufficiently powerful to translate that resentment into effective resistance.'

In other words there must be justice in any system of reparations. It should not lead to greater issues than the immediate need for payment.

The type of reparation described in the foregoing paragraph relates to that between warring states, with the vanquished having to compensate the victor for human suffering, damage caused etc. It so happened that the loser in World War One, Germany, was largely responsible for initiating the War. What would happen if the victor in war was the prime mover in initiating it?

However the concept of reparation has moved along in the last century to acknowledge compensation to individuals or groups who have been wronged or endured undue suffering at the hands of another. To be meaningful, reparation does not imply only financial compensation. It is a wholesome act including a formal apology acknowledging wrongs, together with seeking the truth of what happened, why it happened, reconciliation between the parties and a commitment to improve relations between them. In the current context of the BLM movement, indeed an important part would be to acknowledge that racism occurs, even to a minor extent in society, working towards reversing it and moving forwards as an inclusive, tolerant and equal society.

The example that immediately springs to mind is the act of reparation by Germany following the Holocaust that occurred during World War

Two. Nazi Germany was not only responsible for the deaths of over six million Jews in extermination camps in Europe. There were in excess of 20 million slave labourers working in German industries during the war. This was about a quarter of the German workforce at the end of the war. The matter of reparation was problematic both for the German and the Israelis. To the latter, the thought that the murderers of yesterday could somehow become a respected and accepted nation in the world was intolerable. To accept compensation from yesterday's killers was unthinkable. In effect, negotiations between Israel and the new state of West Germany were conducted in secret, to protect the negotiators. There were many in Germany too who did not think that compensation to Jews and the state of Israel was due. Many in German public did not think they were responsible for what was done by the Nazis in their name. At the outset, the leaders of Israel were not even prepared to enter into negotiations with the Germans, who only seven years earlier had been their killers; they were nothing short of gruesome murderers with whom any discussion was unacceptable. Discussion between the two parties eventually started in the Hague in Holland in 1952. Chancellor Konrad Adenauer of Germany started the negotiations with a figure of four billion German marks as a sum in compensation to Israel. One may question the reason for the readiness of the Germans to address this issue. There was an ulterior motive and it was this. West Germany, as it was then known, was driven by a desire to be considered and admitted as a member in 'proper standing' among the nations of the world. Was there genuine contrition here? Who knows? But there was a starting point in the negotiations. David Ben-Gurion (1886 – 1973), founder and first Prime Minister of Israel in 1948 asked, quoting *Kings 21:29*, 'Have you murdered and also inherited?'. There was a powerful need, irrespective of motives, for Germany to confront its past and enter into discussions about reparations.

The position of East Germany in these negotiations was interesting. East Germany was under the Soviet sphere of influence after World War Two and was in effect under the control of the USSR at the time. Moscow did not accept that the German people as a whole were responsible for the holocaust. There was no admission of responsibility and from all accounts it appears that East German culpability for the Holocaust was effectively swept under the carpet.

However and finally agreement was reached where West Germany agreed to pay Israel in goods and services amounting to 3.5 billion German marks, over a 12 year period. In addition West Germany agreed to return property seized by the Nazis to their legal owners. A sum of 450 million marks was earmarked to compensate owners of property compulsorily taken by the Nazis. By 1956 West Germany was paying over 85% of Israel's state revenue.

In 2013 Germany agreed to pay $1 billion for the care of elderly Holocaust survivors; this is 65 years after the end of World War Two. Then again take the case of the Remembrance, Responsibility and Future Foundation (Stiftung Erinnerung, Verantwortung und Zukunft; or EVZ) which was established in 2000 with the objective of paying compensation to former forced labourers in Nazi concentration camps. There were eight and a half million forced labourers and four and a half million prisoners of war who were forced to work in German factories. They were in effect slaves of the Nazi administration.

The important catalyst for all of this was the view of Konrad Adenauer who said ' In the name of the German people, unspeakable crimes were committed which create a duty of moral and material restitution'.

The wholesome nature of reparations by Germany are seen by its other acts. It enshrined in its 1949 Constitution the outlawing of symbols of and propagation of hatred against any sections of its community and assured asylum to people from around the world fleeing war and persecution. Witness how in 2015 Germany overcame European bureaucracy on immigration and let in one million asylum seekers from Syria.

Because of the sensitive nature of the word 'compensation' the words 'reparation' and ' restitution' were used. Most Jews could not contemplate or accept compensation for the deliberate, institutionalised murder of millions of their fellow Jews.

Important features stand out in any description of reparations by Germany to Israel in the aftermath of World War Two. The chronological proximity of the human horrors of the Holocaust to the survivors is one obvious and critical factor. Memories were fresh and painful; events were literally in real time. This contributed to the apparent revulsion of survivors in Israel and Jews elsewhere in the world to entering into any discussion with those whom they rightly perceived to be the murderers of their family members and their race. This was accentuated by the extent of the murderous activities, the industrialised killing in gas chambers etc that were revealed at the conclusion of the war. How could the two parties ever have anything in common or be able to sit around the table at discussions? The moral imperative was recognised early on by Chancellor Adenauer, even though the German population was opposed to being held to account for the atrocities of their leaders. Germany was also a broken, devastated nation at the end of the war and how could it be made to pay reparations in those circumstances? Israel was equally but in a different way a nascent nation getting on its feet. The financial payments which made up the reparations was a benefit to the young Israel.

Secondly it was painful yet relatively easy to identify victims and their families which made the logistics of reparation easy.

The wholesome nature of compensation by Germany is seen in its acceptance of what it inflicted on another people and it continues being involved in the process of reparation and reconciliation. It continues its acts of contrition and reminds its people never to forget. One cannot ask more.

Would Israeli citizens of today or say in a hundred years from now clamour for compensation of activities during World War Two and the Holocaust? And would they do so with the same vigour and conviction as the world has seen in the past 70 years?. Whom would any reparation be paid to and what use would any financial contribution be put to? How would monies be disbursed? And would descendants of those who died in the Holocaust be reimbursed for the sufferings and death of their ancestors? Would this be seen as a just compensation for wrongs of centuries ago or would it be a virtue signal? Once payment is made, is the matter closed?

A not too dissimilar situation occurred with South Africa's Truth and Reconciliation Committee which was established in 1996, after the end of apartheid in the country. Its objective was to look at human rights violations, identify areas for reparation and consider applications from persons for amnesty. There were over 19000 cases of gross human right violations and another 2900 identified through the amnesty process. Of a total of 7111 applications for amnesty 5392 were refused, some were withdrawn and only 849 were eventually granted amnesty. As Varushka Jardine wrote in 2008, 'As a country we would have been much poorer had the truth not been told. I believe it was truly a necessary part of our history'.

Here again the proximity of events to victims not only helped reparation but also some reconciliation. Why some reconciliation one would ask? The immediate response to that would be what some persons may find offensive – that money cannot wash away sins when crimes were committed.

In both Germany and South Africa, events occurred at a time in human development and progress when there was an evolved concept of human rights. The end of slavery and the words of Thomas Jefferson in 1776 are often quoted – 'We hold these truths to be self-evident, that all men are created equal, that they are endowed by their Creator with certain unalienable Rights, that among these are Life, Liberty and the pursuit of Happiness'. Whatever was meant by Thomas Jefferson and however it was applied is not immediately relevant here ; the concept of rights was articulated and recognised.

Many would find it unjust to be blamed for actions of their predecessors or as in the case of slavery, events that occurred centuries ago. It could be argued that the sins of the fathers are the sins of the sons. Others would quite rightly rebut this assertion as fallacious and that it amounts to an assault on the fundamental human rights of individuals, to be held to account for the actions of their ancestors. An equally robust argument can be put forward. And it is this - slavery benefitted society and those living today. It could be said that there was an enhanced quality of life as a direct result of the fruits of slavery. Slaves generated economic development in the countries where they were held and made to work. For e.g. in the USA the per capita gross domestic product (GDP) which was $58 in 1800 reached $125 in 1860. The historian Edward E Baptist claimed that about 50% of GDP was from slave related activity. In his controversial book, 'The Half Has Never Been Told: Slavery and the Making of American Capitalism', he claims that slaves were the engine that drove the economic boom of the cotton years in America; cotton was a prime world commodity at the time. The book, however, was not universally well received. It was described as being critical of American capitalism of the time. One wrote 'Mr. Baptist has not written an objective history of slavery. Almost all the blacks in his book are victims, almost all the whites villains. This is not history; it is advocacy.' The comment drew much satire for e.g. 'Mandela's Long Road to Freedom downplays the contemplative benefits of a lengthy Robben Island sabbatical.' And 'Sadly, the Bible is biased against Pharaoh, preferring rebels led by a turncoat with no sense of direction'.

Baptist's book was reviewed in the Journal of Economic History by Eric Hilt who wrote 'much of its economic analysis is so flawed that it undermines the credibility of the book.' And maintained that the contribution of cotton to the proportion of GDP at the time was an error and was 'overstated'. However cotton was an important world commodity and its value and primacy of the time can be seen from the example of the town of Natchez in Mississippi which was, at that time, the cotton capital, had the most number of millionaires in the world. It could be said to have been the Silicon Valley of the day.

Nothing, however, detracts form the essential conclusion that slavery contributed to great economic productivity and in the case of the USA, to its dominant economic position of today. Large companies like Lehman Brothers, and New York Life Insurance Company were involved in slavery.

Armed with these facts, contested thought some of them may be, one can make a case that the quality of life of people in the USA today is directly associated with the benefits brought to the economy by slavery in centuries gone by. And this resulted not only from the physical labour of slaves. There was also the 'equal but separate' development of blacks and whites which allowed the latter to progress while the former stagnated. The legacy of these policies is the poor quality of life of blacks of today – education, housing, job prospects etc. One cannot leave out the less than optimal social fabric of blacks that perpetuates their lower standard of living, almost to an institutionalised degree. This latter has to change too.

Reparation for slavery poses many problems not least because of what happened centuries ago and the lack of proximity of events to survivors. Unlike the Nazis or the apartheid regime in South Africa where there were identifiable perpetrators, there are no readily identifiable persons now. There are survivors of slaves and of slave traders. The nations involved in the slave trade are known. Slavery, especially on the west coast of Africa was a commercial enterprise where there was a need to source labour to work the sugar- cane fields in the Caribbean and the cotton fields in the Americas. The crucial, mostly unanswered question is how these slaves originated. Slavery was endemic in Africa and 'slavery' as is commonly understood and used started with Portuguese who saw slaves as a readily available source of human capital for work. Now this leads to an area fraught with difficulty. Does one look only at the trans-Atlantic transport of slaves? Or does one look at slavery and especially African slavery in its entirety – trans- Saharan and East African. Also is needed a review of the activities of the slave catchers in Africa and the countries that thrived on slavery, to consider the aspect of reparations. If the answers to these are in the negative, one has to ask why? The slave catchers were pursuing their business as was happening in Africa at the time that the Portuguese originated trans-Atlantic transport of slaves. Should their descendants be identified and prosecuted? If the answer to this question is negative, then why not?

Th African man's part in slavery cannot be ignored in any discussion on the subject and so also in any consideration of reparations.

If one were to resolve the foregoing issues one then has to consider who one pays reparations to. How does one identify victims of slavery? It is a fact that descendants of slaves in America, the Caribbean and elsewhere have progressed better than most of their compatriots living in Africa. They have benefitted from the improved economies of their adopted countries. Would they contribute to payments of reparations? It is known that the poverty rates among blacks which was at 87% in the 1940's declined to 47% in 1960 and dropped another 18% in the next 20 years.

One has seen that many expatriate Africans are reticent about contributing to the development of Africa. Most Americans do not support payments in cash as compensation for slavery.

What about other aspects of slavery? If BLM is to mean anything it has to be about black lives across the world and not only about a narrow spectrum of black people. The trans- Saharan and especially the East African slave trade are largely hidden or less frequently discussed subjects.

At a United Nation conference on racism in 2001, some delegates attending wanted the slave trade that existed between Africa, Europe and the Americas acknowledged as a ' double Holocaust'. 'Holocaust' is a specific term which refers to the genocide of Jews in Europe during World War Two. It is not a generic word that may be applied to any other situation, however evil or depressing that may be. In this respect describing slavery as a holocaust is unwarranted. But in this claim one also recognises its selective nature. There is no acceptance that slavery was endemic in Africa or any mention of the two other aspects of African slavery – trans-Saharan and the slavery which occurred on the East coast of the continent. Senegal's then President Abdoulaye Wade (1926-) said 'I am opposed to demanding financial recompense, ...Slavery, the subjugation of a people for three centuries, cannot be evaluated in billions of dollars..... It is absurd... that you could pay up a certain number of dollars and then slavery ceases to exist, is cancelled out and there is the receipt to prove it,' he added......'we still suffer the effects of slavery and colonialism, and that can not be evaluated in monetary terms. I find that not only absurd, but insulting.' These words appear to sit in accord with the words of Brandon Haber in the *'Handbook of Reparation'* which states ' There should not be anything in a reparations program that invites either their designers or their beneficiaries to interpret them as an effort to put a price on the life of victims or on the experiences of horror. Rather, they should be interpreted as making a contribution to the quality of life of survivors'.

Wade made the point that Africans had themselves owned and sold slaves and asked the rhetorical question 'Should they also pay up?'. This is the painful issue that has been raised by many writers.

Wade continued 'Some of us have forebears who may not have sold slaves, but had slaves in their armies. I am talking about my own ancestors, who had 10 000 soldiers at that time, of which two thirds were slaves.' The recognition of endemic slavery in Africa and trading in slavery by African themselves needs to be confronted. How many Africans today have ancestors who were slave owners and slave traders?

The author Sandra Green wrote 'While 11 to 12 million people are estimated to have been exported as slaves from West Africa during the years of the slave trade, millions more were retained in Africa. 'It's not something that many West African countries talk about,'.

The renowned black author Zora Neale Hurston wrote 'the white people held my people in slavery here in America. They had bought us, it is true, and exploited us. But the inescapable fact that stuck in my craw was: My people had sold me … . My own people had exterminated whole nations and torn families apart for a profit before the strangers got their chance at a cut. It was a sobering thought. It impressed upon me the universal nature of greed.' And we might add, the universal nature of slavery.'

Europeans did not invent slavery. They came upon it and used the institution of slavery in Africa to their advantage. In his bock '*The African Slave Trade*', Basil Davidson wrote ' The notion that Europe altogether imposed the slave trade on Africa is without any foundation in history … . Those Africans who were involved in the trade were seldom the helpless victims of a commerce they did not understand: On the contrary, they responded to its challenge. They exploited its opportunities.' Slavery was a win- win situation for all parties who were involved, except for the slaves and their families.

The American author, Thomas Sowell wrote, 'more whites were brought as slaves to North Africa than blacks brought as slaves to the United States or to the 13 colonies from which it was formed. White slaves were still being bought and sold in the Ottoman Empire, decades after blacks were freed in the United States.'

Two prominent Ghanians paint a telling picture of the slave trade in Africa. The diplomat Kofi Awoonor wrote 'I believe there is a great psychic shadow over Africa, and it has much to do with our guilt and denial of our role in the slave trade. We, too, are blameworthy in what was essentially one of the most heinous crimes in human history.' That the African himself played a part in this so-called 'heinous crime' is largely ignored - no, these uncomfortable facts are airbrushed for a single narrative that portrays the European as the villain and the black man as the victim. Meanwhile the politician Samuel Sulemana Fuseini admits that his Asante ancestors accumulated great wealth by capturing his fellow Africans and selling them into slavery.

In 2000 the President of Benin, Mathieu Kérékou, publicly apologised for his country's role in the propagation of slavery saying 'selling fellow Africans by the millions to white slave traders'. Africans are acknowledging their role in slavery and are pleading for forgiveness.

The film director, Roger Gnona M'bala from the ivory Coast said ' It's up to us to talk about slavery, open the wounds of what we've always hidden and stop being puerile when we put responsibility on others ... .'

The part played by Arabs in the trans-Sharan and east African slave trade is concealed and seldom talked about. It is estimated that between the 7th and 19th centuries more that 14 million black slaves were transported across the Sahara.

In the book 'Le Génocide Voilé' (' he Veiled Genocide'), the author Tidane N'Daye who is Senegalese, described the horrors of the East African slave trade which was dominated by Arabs. Arabs considered blacks to be inferior. This is probably the first occasion when race came into slavery. The Atlantic slave trade was a commercial venture and not, at least initially, based on race but on the ability of slaves to work the fields and plantations. It is estimated that 80 % of the slaves in the trade in the east coast of Africa died. 17 million males were castrated. Both perpetrators and descendants of slaves are in denial. These sobering and painful facts are compounded by silence of Black Americans; it appears to be a taboo subject.

Taking the totality of the African slave trade into consideration, one wonders who needs to participate in reparation payments and who are the potential recipients of reparations. There were several actors in the slave trade with Europeans being the conduit for transport of slaves across the Atlantic. Are the latter to bear any potential cost of reparations for a segment of the slave trade? That would be discriminatory to the many millions who suffered in the trans-Saharan and East African slave trades.

An interesting conundrum arises if America were, hypothetically, to accept the suggestion by many, including the activist Te-Nehisi Coates, that 14 trillion American dollars be paid in reparations. Would such a transaction silence the BLM movement and others who clamour for reparations? Or would additional amounts of money be needed? And of course the thorniest question is what the money would be spent on. Paying it to black people would be utterly ineffective. It would be like saying 'here's some money as you are the descendants of slaves; accept and remain silent about slavery hereinafter'. Insulting as a such a gesture would be, as implied by Abdoulaye Wade, it is not likely to change anything, especially if the payer expects silence and that the issue of slavery would suddenly disappear. And there is the matter, painful as it is to repeat, that descendants of slaves in America and in Europe have done better that their compatriots in Africa. They have more material possessions, better access to medical care, pensions and greater opportunities for their children, to name but a few, than those living in many parts of Africa. The ridiculous and apparently offensive matter arises - has not slavery of the ancestors benefitted their descendants? The same could also be said about the slave-catcher and trader in Africa. Their descendants in the developed world have, on average, done well with a better standard of living and greater opportunities for their children. Could it be that slaves unintentionally invested their ordeal for the benefit of their descendants? This is not meant to sound as slavery having been an acceptable or beneficial proposition. Nothing could be further from the truth, considering the appalling suffering that slaves endured.

Perhaps the words of Robert Johnson need serious consideration at this stage. Johnson, 74, is the founder of Black Entertainment Television (BET) and he is reputed to be America's first black dollar billionaire. In 2020 he said 'Is $14 trillion too much to ask for the atonement of 200 plus years of brutal slavery, de facto and de jure government-sponsored social and economic discrimination and the permanent emotional trauma inflicted upon black Americans by being forced to believe in a hypocritical and unfulfilled pledge that 'all men are created equal?' The transfer of wealth, Johnson believes, would help to correct the inherent inequalities in society that places blacks at disadvantage. He went on to say that reparations would be the 'affirmative action program of all time'.

There is considerable merit in the viewpoints of Robert Johnson. There is little doubt that improved housing, education and access to better healthcare are likely to make considerable strides in levelling up while increasing ambition and the personal aspiration to achieve. But one cannot ignore the words of Barack Obama. The need for domestic social capital is paramount; this is not likely to change much with reparation unless there is a profound, dedicated and sustained commitment to the family unit and the guiding hand of parents in the formative years in the lives of children.

Where Robert Johnsons' proposal falls flat is the suggestion that about 40 million African-Americans would get $350,000 cash each, spread over 30 years. This is equivalent to about 11,700 dollars per year per black person in the group of 40 million that he identifies. One is bound to ask what this amount of approximately 1000 dollars per month would achieve? The fact, as he says, that the black man understands cash is not helpful here, especially if it is squandered and does not make any significant improvement in the quality of life or in the equality and inclusivity of blacks in society. Blatant cash transfer can never be a logical answer. Nor can any other form of wealth transfer, based on cash. Professor David Abulafia of Cambridge University in the UK said ' Large cheques aren't going to alter the past, which is always more contentious than activists like to think'. Simplistic monetary proposals driven by a sense of wokeism, where the black person is the victim and the white person is the villain is never likely to address the issue of reparations or indeed improve the life of blacks. What is needed is the reversal of any institutionalised disadvantage in terms of access to good housing, education etc. How did Robert Johnson himself or Barak Obama or Oprah Winfrey succeed if not by education, hard work, dedication and perseverance. These are aspects of life that need to be instilled early on in life of young blacks– hence the value of a good home where responsibility, accountability etc are not only practised but also taught to offspring. In one or two generations one would see the green shoots of a new, vibrant, responsible and inclusive society. If reparation is to mean anything it must be not only an acceptance that slavery was wrong and abhorrent, although it was not perceived as such at the time. But also there has to be an acceptance and a willingness to use reparations as means of providing all in society the same opportunities and quality of life. Described in these terms reparations or whatever else one may choose to call the program, are likely to be more acceptable to the average person, who ultimately has to pay for the scheme. These persons are quite right to state that they are not responsible for the acts or omissions of their ancestors and predecessors. As a You-Gov poll in 2016 showed that '80% of Americans over 69 years of age opposed reparations'. In the case of millennials, only 40% agreed with the idea of paying reparations and 11% were unsure.. The rest were opposed to reparations. The topic of reparations is also a highly political issue in the USA. – 55% of Democrats support a study of reparation payments while only 14% of Republicans support it. Individuals feel strongly about being responsible for the actions of their predecessors at a time when slavery was not considered an immoral act. There is considerable justification and support for this view. In fact the Bible lends weight to this view in Ezekiel 18:20 – ' The son shall not suffer for the iniquity of the father, nor the father suffer for the iniquity of the son. The righteousness of the righteous shall be upon himself, and the wickedness of the wicked shall be upon himself'.

Stuart E. Eizenstat was a special representative of the President of USA and Secretary of State on Holocaust-era issues from 1993 to 2001. He said that 'reparations in the form of cash payments for descendants of slaves are not the way to right this grievous wrong……. reparations are complicated, contentious and messy, and work best when the crime was recent and the direct victims are still alive. Based on my experience, I believe that trying to repay descendants of slaves could end up causing more problems than reparations would seek to solve and that there are better ways to end racial disparities.' This was best illustrated in a class action in 2002 where JPMorgan Chase and other companies were named. The case was a claim for reparations. The case was dismissed with the judge ruling that the claimants had failed to demonstrate a clear link between themselves and the companies named in the action. A similar action claiming the sum of $1bn brought by Ed Fagan, a human rights lawyer, against Lloyd's of London, RJ Reynolds and FleetBoston was withdrawn.

The report – '*SIERRA LEONE REPARATIONS PROGRAM -The Limits of Good Intentions*' of 2010 provided some basis for the reparations program in that war-torn country . These were –'to respond to the needs of victims, promote healing and reconciliation, restore the dignity of the victims and to restore civic trust'. It is possible and indeed desirable to extract from this document the essential need to identify victims, as was apparent after World War Two. Victims need compensation for sufferings endured; this does not extend across several generations to the descendants of slaves. The latter are hardly victims of slavery. They may be victims of racism but that too is improving as the words of Thomas Sowell make clear. That there is more to travel in the journey of reducing racism and addressing equalities is without doubt the pressing need for many societies.

Wrongly managed, the issue of reparations is likely to be a continuing source of friction and resentment that is likely to feed into white supremacy ideas and into those who propound the ridiculously titled 'Great Replacement Theory'.

What would a black person or family do with their money? In 2006 Matthew Corbin from Cheyney University Pennsylvania wrote a thought provoking article – *'5 Reasons Why Black People Are Still Broke'*. He listed the following – they overspend, do not support black businesses, don't know how to invest or how to save, and are not working hard enough to get out of poverty. The black person is described as wanting to emulate his richer black neighbours even if he cannot afford it. This leads to overspend and a spiral of debt. What is interesting is that they would spend money that they cannot afford on goods from white businesses rather than from black-owned shops, thinking the latter are too expensive. Their ability to save an invest for the future is limited. They are therefore in a trap of their own making while continuing to tighten the financial noose around themselves . The same views were expressed some years earlier by Bill Cosby and Alvin F. Poussaint in their book *'Come on, People: On the Path from Victims to Victors'*. They ask for e.g. why a black parent would spend $500 on sneakers for their children than on educational toys that would benefit them. So what would $1000 per month on proposed reparation achieve? More sneakers, more designer goods, less education and increasing poverty and desolation. Teaching black people and all people life skills must surely be more important than giving them money. 'Give a man a fish and you feed him for a day; teach a man to fish and you feed him for a lifetime'.

This is what Ta-Nehisi Coates, American journalist, told the Congress of the United States of America in 2019 – 'The typical black family in this country has one-tenth the wealth of the typical white family. Black women die in childbirth at four times the rate of white women. And there is, of course, the shame of this land of the free boasting the largest prison population on the planet, of which the descendants of the enslaved make up the largest share' That this is a sombre statement is without doubt. But set against the words of Barak Obama, Matthew Corbin, Bill Cosby and others one is obliged to ask whether there is a lot missing in what was said by Coates. Why? Is it slavery alone or is it the fundamental inequalities in society that consign not only blacks but also others to a situation where there is under-achievement, poor health etc. But by far the significant numbers of blacks in prison as alluded to by Coates begs the question again – why? Why would a black child or youngster prefer to be part of a gang than go to school? Why would they prefer a gun to a toy or a book? Why does the black person choose a sub-optimal standard in life than aspire for the highest and the best? Coates acknowledges that monetary recompense cannot be the sole answer. That there is an acknowledgement of the negative impact of slavery would be a satisfactory starting point. Thereafter addressing the issues that are fundamental to and drive under-achievement must be the imperative. One would find it difficult if not impossible to agree with Coates that the majority of Americans frown on the success of black people. They are acclaimed, as can be seen by the overwhelming support for the views for e.g. of Barack Obama. One would have been unlikely to have achieved the position of President of the USA if one were to agree with Coates.

What is singularly missing from Coates' views is a clarion call to black leaders, opinion-formers, influencers and those who are successful in all walks of life, to address other blacks to seek personal emancipation through effort. Don't wait for reparations or handouts – reach for the stars yourselves!. As the tennis champion, Serena Williams said ' You have to believe in yourself when no one else does……… It doesn't matter what your background is or where you come from, if you have dreams and goals, that's all that matters…… Growing up I wasn't the richest, but I had a rich family in spirit…..'

Would it not be better to have a reparations narrative based on the inherent and patently visible inequalities in society? A humane society would strive to see all persons treated as equals. While acknowledging that slavery was wrong, society does not have to atone for it now. On the contrary it is the job of leaders to inform and educate the public that slavery led to the birth of inequality. While large strides have been made in recent years, society has a moral duty to all it's citizens, blacks, coloured, white, that they are included in the same opportunities that should be open to all. This will then place an equally moral burden on all to participate in an equal society and to bear the responsibilities associated with equality. Funds spent in such programs would right the wrongs of the past, but most importantly demonstrate and practice equality in society.

Successful blacks have amply demonstrated that opportunity is there. What is lacking in the many is the desire to achieve and the drive to get there. This is where black and coloured leaders have a prominent part to play. The few who have achieved must reach out to the many who are disillusioned and may feel disenfranchised, to come in to the fold and play their full part.

Here now is a question the devil's advocate may pose? Supposing it was hypothetically agreed that financial reparations would be paid to blacks who are descendants of slaves. How would those blacks who have succeeded and are doing well, through their own effort and application, feel about the proposal? It would seem that a successful descendant of a slave would then have agreed to pay not only themselves in being a descendant of slaves, but also to contribute to less successful descendants of slaves. That brings into focus why some blacks, despite the injustices of the system, have strived and been successful while others, one may conclude, have not been as assiduous as the former. Should not society be considering the reasons for the latter rather than making a blanket statement of reparation? One may now discern why the majority of persons would not, in all likelihood, support a system of payments to Individuals. This is also apparently so of successful blacks. The blanket transfer of wealth is never likely to improve the lost of impoverished blacks. In medicine it is said that diagnosis precedes rational management. So also it is in the situation of disadvantage blacks. Address black disadvantage and the causes of black disadvantage and one may then begin to make some progress.

What about coloured persons? When attempting to address disadvantage one needs to look at the situation widely and not confine oneself to a select group, however deserving, special or meritorious the clam of that group may be. For herein lies resentment and racism. All those who are disadvantaged need help. In trying to reverse black disadvantage one may envisage a wider movement of improvement to the benefit of society as a whole.

The author and broadcaster Afue Hirsch quoted Sir Henry Beckles, historian and vice-chancellor of the University of West Indies, about the 'pandemic of chronic disease' in the West Indies as being linked to slavery. The region is recognised as having a high rate of hypertension and is a leading area in the world for diabetes related amputations of the limbs. Sir Henry Beckles is quoted as saying that 'for 300 years the people of this region were forced to consume a diet based on what we produced, sugar'. Sugar was a food substance in much demand at the time and was produced in vast quantities in the plantations of the West Indies using slave labour. These facts are not in doubt. Sugar is sweet and most would like it, as any child knows. But to extend that to compulsion in consumption, is to stretch the matter to incredulity. Diabetes was a feared disease because it was invariably fatal at the time. The discovery of insulin by Frederick Banting and his assistant Charles Best in 1921 helped transform the lives of those with the disease. Medicine is even now learning and discovering more about diabetes. Despite the vast advances in knowledge about diabetes and practice, even to this day about 170 amputations take place in the UK every week for the complications of diabetes. One is bound to ask what the government of the West Indies is doing about the problem rather than attributing it to slavery.

The same may be said about hypertension or high blood pressure, which is referred to in the paper by Hirsch. Hypertension is a common worldwide problem and again to relate this to slavery is without substance. In a paper in 2015 titled *Disparities in hypertension among black Caribbean populations: a scoping review by the U.S. Caribbean Alliance for Health Disparities Research Group (USCAHDR)* written by Aurelian Bidulescu, Damian K. Francis, Trevor S. Ferguson and colleagues it was shown that hypertension was commoner in Caribbean blacks than in West African Blacks or Caucasians. Considering that many slaves came from West Africa, it begs the question why they do not have the same rate of hypertension as Caribbean blacks. The link with slavery is non-existent. Bidulescu and colleagues wrote that the social and economic situation in groups of people taken together with the provision of health care, politics and the legal framework in a country is needed for improvement and for changes to be seen in health of the population. They went on to write that there is a complex interplay of factors which must consider social and cultural factors.

The Barbados Studies of Amputation in people with diabetes of 1999 shed light on the problems of health in the West Indies. With one in 100 people with diabetes having an amputation, this ranks as one of the highest in amputation rates in the world. One in three of those who have an amputation would likely die in the next year. At 5 years only 60% would survive after a minor amputation i.e. of a toe. In the case of a major amputation, only a third of amputees would be alive at 5 years after an amputation below the knee while only 10% would be alive at 5 years after an above- knee amputation. These are horrendous survival statistics which paint a picture of grave threat to health of the people in the region.

It is heartening to note that the burden of non- communicable diseases (NCD's) was recognised in the Caribbean when the Caribbean Heads of Government responded in their report of 2007 *'Uniting to Stop the Epidemic of Chronic Non-Communicable Diseases'* This was a belated acknowledgement that NCD's had been described by the World Health Organisation (WHO) as a worldwide problem threatening global health. It is not unique to the Caribbean or linked in any discernible way to slavery. The report identified tobacco use, unhealthy diet, physical inactivity, and alcohol excess as the major threats to a healthy life which lead to hypertension, obesity, diabetes and heart disease. Control of these risk factors, therefore, would, according to the report, reduce the incidence of all these diseases including cancer. Half of the people in the Caribbean are described as not doing any physical activity whatsoever and the report refers to them as 'couch potatoes'. One now had a blueprint for reduction in NCD's and the risks of complications from them.

Considering that these countries have been independent since the 1960's - Barbados gained its independence in 1966, the Bahamas in 1973, Grenada in 1974, Dominica in 1978, St. Lucia and St. Vincent and the Grenadines in 1979, Antigua and Barbuda in 1981 and St. Kitts and Nevis in 1983 – it is wholly appropriate that the respective governments worked to improve healthcare rather than falling back on slavery as an excuse for, at best, limited intervention in the area of public health.

It is possible to bring about change in health, education etc. Take the example of North Karelia, a province of Finland. In the early 1970's it had one of the highest death rates in the world from heart disease. A project was launched with the community and the WHO, 'North Karelia Project', with the objective of bearing down on the number of deaths from heart disease. The project acted on smoking, the consumption of fat and encouraging people to eat healthily including fruit and vegetables. This was not a didactic exercise where information was disseminated to the public. It was an active process where researchers reached out to the public – talking to them, organising meetings and discussions in schools, social clubs, church congregations etc. The project lasted 25 years and was a success. As the Director of the North Karelia Project, Professor Pekka Puska, said simply giving people information was not adequate. There had to be active participation of the team with the community. Behaviours changed, smoking declined together with acceptance of healthy eating habits. The results at the end of 25 years were impressive with 71 less deaths per 100,000 men. Since the project concluded the people of North Karelia continue to enjoy good health with a much reduced risk of dying from heart disease and cancer.

North Karelia has shown that it can be done. What is needed is the will to deliver. The experience of North Karelia provides a glowing example of how monies may be invested to improve the health of blacks and bring them to the level of health enjoyed by others. And if it can be done for health so too can great strides be made with education, housing etc. Here is a viable project in reparations. Money without focus can never be an answer; it is doomed to failure.

Reparations have been tried in the past in the USA. The Indian Claims Commission of 1946 awarded $848 million to 176 different Native American tribes for lands that had been taken from them. Similarly Japanese- Americans who had been interned during World War Two received a payment of $20,000 per person in an internment camp.

Two other examples are important and relevant here as they do not involve the payment of monies to specific persons. Georgetown University in Washington DC once owned 272 slaves. It has decided to offer scholarships to descendants of those whom the University had enslaved. In March 2021 the town of Evanston, a suburb Chicago in Illinois, was the first city in the United States to offer reparations. It proposed to provide 'qualifying black households' financial assistance for home ownership and home improvement grants. Would these two descriptions serve as examples of meaningful reparation for slavery? The obvious answer is no. Georgetown University is not compensating the slaves for their suffering but acting out of its sense of morality to help descendants of slaves. But there may be others who are equally or more deserving of the University's help? Does it wash the guilt of the University? Again, not but it makes them feel good. Would it not have been better, in the name of it's past association with slavery, to have used money to enhance the lives of all deserving students? In the case of Evanston, again, would it not have been prudent to use monies to generally improve housing for those most deserving of help?

Perhaps one of the most historical acts in reparation occurred on 16th January 1865 when Union General William Tecumseh Sherman issued Field Order No. 15. This was a proclamation that lands confiscated and which amounted to 400,000 acres would be awarded to newly freed black people. The land was split into parcels of 40 acres each. This was arable land which included rice fields. The new owners had right to the land and title to it would follow from Congress. Military protection was provided for the new land owners. This act of reparation followed discussion with black leaders who emphasised that their people needed land and expressed their desire to live in communities on the land. General Sherman subsequently ordered that army mules be given to the new settlers. The program gained the name of '40 acres and a mule' The lands were renamed Sherman Land by the grateful blacks. During the initial discussions, blacks were asked what they wanted. 'Land' came the universal reply, continuing 'The way we can best take care of ourselves, is to have land, and turn it and till it by our own labor ... and we can soon maintain ourselves and have something to spare ... We want to be placed on land until we are able to buy it and make it our own.' Unfortunately this program did not last long. It ended soon after the assassination of President Abraham Lincoln in April 1865. Andrew Johnson who succeeded Lincoln as President revoked the program and returned the lands to their white planter owners. What the program showed during its short life was that it was possible to provide material reparation, as opposed to financial compensation, which can make a difference to blacks. It would induce them to use their industry and resourcefulness to progress.

In 2005, America's second biggest bank, JP Morgan Chase, apologised for its involvement in the slave trade. Two of the banks it acquired, Citizens' Bank and Canal Bank in Louisiana, accepted slaves in lieu of loans, which they had made to plantation owners, when the latter could not meet their debts to the banks. It is estimated that between 1831 and 1865 the two banks had accepted about 13000 slaves as collateral. While offering its apology to the African-American Community, JP Morgan Chase also established a $5m college scholarship programme for black students in Louisiana. This was done to 'both acknowledge the past and improve the future'.

What these examples demonstrate is that personal financial reparation to individuals is not necessary or even desirable. Material assistance that could make a difference to the life of blacks by enhancing their life skills is a better investment that could help chart a journey towards equality.

There can be no greater and more fitting reparation than the recognition of what happened regarding slavery, by all the descendants of those involved in the slave trade. Slavery was a stain on humanity. The fact that it has been present from time immemorial is no justification for a failure to recognise now that it was an evil, although it was not perceived as such at the time. Slavery was legal at the time it was practised and continued in some countries until recently. Mali, for e.g. has a long history of slavery. The French abolished slavery in Mali in 1905 but the practice of slavery continued. The practice of 'descent based slavery' continues to this day, where the descendants of nobles and slave holders still consider the descendants of slaves as still being slaves themselves. September 22nd is Independence Day in Mali. On that day in 2021 in the western city of Kayes, young people were publicly celebrating Independence Day when they were set upon by descendants of the slave-holding class using machetes and sticks. Several were wounded and at least one person died in the attack. The social class structure is very much alive in Mali to this day and descendants of slaves remain in the lowest stratum of this hierarchy. The persistence of social strata allows 'descent based slavery' to persist. Members of the slave class cannot occupy positions of prominence in society or even be in public service. They cannot be lawyers, judges, town councillors, mayors etc. Discrimination is rife in Mali society. Successive

Mali governments have not been vigorous enough in stamping out the practice of 'descent – based slavery'. There is the risk that marginalised members of society may find refuge in terrorist groupings, as a result of the sense of being disfranchised. Yvan Guichaoua, from the Brussels School of International Studies at the University of Kent, states that the al-Qaeda-linked Jama'at Nusrat al-Islam wal-Muslimin (JNIM) movement in the area could take advantage of the cracks in society which 'descent-based slavery' provides.

Slavery was part of African culture. In many other cultures too, worldwide, slavery or variations of it have been a part of society. A desirable and wholly appropriate act of reparation would be when descendants of slave holders, slave traders and slaves were to meet in a joint act of contrition and understanding of what happened centuries ago. This would give life to the words of Martin Luther King. There is no doubt slave traders and slave holders were jointly involved in many aspects of slavery. Where then does financial reparation come into the discussion? Payment of money devalues what happened and reduces slavery to a market place and the slave to a commodity yet again, which can be equated with finance. Does it not equally reduce descendants of slaves to commodities, tradeable for money? One is reminded of the words of President Wade of Senegal when he denounced financial reparations. Does he know something about slavery which is not recognised or is difficult for others to accept? One is, sometimes, at a loss to understand the deeper meaning of what he said.

Any study of reparations would be incomplete without reference to the unusual and bizarre situation of Haiti. The country declared independence from its colonisers, the French, in 1804. Haitians revolted against those who were their slave masters. Haiti is the first and only independent nation to be born after having thrown off its shackles of slavery. But its freedom was short-lived. Come 1825, with King Charles X on the throne in France, the French were back, demanding payment from the Haitians for their freedom or, in their poverty and powerlessness, to face the prospect of war with the French. The demand was for 150 million French francs to be paid in five annual instalments. There was no way the nation that was impoverished then, as it is now, could pay this colossal sum. The French knew it and conceived of a cunning way to ensure payment. Borrow

Reparations

the money from a French bank; fast forward to Rwanda fir a similar arrangement.. The payments made by Haiti to France varied in total from 21 billion to a 100 billion dollars. The loans obtained from French banks had to be repaid with interest. This was also the same money which deprived the country of development and pushed it further into debt and into poverty. It is recorded that the Paris-based bank, Crédit Industriel et Commercial, gained massively from its deals in Haiti. The Haitian historian, Georges Michel, wrote that the French were aided by local people who helped rob the country of its resources. Transparency International wrote that Haiti is one of the most corrupt nations of the world. Of a loan made to Haiti by France in 1875, bankers helped themselves to 40% of the amount.

François Duvalier, who was known as 'Papa Doc', ruled the country as dictator from 1957 to 1971. He was followed as President by his son, Jean-Claude Duvalier, called 'Baby Doc', from 1971 to 1986 when he was overthrown from power. 'Baby Doc' continued his father's practice of corruption, embezzlement and what amounted to 'state capture'. On 7th April 2003, the then President of Haiti, Jean-Bertrand Aristide, made a claim for reparations which came as a shock to France, who had tried to keep the matter under wraps. Most of what happened in the 19th century in France's involvement in Haiti was not known to the public; it was not taught in schools. France's role in Haiti was airbrushed from history. Aristide was whisked out of Haiti in an attempt to silence the matter.

Haiti was the first and only country in the world to pay reparations to its colonisers, it's slave-masters - the French! And the French tried everything in their power to conceal this fact. When the French Ambassador in Haiti at the time, Yves- Gaudeul heard the claim for reparations he called it 'explosive...... we had to try to defuse it'. The French set to work to remove Aristide from power. A later French Ambassador, Thierry Burkard, said that France and the USA organised a 'coup' to remove Aristide from power and it was 'probably a bit about' his call for reparations.

However, one has to be fair to Ambassador Gaudeul who wanted France to be open and transparent about the matter, claiming 'I didn't understand how we could be so stupid'. 'It's never taught; ...It's never explained' said a former French Prime Minister Jean-Marc Ayrault, who continued 'All French people are affected. Yet, French students don't learn about it and few officials discuss it'. This, from a nation which prides itself on its claims for liberty and the freedoms of peoples around the world.

'We were very disdainful of Haiti' Mr. Gaudeul had said. 'What I think we will never forgive Haiti for, deep down, is that it is the country that beat us.'

Despite being independent, France worked to ensure that Haiti remained dependant on it; Haitian independence in name only. The French historian, Jean-François Brière, called the arrangement of payments a 'meta-slavery' which prevented Haiti from asserting itself as an independent nation.

One wonders why Haiti was treated this way, not only by the French but also by the Americans who collaborated actively with the French, especially in removing Aristide from the scene. Slaves rising against their masters was an existential threat to the latter and to the whole edifice of slavery. The powers of the time, especially the French were not going to let the Hattians get away with it. Both the latter's independence and Haiti's claims for reparations were affronts to the perceived superiority of France. How could the powerless slaves rise up against the French, or so the latter thought. It was a threat that most slave holders feared. Slaves had rebelled on slave ships and they had run away from the lands in which they were held and worked. But never had a nation of slaves risen up against their colonisers who were nothing but slave masters. This was a situation worse than a colony of an empire, fighting for independence. This was an outright rebellion against those who owned the people who were slaves, not the 'locals' as some colonisers would refer to people in colonies and dominions of an empire. How dare they rebel in this manner? Or so the French thought. A consideration foremost in the minds of slave owners of the time was whether this rebellion would spur other slaves to act in a similar manner. There was also the need for labour to work the fields.

In a speech in 2015, France's then President, Francois Hollande admitted that Haiti's ransom payments to France was called 'the ransom of independence.' To resounding applause by the attending crowds which included African heads of state, he said 'when I come to Haiti, I will, for my part, pay off the debt we have'. Did he really say that! Michaëlle Jean, the former secretary-general of the International Organization of la Francophonie said that the statement of Hollande was so 'immense that people cried'. Did he really, really say that? It would be the first instance of admission of past wrong doings by a head of state and what seemed to sound like an acknowledgement of the need to pay Haiti reparation for past French deeds. But above all, it would have been repayment to Haiti of money that was morally and illegally taken from it. This was a wealthy country literally bleeding a far poorer desperate nation of its meagre resources. Marlene Daut, a scholar from the University of Virginia called it 'the greatest heist in history'. Surrounded by French gunboats, a newly independent Haiti was forced to pay its slaveholders, reparations. You read that correctly. It was the former *slaves* of Haiti, not the French *slaveholders*, who were forced to pay reparations. Haitians compensated their oppressors and their oppressors' descendants for the privilege of being free. It took Haiti more than a century to pay the reparation debts off.

Alas that is not at all what Holland meant. In classic double-speak, one of his aides issued a follow up statement saying that what Hollande 'really meant' was only about a 'moral debt'. There it is – slaves paying their wealthy slave holders a ransom for their independence! And a century later the slave holder using words to pay a moral debt!! Morality, if there is any left, remains hollow without concrete action. This is the most perverse example of reparation payment – reverse reparations from the impoverished to the fabulously wealthy. This is a startling example of slavery and theft on a single nation – and all because it sought freedom. Liberté, égalité, fraternité - where art thou? The Haitians were in need of you.

One is reminded of the morality of the French in bombing and sinking the Greenpeace ship, The Rainbow Warrior, in Auckland harbour in 1985. That is another story of French duplicity and paucity of meaningful morality.

But as a nation of freed black slaves, Haiti was a threat to the existing world order. President Thomas Jefferson worked to isolate Haiti diplomatically and strangle it economically, fearing that the success of Haiti would inspire slave revolts back home. With the invention and spread of the 'cotton gin', slavery was becoming much more lucrative at the very same time a free Haiti was coming into existence, and slaveholders in the United States and other countries clung to and expanded the inhumane means of production. Haitian success was perceived as a threat to this system for decades, and the United States didn't officially recognize Haiti until 1862, as slavery began being abolished.

The 'cotton gin', which meant cotton engine, was invented by Eli Whitney (1765–1825) and patented in 1793. The engine allowed for the rapid separation of cotton from its seeds. Prior to the invention of the 'cotton gin', separation of cotton fibre from its seed was done manually. The cotton engine made it much easier and separation of fibre from seed was on a lager scale than could be done manually. Far from relieving the need for manual labour i.e. slaves, the invention of the 'cotton gin' paradoxically increased the need for slaves. They were needed to harvest more cotton and bring it in for separation. The lager amounts of cotton seed produced by the machine needed slaves to replant them to produce more cotton or to be used in the production of cotton-seed oil. Freedom for slaves would hamper productivity and the economy.

RISE OF THE PHOENIX

The phoenix is a bird in Greek mythology which arose from the ashes of its predecessor. A phoenix is used as a motif or emblem by many organisation; a symbol of resistance, persistence and eventual success. The flag of San Francisco has a phoenix in its centre to symbolise it rise from the earthquake of 1906 and resulting fires in the city. Coventry University in the UK has a phoenix rising our to from the ashes on its flag and Coat of Arms. The crest of Coventry City Football Club has a phoenix rising from the ashes in memory of how the City of Coventry was rebuilt after the blitz by the German Luftwaffe in World War Two.

Teal Swan (1984-), an American author and influencer, wrote 'Here in this suffering, all previous beliefs are called into question. They are consumed in the fire sparked and fuelled by our own illusion. The pain becomes the ashes we are now entombed in. It is only when we find ourselves at this most imprisoned of junctures that we emerge again, the phoenix of our very life which is ever so much more beautiful than the last one.' It is what is implied in the words of the American author and Taoist philosopher, Min-Dao Deng 'Whether we remain the ash or become the Phoenix is up to us.'

When one is beaten one can stay down and wail in sorrow. Or one can stay down and become a victim. Blame all one's failures on the lowness of one's life and the poor deck of cards that life has given one. This is an easy path but leads to suffering. As Christian said to himself on meeting a hill on the way to the Celestial Gate in the book, *'Pilgrim's Prog*ress' by John Bunyan – 'Better, though difficult, the right way to go; Than wrong, though easy, where the end is woe'. The latter path of victimhood is a never-ending and distressing circus of suffering, depression and dependence. Until one confronts oneself and reckons with what is happening. Of course the alternative is to strive for better. One can take a long, hard look at one's personal psychological mirror and take account of the positive attributes that one has, for there always are. They may be submerged by the misery of the situation, but the latter is to a large extent caused by one's own thinking. If one were to only recognise negative attributes as one's enemies and deal with them, one is then on the path of working with all that is positive that one has. As Arnold Schwarzenegger, the actor and former Governor of California once said 'No matter who you are it's the simple things in life that lead you to believe that you can achieve anything'. It may need a modicum of talent, but it was said that 'hard work without talent is a shame but talent without hard work is a tragedy'. One needs a goal, motivation to move forwards and then personal application. One may not get there but one would, nevertheless, have achieved a lot in the process. By application or hard work one needs to separate volume of work from its quality. It is working harder while being smart at it that helps one to make progress, in other words smart, hard work. It is an amazing fact that as one applies oneself, one discovers more about oneself – strength, courage, persistence and most of all a degree of personal resilience which would stand oneself in good stead as one's personal future unfolds. On the journey one overcomes obstacles, big and small, but the focus always remains the goal. The late great boxer Muhammed Ali said 'It isn't the mountains ahead to climb that wear you out, it's the pebble in your shoe.' The inner courage and personal conviction to overcome the obstacles, while keeping one's goal in focus at all times, helps one to get there; to achieve. Rabindranath Tagore, the author from India, wrote 'The traveller has to knock at every alien door to come to his own, and one has to wander through all the outer worlds to reach the innermost shrine at the end.' When ambition and the flames of desire burn within oneself, and the goal is always in sight, ' the journey home is never too long'.

The life of Andrew Jackson Young Jr. (12.03.1932-) is interesting for his progress from the place of his birth in New Orleans, Louisiana, USA. Being from a middle class family, his parents (father was a dentist) tried to provide the best for the family while protecting the children from the harsh realities of being black and segregation of the time. Young Sr. hired a boxing coach to teach his children how to defend themselves. Interestingly, and this is a feature that is encountered by blacks in the USA when discussing their ancestors in Africa, the young Andrew was surprised by the attitude of his parents and other middle-class blacks, who did not help their less fortunate blacks more, than they were seen to do at the time. Andrew Young was a close associated of Dr. Martin Luther King Jr. In his early life Andrew was a pastor and was active in encouraging blacks to register for and vote at elections. He became a congressman from Georgia and a Mayor of Atlanta, Georgia. He was the first African – American to hold the position of United States Ambassador to the United Nations, having being appointed to that post by President Jimmy Carter in 1977.

Thurgood Marshall (1908 – 1993) was a lawyer and civil rights activist who was the first African – America to become a Justice of the Supreme Court of the United States of America . Both his parents were descended form slaves; his father was a porter on the railways while his mother was a teacher. At the outset he wanted to study medicine but eventually his choice was law. He wanted to attend his local law school, University of Maryland School of Law, but he was prevented form applying because of the segregation laws of the time. He went to Howard University School of Law, and graduated first in his class achieving LL.B magna cum laude. It is said that his mother had to pawn her engagement and wedding rings to meet the bills for his education. He was appointed to the United Sates Court of Appeals Second Circuit in 1961 by President John Fitzgerald Kennedy. His nomination for associate Justice of the Supreme Court of the US went to the Senate for ratification. He was voted 69 to 11 in favour with 37 Democrats and 32 Republicans voting for him. Ten Democrats and one Republican voted against him. A significant achievement of Thurgood Marshall was a greater collaboration between the Federal Bureau of Investigations (FBI) and the National Association for the Advancement of Coloured People (NAACP). He was also the first African-American Solicitor-General of the United States when President Lyndon B Johnson appointed him to the post in 1965. A statue of Marshall is to be found in the Lawyers Mall close to the Maryland State House and another is located in the building of the federal courts system in Capitol Hill Washington.

In 2003 the United States Postal Service issued a stamp in memory of Marshal in its Black Heritage series of stamps.

The most famous ruling of Thurgood Marshal was in the case of Brown v. Board of Education of Topeka, Kansas in 1954. Marshall ruled that the racial segregation of children in schools was unconstitutional and that the policy of 'separate but equal' education was not equal at all.

Review of the lives and work of Andrew Young and the Late Justice Thurgood Marshall shows not only their dedication to the cause of civic rights and equality but also their single-minded determination to work at and achieve their chosen goals.

The Nawab of Pataudi Sr (1917-1947) whose real name was Iftikhar Ali Khan was the eight holder of the title of Nawab. Nawab was the title given to a governor in India during the Mughal times. Pataudi is a town in Haryana State in India. A dedicated cricketer he played Test cricket for both India and England. His son, Nawab of Pataudi Jr. (1952-1971), Mohammed Mansur Ali Khan, was the ninth and last holder of the title of Nawab of Pataudi. He too was an ardent cricketer who played for Winchester College in England and for Sussex and Oxford. Despite the loss of vision in one eye following an in injury which sliced the eye in a car accident in Hove, West Sussex, UK, in July 1961, he was able to perform as a successful batsman and was the captain of the Indian Test cricket team.

The work of the late Thurgood Marshall and later Andrew Young occurred at the time of segregation and considerable difficulties for blacks in the USA. The Jim Crow laws were in operation; these forced the separation of blacks and ensured that they were banned from some places. That Thurgood Marshall and Andrew Young pursued their careers and contributed in many and significant ways to the USA and society are a tribute to their focus and determination to rise above the difficulties that they encountered and which were not of their own making. The same may be said of the Nawabs of Pataudi, father and son. They lived in the United Kingdom at the time when, what was popularly known as, 'colour bar' was in operation. Colour bar is defined as a 'social and legal system in which people of different races are separated and not given the same rights and opportunities.' It was not uncommon to see in post-war UK, notices in shops, restaurants etc saying 'No blacks, Irish or dogs'.

Two other person noteworthy of mention are Condoleezza Rice (1954-) and the late Colin Powell (1937-2021). Born in Birmingham, Alabama, Rice can trace her ancestors to the times of the Antebellum period when slavery was rife and attempts were made to defend slavery as being for the good of the slaves. At that time there were about 700,000 slaves or the equivalent of one in six or 18% of the population. Rice claimed that she is 51% African, 40% European and 9% Asian. Her mitochondrial DNA can be traced to the Tikar tribe in Cameroon who can be traced back to the eleventh or twelfth century. In her book *'Democracy; Stories from the Long Road to Freedom'*, she describes her great-great -grandmother on her maternal side as having borne five children from different slave owners. Her ancestors were share-croppers; this is an arrangement between a landowner and tenants who are allowed to use the land for crops, a share of which is returned to the owner.

Condoleezza Rice was US National Security Adviser from 2001 to 2005. She then became the first female African – American Secretary of State of the USA and was appointed to the position by President George W Bush. She served in this position from 2005 to 2009 and was replaced when President Barak Obama took office. Rice then returned to academia In Stanford University as a professor of political science.

The late Colin Powell was born in New York to immigrant parents from Jamaica. His father was a shipping clerk and mother a seamstress. He started his life as a soldier in the Reserve Officer Training Corps (ROTC) and continued from there on as a soldier in various capacities for 35 years. He had two tours of duty in Vietnam, the first being cut short by infection in a leg from stepping on a booby trapped stake. His second tour was in 1968 as a major. He was accused of attempting to whitewash the My Lai massacre of innocent civilians by American soldiers in Vietnam in 1968. He became National Security Adviser under President Ronald Regan in 1987 and Chairman of the Joint Chief of Staffs under President George W Bush. He was made a 4-star General in 1989. Of his time with the ROTC Colin Powell said 'I found something that I liked, and that was ROTC,

Reserve Officer Training Corps in the military. And I not only liked it, but I was pretty good at it. That's what you really have to look for in life, something that you like, and something that you think you're pretty good at. And if you can put those two things together, then you're on the right track, and just drive on'.

Turn now to recent history and one encounters President Barak Obama (1961-). He was the first African – American President of the United States, serving two consecutive terms as its 44th President from 2009 to 2017. He was born in Honolulu to a Kenyan father and an American mother. Obama's father was in the USA pursuing his education when he married his mother, Stanley Ann Dunham. Barak's parent divorced in 1964 following which Obama Sr. returned to Kenya. Barak Obama Sr. died in an motor accident in Kenya in 1982 when Barak Obama Jr. was 21 years old. In 1965 his mother married an Indonesian and the young Barak and his mother went to live in Indonesia. When he was six years old in 1991, Barak Obama returned to Hawaii to live with his maternal grandparents. His mother died of uterine cancer in Honolulu in 1995. Obama's' exposure to many cultures and growing up in Honolulu, which was multicultural, impressed upon him the presence of diversity and the need for tolerance of others. However in his time at school he was also awakened to the tension of racism despite growing up in a multi-racial society and attending Punahou, described as an elite school in Honolulu. He however kept his tensions in check and presented himself as a well mannered disciplined student. He was, by all accounts, bright and dedicated to his studies. He went to Harvard Law School in 1988 and graduated with a <u>Juris Doctor *magna cum laude*</u> (Doctor of Law or of Jurisprudence with distinction) in 1991. Barak Obama credits his Indonesian step-father, Lolo Soetoro, with having taught him some hard facts of life. One day the young Barak, when living in Indonesia, returned home from school with a 'egg-sized lump' on his head. This came about during a fight with a boy about a friend's stolen soccer ball. Barak was hit on his head with a rock, hence the lump.. The next day father and son donned boxing gloves and sparred. Soetoro said 'the first thing to learn is to protect yourself- 'Keep your hands up ……You want to keep moving, but always stay low—don't give them a target'. When Obama accidentally let his defences down, he felt the force of his father's gloved fist on his jaw and heard his father's voice 'Pay attention'. Obama described this event in his book *'Dreams from my Father'*. Later on father and son discussed life and the difficulties likely to be encountered in the world. Soetoro said 'Men take advantage of weakness in other men. They're just like countries in that way. The strong man takes the weak man's land. He makes the weak man work in his fields. If the weak man's woman is pretty, the strong man will take her.' And then he posed the question to Barak 'Which would you rather be?' This has been a perennial question for Barak Obama. He appears to have reflected on it during his life. Obama said about what he learned from his stepfather – 'I remember that very vividly, and my stepfather was a good man who gave me some things that were very helpful'. Obama told journalist Jon Meacham in 2008 'One of the things that he gave me was a pretty hard-headed assessment of how the world works.' His mother and stepfather divorced in 1980 and the latter died in 1987 of liver failure at the age of 52 years.

A reading of Barak Obama's childhood days portrays the many changes he was exposed to – living in Hawaii, moving with his mother to live with his stepfather in Indonesia and then returning to Hawaii. During all these changes it appears that the young Obama's education was not disrupted; along the way he learned Indonesian and also about different people and cultures. These helped fashion his sense of values in later life and come out clear in his books. His book '*The Audacity of Hope*' is a plea for inclusivity amidst all the tension of society – politics, racism, terrorism etc.

Barak Obama said ' I was a black man who was brought up without a father and I know the cost that I paid'. However it would appear that he had some compensation for a brief period in his younger days from his Indonesian stepfather. He, nevertheless, is passionate about the presence of a father in the lives of children. In 2008, as a potential candidate for the Presidency of the USA and as the first black candidate, he spoke on Father's Day in Chicago saying that too many black fathers were missing from the home and from the lives of their children. They were behaving like boys and abrogating their parental responsibilities. He rattled off sobering yet pertinent statistics which showed that children who grew up without fathers were five times more likely to live in poverty, nine times more likely to drop out of school and twenty times more likely to go to prison. They are 'more likely to have behavioural problems or run away from home or become teenage parents themselves'. He asked the question which could be asked in London and other inner city areas of England 'How many times in the last year has this city lost a child at the hands of another child?'

To all those who say men are not necessary one could rapidly reply by asking them to look at Ukraine. In the absence of men the country would have collapsed very soon after the invasion by Russia. But the country battles on putting up a fight like no other and earning the respect of the world for its bravery and its defence of basic values. One has only to glance at images of Ukrainian women and children leaving for safety by train. The stations are also full of men with tears in their eyes waving goodbye and kissing their women and children through the steamed up windows of the railway carriages. As the trains pull out of the station, the men head back to the front line to defend their country, their families and their values. And they fight and die in the hope that they would be reunited with their loved ones. While one may imagine the monument in Mamayev Kurgan shedding tears of sorrow for Russia's barbaric invasion of its peace-loving neighbour, the sons of Ukraine shed their blood for their country and their values. This could not have happened in the absence of men. The heroism of the men of Ukraine would be written in blood as they fight for their women and children. Whither Ukraine sans men ?

One may again recall the words of Barak Obama on that Father's Day in 2008 'Of all the rocks upon which we build our lives, we are reminded today that family is the most important. And we are called to recognize and honour how critical every father is to that foundation.'

Bernard Francisco Ribeiro (1944-)was born in Achimoto, a town in Greater Accra in Ghana. After migrating to the UK he was educated at Dean Close School, Cheltenham, in Gloucestershire, and read medicine at Middlesex Hospital Medical School in London. He became of Fellow of the Royal College of Surgeons of England in 1972 and was made an honorary Fellow of the American College of Surgeons in 2008. For his services to medicine, he was appointed a Commander of the Order of the British Empire (CBE). This was followed by being appointed a Knight Bachelor in 2009.He was elevated to the House of Lords and became a life peer in 2010 and assumed the title of Baron Ribeiro, of Achimota and of Ovington of Hampshire, a county in England. He was President of the Royal College of Surgeons of England from 2005 – 2008.

Narendra Babubhai Patel (1938-)was born in Lindi, a town on the Indian Ocean coast of the then Tanganyika, which is now Tanzania. He studied medicine in the University of St.Andrews in Scotland and worked for over 30 years as an obstetrician and gynaecologist in Ninewells Hospital, Dundee, also in Scotland. He became a Knight of the Realm as Sir Narendra Patel in 1997 and was created a life peer in 1999, taking the title of Baron Patel, of <u>Dunkeld</u> in <u>Perth and Kinross</u>, in Scotland. He was President of the Royal College of Obstetricians and Gynaecologists from 1995 to 1998.

Sir Sabaratnam Arulkumaran (1948-) was born in Jaffna, a town in northern Ceylon, now Sri Lanka. He was educated in schools in Jaffna and graduated in medicine from the University of Ceylon in 1972. He specialised in obstetrics and gynaecology and became a Fellow of the Royal College of Obstetricians and Gynaecologists. He is an honorary fellow of several international colleges and societies of obstetrics and gynaecology. He was President of the Royal College of Obstetricians and Gynaecologists from 2007 to 2010. In 2012 he became President of the International Federation of Gynaecology and Obstetrics. And from 2013-2014 he served as President of the <u>British Medical Association</u>. He was appointed Knight Bachelor in 2009 for his services to medicine.

Acknowledged as one of the most technically competent gynaecological surgeons in the post-war era was the late Sir Rustam Moolan Feroze (1920 - 2010) of Kings College Hospital in London. He was knighted for his services to medicine in 1983 and served as President of the Royal College of Obstetricians and Gynaecologists in 1981.

Those who have read the 1991 book by Robert Kanigel, 'The man who knew infinity' or seen the film by the same name cannot but marvel at the sheer doggedness of Srinivasa Ramanujam. A mathematics genius without much training in the subject, he confused leading mathematicians of the day by his theorems and his understanding of number. He was born into a

Tamil Brahmin family in Mysore in India. He later moved to Madras, now Chennai. He was a child prodigy in mathematics who devoted his short life to the subject, to the exclusion of other subjects which he, not infrequently, failed in his school examinations. He was invited to Cambridge by a leading mathematician at the time, Professor G.H. Hardy. Hardy said of some of Ramanujam's work 'defeated me completely; I have never seen anything in the least like them before'. A devout Hindu, Ramanugam refused to leave the land of his birth. He was eventually persuaded to travel and spent five years in Cambridge. Srinivasa Ramanujam became one of the youngest Fellows of the Royal Society and the first Indian to be elected Fellow of Trinity College, Cambridge. He died at the age of 32 years, probably from hepatic amoebiasis.

What was it that propelled these persons to the pinnacles of their respective careers? Sir Rustam Feroze lived, studied and worked at the time of 'colour bar' – a period of extreme discrimination in the UK! Achievements were possible because of the one common factor they all shared – they maintained focus, worked and were dedicated and had indomitable spirits to help them overcome any obstacles that they encountered in their lives journeys. Perseverance was likely to have been a common attribute. How do these qualities sit alongside the equality, inclusivity and wokeness of today? One is reminded of the words of the poet, Henry Wadsworth Longfellow, which are relevant here:

> 'The heights by great men reached and kept, were not attained by sudden flight, For while their companions slept, they were toiling upwards through the night'

Not only individuals but also organisations and countries can achieve high standards in what they set for themselves. A simple example would illustrate this point. One returns to Rwanda and its management of AIDS. During the Rwandan genocide and its aftermath, health care was virtually non- existent in many places in the country. There was hardly any care for HIV/AIDS. Partners in Health (PIH) worked with the Rwandan government and with assistance from the Bill and Melinda Gates Foundation to set up the Rwandan University of Global Health Equity.

Partners in Health (PIH) is a not for profit international health organisation which works to provide health care in poorer countries. It works with local departments of health and health ministries to improve health by building clinics and hospitals, improving the quality of drinking water, provision of food, training personnel etc. Its success is derived from the long term partnerships it builds locally where ever it is working. Its work in Haiti led to a remarkable project, the Zanmi Lasante Sociomedical Complex. This involves a hospital, radiology facilities, women's health, children's ward etc. And it all started as a small clinic from where it grew to the complex that it is today. When an earthquake struck Haiti on 12th January 2010, PIH was well placed to mobilise and provide health care support for displaced and ill people. It set up satellite clinics in four camps to provide care while supporting staff at the General Hospital in Port-au-Prince, the capital of Haiti.

The experience gained in Haiti allowed PIH to work with the government of Rwanda in setting up clinics designed for primary medical care where HIV/AIDS could be managed.

PIH initiated the University for Global Health Equity which provides a 2 year part-time masters degree in global health delivery. The University officially opened in Butaro in 2019.

PIH was set up by Paul Farmer, Thomas White, Ophelia Dahl, Jim Yong Kim and Todd McCormack. Sadly Paul Farmer, who was a visionary, passed away in February 2022. Their work in Rwanda contributed to the steepest reduction in the world in AIDS related deaths in children under the age of 5 year – a reduction of 70% in the numbers of deaths. PIH worked with local communities to train a group of 45,000 healthcare workers who provide primary care for diarrhoea, malaria, family planning, ante-natal care and vaccinations.. The number of people treated for AIDS in Rwanda rose from zero at the conclusion of the conflict to 108,000.

When one reviews the achievements of those listed in the previous paragraphs and many others who have risen against obstacles, one cannot escape the separation of slavery from racism. These are two different entities. The descendants of slaves have been exposed to racism but one is hard pressed to attribute all attenuated development and under- achievement to slavery. Racism, institutionalised and personal, has been a persistent thorn in the side of many peoples lives. But even with racism being ever-present, that people arose and progressed, raises many questions about how they achieved against the odds ranged against them. An important ingredient in the lives of all persons is social capital. What is social capital? It is a combination of several facets of existence that contribute to a person's development. These include trust, interpersonal relationships, values etc that encourages and allows people to identify with social groups, be accepted in them and to function as a cohesive society. Much of what is called social capital arises in the home. Take for example values. What values does an individual acquire and personally develop as they progress through life? The seeds of values are planted at home – responsibility to parents, siblings and others, courteousness, learning etc. Even an aspect as simple yet much ignored as punctuality is instilled in and acquired in the home. Elementary these may be, but they are the building blocks of other values. In the home is found the scaffolding for the future law-abiding, god-fearing, responsible, caring person. On this foundation is built other values – respect for and interaction with adults, avoidance of conflict, the importance of compromise in resolving differences of opinions, the futility and hence avoidance of violence etc. One can go so far as to say these attributes cannot be acquired elsewhere unless the rudiments have been learnt and acquired in the home. The social scaffolding from home leads to greater acquisition of social skills accompanied by the ability to 'learn how to learn' new social skills through the travails of life.

Adversity in life is never a reason to jettison social skills. On the contrary, they remain useful to help surmount life's crises. The response to adversity determines how a person progresses. One common response is victimhood. Victimhood is an extreme negative feeling, as it shuts doors that allows one to see the much greater positive aspects and strengths that one undoubtedly has. It incarcerates one in a prison of thought that is reinforced by others who purport to care. In all the cases described in the previous paragraphs, victimhood was either absent or its presence was momentary. Victimhood seeks to apportion responsibility to others, which may be the case. But it is much worse than that – it encourages helplessness and waiting for others in society to right any wrongs, which may not be forthcoming. It is far better to break away from one's prison and look at one's inner strengths and values and so devise a means for dealing with adversity. As Thurgood Marshall's mother did – pawn her jewellery to pay her son's school fees. Or Srinivasa Ramanujam who persisted with his interest in mathematics. He had no ambition of leaving his home village, let alone his country. He had a deep and abiding interest in mathematics, which he pursued to international recognition.

Victimhood is an obstacle to progress. It prevents positivity in an individual confronting adverse events and denies the person the ability to take ownership of their problems. No ownership equates with the absence of personal responsibility and subservience to the negative event; the result is inactivity and continuing victimhood.

What all the people in this chapter displayed in abundance was resilience and perseverance.

For a phoenix to rise from the ashes of adverse situations, one needs ownership, perseverance and resilience. These attributes together can surmount most odds in life. The greatest asset that a person has, is belief in oneself. The journey may be long, as often it is; it may be tortuous as it has to be, in circumventing obstacles. There may not be an end in sight, but it, most certainly, is there for one to behold, if only one has both sight and vision. Personal achievement is limited only by one's imagination. Dare to dream! Reach out to the stars and don't let oneself be consigned to mediocrity, which is but one step from incompetence, inefficiency and under-achievement.

What is happening in Britain is the almost malignant resentment held by the left of the political spectrum, on hard work and aspiration by persons, especially of they do not share the same views. One reads the ridiculous description of some as being not 'real blacks' for not sharing the politics of the left, which see everything through the narrow telescope of colour, race, victimhood, and now sex and gender. So for example Sajid Javid, the first non-white Home Secretary of the UK was described as a 'coconut' by activists. Similarly the Ghanaian Chancellor of the Exchequer, Kwasi Kwarteng was described by a left wing MP as follows – 'If you hear him on the Today programme, you wouldn't know he's black.'. Not only was this a racist comment, rightly denounced by the leadership of the Labour Party, but it also betrays the inherent racism which sees and reduces all things to a matter of race. In so doing racism is kept alive by non-whites themselves. As Ron Liddle wrote, one may only be a true black if one subscribes to a set of views. Therefore, wrote Liddle, Tony Sewell, Trevor Phillips, Zadie Smith and Sir Trevor Macdonald were recently excluded from a list of '100 Great Black Britons'. This says much about the groundswell of racism propagated and maintained by some in the black community.

Interrogate your teachers, question elders and parents, seek answers. Refuse to blindly accept that which is said or written. Thereby one gains knowledge which is based not only on what one has heard or read, but the knowledge that is embellished by curiosity. Remember, knowledge is power and use it to enhance oneself and to set oneself free. Gloria Steinhem wrote – 'the truth will set you free, but first it will piss you off'; it certainly does and it would be the day of reckoning and the dawn of personal enlightenment. One would be surprised by what one learns and which may be at variance with what one was told or even taught. Be your own teacher and become a lifelong learner. An old African proverb may not be out of place here – 'not to know is bad; not to wish to know is worse'.

Soon one learns that there is no single storyline.

WHITE CROCODILE, BLACK CROCODILE, NEW SLAVERY FOR OLD

Some years ago, appearing on British television with host, Sir Michael Parkinson, the late, great Muhammad Ali asked 'why is Jesus white with blue eyes?'; 'why are angels white?'. He asked, 'mamma, when you die, would you go to heaven?' - 'naturally' came the reply.. 'what happened to all the black angels?.... I know, the white angels are in heaven while the black angels are in the kitchen preparing milk and honey'. 'And Tarzan, King of the jungle; Tarzan is on the trees talking to the animals in the jungle, but the African man cannot talk to the animals.'

This interview is worth visiting because important philosophical questions are asked by arguably the greatest person who lived in the 20th century – sportsman par excellence, black activist, politician and poet.

That black lives matter is incontrovertible. That awareness needs to be increased about police brutality is a matter of urgency. And that discrimination in all forms and against all people and groups, not only blacks, needs to be severely reduced if not eliminated altogether. The last statement is qualified as it is obvious to even an elementary observer that total elimination of discrimination is an utopian dream as would be the achievement of unrivalled equality. But if there is continuing work towards that destination, the journey is all the more worth and productive. People will have impressions and biases – one cannot eliminate thought.

The death of George Floyd in May 2020 at the hands of the Minneapolis,

Minnesota police in the USA not only triggered riots but yet again raised awareness of police brutality towards black people in the USA. It could be compared in its seismic effect with that of Colin Kaepernik. Following on, there undoubtedly needs to be re-education of police officers on lawful and humane means of interactions with the public, be this interrogation or arrest. There is no place in the police for violence or thuggery.

This is about more than discrimination against blacks, but about discrimination against a minority ethnic group and indeed against anyone. The late Mr. Floyd died because a police officer placed his knee on the neck of Mr. Floyd for seven or eight minutes. The police officer, Derek Chauvin, continued to place his knee on the neck and probably compressing and compromising his windpipe, even after George Floyd pleaded saying that he could not breathe; 'I can't breathe' he said. Chauvin was convicted of murder and manslaughter, apart from a gross violation of the civic rights of George Floyd. What happened to the latter is strangulation by any definition of the term and cannot be misconstrued as the restraint of a potential criminal. Such a procedure should never have been in the repertoire of any police force or law enforcement agency. This is all the more ugly that such inhuman restraint was deployed by police in a liberal, democratic country. One would expect such extreme controlling behavior to be part of the arsenal of police officers in a totalitarian state but never, ever in a democracy.

The late Sir Robert Peel is considered the father of modern policing in the United Kingdom. He established the Metropolitan Report on police in London in 1829 based on nine basic principles. Sir Robert Peel was of the view that the police needed to be proactive and preventive in their work; he thought that policing of this kind is likely to be more effective than if it simply reacted to events and was more interventional. One hundred years later, in 1929, President of the USA, Herbert Hoover established the Wickersham Commission to look at policing. The Commission was chaired by the former attorney-general, George W. Wickersham and was set up to review how police worked at a time when there was burgeoning organized crime coupled with police corruption. In his book 'The prohibition era and policing: A the legacy of mis-regulation', Wesley M Oliver, Professor of Law at Duquesne University wrote in 2018 'Intrusive searches for alcohol during Prohibition destroyed middle-class Americans' faith in police and ushered in a new basis for controlling police conduct'…… a presidential commission awakened the public to torture in interrogation rooms, prompting courts to exclude coerced confessions irrespective of whether the technique had produced a reliable statement'. It is interesting to view these two aspects of policing on either side of the Atlantic. Their relevance is about the primary need for a police service in the current climate of frequent calls to defund the police. Consider for example the stop and search laws in the UK. Stop and search or commonly referred to as 'SaS laws' are a preventive exercise. One often hears of the public perception that the application of 'SaS' is based on racial profiling of possible suspects. If one were to return to what Sir Robert Peel intended, namely that policing be focused, implicit in this statement would be evidence based preventive activity by police. Police services across the world have at their disposal vast amounts of data and statistics collected over many decades, related to various aspects of their work- preventive and interventional policing. As would be expected, the information would vary with trends in criminal activities in respective local populations. Properly collected information subjected to valid analysis would provide useful tools to help inform the provision of services by any organization – and policing is no exception to this fundamental rule. Police would use data to analyze where criminal activity or breaches of the law are most likely to occur and by whom, and use this information to inform and direct services. To claim that such laws are biased against blacks and other minority ethnic group may be justified. However, if one were to return to the fundamental principle of policing by Peel, namely that it is a service provided with the consent of the public, then the public needs to have access to information that would reassure it services are directed to where they are needed most. If it so happens that the evidence points to one particular racial group being more likely to commit offences, then any claim that such activity is racially motivated fails. It is incumbent upon the police to provide this information on a regular basis or place it in the public domain, without compromising its operational activities or sources of information.Regular access to this information would help reassure the public that police activities are directed not against a particular group of persons but is focused on keeping the whole community that it serves, safe.

One frequently hears about calls to defund the police. The opposing claims are equally strident in demanding more police presence with information about increasing criminal activity and especially with each reported murder. At face value these two claims are incompatible and are mutually exclusive. Policing exists to keep streets, communities and the nation at large safe. One must ask those who seek to defund the police about precisely what police activities they would wish to reduce or are they claiming a negligible police service? Who would conduct the activities of the police like crime prevention and resolving crimes? Again to return to what Sir Robert Peel implied, one has to ask whether prevention is not better than resolution of crimes, after they have occurred? Who or which organization would provide such a preventive service? The corollary to this question is who would provide the current police intervention after a crime has occurred or when one is suspected? These two aspects need to be there in any society; their absence would complete a serious degradation of policing and result in unsafe communities. They have to be provided by an alternative organization - a police service by another name!

At this juncture, it is timely to return to some of the principles of policing set out by Sir Robert Peel.

The hallmark of good, effective, democratic policing is the prevention of crime without repression of the public. Repression and fear are the instruments of totalitarian regimes. In a democracy, not only must a criminal be judged fairly and remain innocent until proven otherwise, but also the police must be transparent and accountable.

Police need the public's respect - where there is no trust there is no respect and leads to ineffective policing.

The public has to want to cooperate with upholding the law. An increasingly important aspect of cooperation with the police, especially in instances of serious crime, is the extent to which people cooperate with the police in sharing relevant and vital information to help solve a crime. And therefore one sees for eg visible cooperation in the UK where people join in with police in searches for missing persons. This is how it should be- operation for a common purpose - help solve crime but also in prevention. Less force, more cooperation – this is a vital ingredient in policing. Cooperation with police is directly proportional to the trust between police and community. Force, especially unjustified force and investigation based on limited evidence erodes trust and leads to less cooperation with police. Cooperation is as much needed in crime prevention as it is in resolving crimes that have occurred. Cooperation here is vital and often urgent; people who have vital information need to come forward without risk from the police or reprisals from their communities. There is no place for being considered a 'traitor' for sharing vital information which would help keep the community safe. Withholding information is aiding and abetting a crime - and who knows what the next event or who the next victim would be? In such a scenario a community that commits itself to silence also consigns itself to continuing risk. Impartiality and fairness should be the watchwords of policing . No segment of the community must be at a disadvantage and conversely no one must be at an advantage compared to others in the community. Police is of the people, by the people and are for the people; they are the people. It is unfortunate that some sections of black communities refrain from joining the police; doing so would not be a simple cosmetic exercise but is a powerful statement that police are the people in uniform who are there to protect and serve the community. The American civil rights activist, Alfred Charles Sharpton, wrote in 2016 that police should live in the communities they serve. Implicit in this view is that police arise from the community in which they live and serve. They are serving their families, friends and neighbours. Here is an appeal for police officers of all races to come from the community. They, then do not travel to work in a different site but live where they work. Police are then not viewed by communities as an alien force imposed on the community. Such a move, albeit small that it may turn out to be, would pay a handsome dividend in a breakdown of the feelings of 'them' and 'us'; a depiction of 'oneness'. Continuing, Alfred Sharpton emphasized the need for police to be brought to justice for the killing of blacks. But he also stressed that it is equally important for blacks to be held to account for violence against the police. This is important if equality is to be proclaimed and practiced. There is no room for excuses from the police, no more than one can accommodate reasons for violence from blacks against the police. One cannot claim a special dispensation. He lamented the lack of adherence by some in the black community to what the late Martin Luther King said 'That old law about an eye for an eye leaves everybody blind; the time is always right to do the right thing.' One returns to his words of 1963 '.... we must not be guilty of wrongful deeds. Let us not seek to satisfy our thirst for freedom by drinking from the cup of bitterness and hatred. We must forever conduct our struggle with dignity and discipline. We must not allow our protest to degenerate into physical violence but meet physical force with soul force'.

For example in 2020, a clip appeared on YouTube of some persons in London mocking a black police officer of Somali origin. What gained the praise of people was not the ugly manner in which the policeman was being treated but the dignity and restraint shown by the latter. This event serves to highlight the difficulty in trying to recruit police officers from all sections of the community. Some people are deeply hostile to joining the police. This again reduces people to think in terms of a 'them' and 'us' vision of society. This concept could so readily be reversed to a 'we and us' mentality – 'we' the police from all communities being there to serve everyone ('us') equally and fairly. One black police officer wrote that the abuse he received arresting a black man was' pretty exhausting'. It is the same in the USA. A police officer over there wrote 'I swear to god I love this city but I wonder if this city loves me. In uniform I get nasty hateful looks, out of uniform some consider me a threat. I've experienced so much in my short life and these last three days have tested me to the core.' Sadly, a few days later he was one of three police officers ambushed and shot dead in what appeared to be an act of revenge. The recurring criticism of the police by politicians, civic leaders etc are now increasingly unhelpful to the essential debate about the police and give sustenance to the community that sees the police as being alien to their own. Even the Macpherson report of 1999 on policing in London, while claiming that the Metropolitan Police was institutionally racist did not imply that officers were racist. What appears to be needed is less criticism of its own but constructive dialogue to bring stakeholders together in a common purpose and to fashion a robust covenant between police and public. The continuing deaths by knives and guns on the streets of London tell their own harrowing, sad story. While there is much criticism of 'stop and search' laws, very few have devoted attention towards answering the basic question - would some of those who lost their lives be alive today if there was more effective stopping and searching of vehicles? Guns, knives and other weapons have reached the point where they are deployed after being transported through the streets of London. If only they had been stopped and identified before they reached the point of the crime, it may just be that some of those who departed are still alive.

There is a difference between police stopping a person and inquiring and being stopped and searched. The former may be seen as an essential requisite of good community policing directed towards prevention. The person been spoken to is not being stopped and is free to leave. In the case of 'stop and search', police may choose to not only inquire about movements, whereabouts etc of a person but they can also carry out a search of the person and the vehicle that they may be travelling in. This is not an arrest of the person who is not free to leave until the search is concluded or other actions follow. To use 'SaS', police must have reasonable suspicion and must be unbiased in their deployment of the process. This is where there has been much opposition to the process by those who claim that it selectively targets blacks. Additionally of course, the process must be minimally restrictive to the individual ie the police should do only that which is necessary for the purpose. Inherent in the use of 'SaS' is that public are treated with respect and with dignity; they are given the opportunity to put their side of the story and it is incumbent on the police to come to a reasonable, unbiased and fair decision.

'SaS' maybe used when the police have reasonable grounds to suspect that a person has committed a crime, is carrying a weapon like a gun, is in possession of an offensive weapon like a machete or is in possession of illegal drugs. Reasonable grounds for 'SaS' may be dispensed with if it is approved by a senior police officer on the basis that a person is carrying a weapon or likely to use one, has committed a crime or a person of interest is in a particular area.

When one looks at the reasons for 'SaS' it is easy to see that there he is much room for suspicion by the public, that the laws are not being used fairly. This is especially so if people have been stopped and no further action has followed and no evidence of criminality or criminal intent is present.

In the year to the end of March 2000 there were about 18,000 people who were stopped and searched; this is 35% above the figure for the preceding year. The campaign group 'Justice' claim that only 4% of those stopped and searched eventually led to an arrest. One can appreciate the frustration and anger in the black community from the figure that 25% of those searched were black.

There were 577,054 searches in 2020 which led to 13% of arrests ie 74,121. One needs clarification of the rate of errors, because not everyone who has a cause for arrest would be arrested, for eg a small degree of drug possession is likely to be dealt with on the spot by a caution or warning

Police should provide advice and guidance to the public and where needed persuade the latter to avoid crime. Where appropriate a warning may be given to a person. This step may be perceived as a mild one, but it is still an escalation from persuasion. An all-important but often neglected role of police is, while building trust and engendering cooperation, to effect change in behaviour of miscreants and to talk them away from misdemeanor and eventually crime. Change in attitudes and behaviour are at the heart of good, effective policing, But to achieve these objectives, trust is needed. Therefore it is imperative that all sections of the community must be represented in police forces.

Judgement and meting out punishment are never the roles of a police service. Judgement and punishment, where needed, are the work of courts. The role of police is to apply the law fairly and firmly but leave its interpretation, when infringements of the law occur, to the judiciary. The death of George Floyd in the USA is a clear example, if one was needed, where indiscriminate and uncalled for violence was used against a helpless person. The gratuitous violence that was used while he was complaining of distress and pleading for relief, was wholly unnecessary.

The death of Tyler Nichols at the hands of the police on 10th January 2023 in Memphis, Tennessee, USA is in mark contrast to that of George Floyd. Here was a black man pursued, arrested and assaulted by five black officers. He appeared to have been beaten so severely and kicked that he died from internal bleeding. At the time of this writing the result of the autopsy report following the death of Nichols was not available. To have been pulled over by the police for what appeared to have been 'reckless driving' and subsequently to die at the hands of the police is as unfathomable as it is unpardonable. This should have been a simple questioning, if there was sufficient cause, and arrest, if there was justification for it. From what is known, Nichols was pepper sprayed, a stun gun was deployed and he was subsequently beaten to, what one may conclude, was his death. That five police officers had used such excessive force was described by the family lawyer, Antonio Romanucci, as 'savage'. And Memphis Police, which is led by its first woman police officer, Cerelyn Davies, who is herself black, said that departmental policies had not been followed, excessive force had been used and that the officers had ignored their duty of care for Mr. Nichols and had failed to render him aid when it was needed. Cerelyn Davies acted quickly to release footage obtained from the body cameras of officers, to the public. This is in contrast to the delays following the death of George Floyd. She described what was recorded as 'heinous, reckless and inhumane' and that what happened was 'physical abuse' of Nichols. Her words are also relevant and interesting – 'I am a citizen, I'm a mother, a caring human being of this county'. Here is a police officer risen from the community in which she lives and works. This provides her with considerable credibility, in addition to being a black police chief of a force who is now facing accountability, as it should. She talked about a failure of basic humanity and the need for accountability, while pleading for the avoidance of violence.

This was a case of black police officers meting out unjustifiable violence towards another citizen, whatever wrong that person may have or may not have committed. This event, like that of George Floyd and going backward to the late Rodney King in 1991, goes to the heart of the culture of policing, and applies to both sides of that Atlantic. It would appear to the casual observer, and quite rightly so, that the police use their authority with apparent impunity and with disregard for the law. Police use the law and their power to enforce it, not to breach the former, which they are commissioned to uphold and thereby serve and protect the public. Instead, for some police officers, the law is their cover for breaching it. This was most clearly seen in the arrest and death of Sarah Everard on the streets of London on the 3rd of March 2021 by a serving Metropolitan Police officer, Wayne Couzens. Arrested in January 2023 was also Metropolitan Police constable David Carrick, who was described as a serial rapist and abuser. On 25th January 2023 the head of the Metropolitan Police in London, Sir Mark Rowley, said that two to three Metropolitan Police officers would appear in court every week charged with dishonesty, abuse and violence, as he seeks out to conduct a root and branch reform of his officers. A similar exercise has been advised for all police forces in the UK. What these events on either side of the pond reveal is the endemic nature of violence within police services. While there may be a racial element to it, the event in Memphis dispels this as a dominant notion. On the contrary the selection training and retraining of police officers has assumed greater importance, if communities are to be served safely and fairly. There is still much work to be done.

Absence of crime, not visible presence of police is the ideal yardstick of effective policing.

The improvements in life opportunities for black and other minority ethnic persons is clear, despite claims to the contrary. In August 2021, 55 students from Brampton Manor Academy in Newham, London were invited to study at Oxford and Cambridge. This was described by Mouhssin Ismail, Principal of Newnham College Sixth Form as an ' educational renaissance' in the locality. Newham is one of the deprived areas, being the second poorest local authority in England at the time that London hosted the Olympic Games in 2012. While the academic success of the young people is a matter for much celebration – here is a fine example of equality and diversity in real time – the streets are still places of fear, with locals being afraid to walk at night. These were the same streets where the black youth, David Gomoh, aged 24 years, was stabbed to death in April 2020. Not involved in gangs, Gomoh died as a result of a lethal feud between two gangs.

All of the foregoing brings one to the reasons why blacks are in conflict with the law. There is a greater understanding of blacks by whites and vice versa. The 'oneness' is undoubtedly taking shape, at least in the UK and is continuing, but the journey is not complete. It is not the destination that matters; the destination may never be reached because of the inherent biases of all human beings, blacks and whites. But continuing on the journey is paramount and the contribution and commitment of all parties remain crucial. Set against these lofty ideals, violence by the police and against the police only serves to resuscitate the crumbling foundations of separateness. As was written 'The objective is to stop police misconduct – not to kill police '. There is no place for the latter, although justice must be done and be seen to be done without exception.

So, one may ask the rhetorical question, of what black people need to do? These words are in contrast to the title of the book by Emma Dabiri, *'what white people can do next'*. One has witnessed great strides being made in recent years regarding equality of people and in diversity. This is especially so in the United Kingdom. Equality and diversity are incorporated in all aspects of society. They are also reinforced during peoples working lives, keeping awareness alive. This accords with what Alfred Sharpton wrote - 'cultural and sensitivity ' training. It therefore behoves black people to move away from the concept of white people being an 'enemy' of sorts to seeing in society an equality that their predecessors may not have experienced. There needs to be an overriding desire to be part of society and this can only start in the home and with children, who are brought up in the culture of oneness in society. This calls for continuing association with others and in working together with all, towards common ends. Neither blacks nor whites would ideally see the other party as different. And this is what blacks need to do next – work towards 'oneness'.

It is however as relevant as it is important to state clearly and loudly that black people did not create racism no more than the white man created slavery. Racism is the product of one group seeing others as not of their own and even inferior to them. Internal racism may occur even within a single group; see the caste system in some countries and the prevalence of tribal identities in some cultures. It would appear that in some instances the black person is a contributor to their own feelings of inferiority, unjustified as it is, and embellished to a great extent by a powerful victim culture.

Extrication from the old pervasive victim culture maybe seen as an important ingredient In black emancipation. It is an easy part in life to blame the other, even without justification for doing so. But people in all walks of life need to ask themselves what they are doing or not doing to contribute to the status quo of apparent separateness or impression of it. Sit up, seize the moment and take responsibility must be a clarion call to all who are mired in victimhood. Too often victimhood arises in the home, from, that rather unfashionable phrase, 'poor parenting'. No, do not dismiss this phrase; it is at the heart of many of society's problems. When there are two parents committed to the upbringing of children, it is no surprise that victimhood diminishes while responsibility is accentuated. Confront the truth, painful as it may initially be. Gloria Steinem, the American social activist and journalist wrote –'The Truth Will Set You Free, But First It Will Piss You Off!'. The same sentiment was communicated by that great African American poet and writer, Mari Evans (1919-2017), a writer from the Black Arts Movement in USA - ' Speak the truth to the people, talk sense to the people, freedom with reason, freedom with honesty'. Responsibility is born and perpetuated in the home; that actions and omissions have consequences is a vital lesson that parents impart to their children. One cannot travel through life devolving personal responsibility to others or freeing oneself of accountability.

Africans and African-Americans are intelligent, cultured and talented people. With guidance and opportunity there's no reason why they should not flourish. Look at how Asians and Chinese succeed, away from their countries of origin; so why not blacks? From Martin Luther King and Rosa Parks through Andrew Young, Colin Powell, Condoleezza Rice, to the current US Defense Secretary, Lloyd Austin, to name but a few, blacks have long ago shed the metaphorical shackles and achieved positions of prominence. What black people need to do next is to remember and emulate these and other countless, successful blacks. The roll call of blacks who have done well and climbed their respective ladders in life are a reminder and a lesson of what can be achieved if one is determined; if one is prepared to become not the hammer but the anvil. For as George Orwell wrote 'In real life, it is always the anvil that breaks the hammer.'

The story of Guion Stewart Bluford Jr. (1942 -) is one of inspiration. It is an invitation not only to blacks but also to all children and young persons on the threshold of adulthood. Here was a young boy who was interested in model aircraft. Supported by his parents, he developed an interest in airplanes and aeronautics. He pursued his chosen path and obtained a PhD in aerospace engineering. He then joined the US Air Force and flew 144 missions over Vietnam. He did not settle there, as the fires of his ambitions continued to burn with a desire to achieve more. He then opted to become an astronaut and joined the National Aeronautical and Space Administration (NASA), from whence he had the opportunity of four flights into space. He was inducted in 1997 to the International Space Hall of Fame. His words 'don't be afraid to learn… don't be afraid to explore' should remain watchwords for every young person. These words should be on the lips of all parents as they guide their children through their formative years of life.

What then should the black person do? First and foremost must be a burning desire to get on in life, to be law-abiding citizens and to try and emulate their predecessors and others.

The inevitable and mandatory starting point in attempting to answer many of these questions must, of necessity, be the home. What in the home warps and distorts the views of a young person, eliminates or blunts ambitions and encourages gravitation to the lowest common strata of society? If the basic building blocks of respect and learning do not come from the home it is not likely to be acquired to any meaningful extent from elsewhere. The home provides the place for incubation of views, morality and social norms. And the incubator is not the four wall of the home but the guidance of two parents. Loose the incubator or jettison the incubation periods of development and the young person maybe lost forever. This does not, in any way, mean that a young person could not use their intuition and their inherent abilities to get back on the track - of course youngsters do; they are resilient and innovative. Don't let them use these faculties in a misguided manner. But equip them and they would achieve better. President Obama alluded to this in what he said. The Lammy review also refers to this; in the year preceding the Lammy review 55,000 young persons were found guilty in courts in the UK, but only 189 parenting orders were issued. Parents have an important part to play in the development of their children and an equally important responsibility when their children come across the criminal justice system. In many ways it may be said that a young person who enters the criminal justice system is reflection of the failure of parents and the home. Young persons are brought before judicial systems not because they were born criminal but they were brought up so - often due to neglect in providing basic care. Parents guard and guide their offspring. The Guardian newspaper journalist, Gary Younge, wrote about how his thoughts turned to the life lessons taught by his mother. An interesting and hilarious account of what one Ukrainian soldier on Snake Island shouted back to Russians who demanded their surrender was obscene and could not be printed. But it immortalised the will of the Ukrainians in protecting their homeland. The soldier who uttered the profanity did not want to be identified as 'he doesn't want his mother to know he's been swearing'. This simple story highlights the bond between mother and son and what the latter had been taught by the former!.

The absence of parenting is lamented by the journalist Rod Liddel of the Sunday Times in the UK. He writes about the wrong lifestyle choice of having a baby if one is not prepared, as a parent, to invest time and effort in nurturing one's offspring. Home time is quality time as far as development of children is concerned; many skills, thoughts etc are imparted and learned. So it comes about that parents now subcontract this important role to others – especially to teachers who are in no position to provide what caring parents can. Teachers are there to teach. One often encounters, in the classroom, an inevitable bifurcation of children into those who learn and progress and those who fail to do so and stagnate. Soon the seeds of tomorrow's juvenile delinquency are sown. Liddel also writes about instant gratification which seems to be the normal for many children and adults. The here and now is what matters – but does it? Reckoning does come and it may be too late.

Some statistics from the USA make for sobering reading. For black men between the ages of 15 to 30 years of age, the main cause of death is homicide with over 90% of those, being murdered by other black people. Similar startling statistics show a high suicide rate and high school drop out rate leading to a high unemployment rate. And it is no surprise that a significant proportion of relatively young black people are in or have been to prison.

Young persons may grow up in an environment and culture of limited guidance from adults and parents, domestic violence and criminality. Left to their own devices it is not surprising that some of them would gravitate towards groups who are involved in low grade communal criminality. They are now only a step towards violence and greater criminal activity. One can imagine the birth for example of the county lines drug system in the UK and how it provides an attractive and apparently lucrative part-time employment to youngsters. Whereas most parents would like their young children to get used to a work ethic by having some job, other youngsters may find criminality an attractive proposition. Having a job, for example as a paper delivery person or working part time elsewhere, is an important training ground. It instills within youngsters not only a work ethic but also other professional values like punctuality, responsibility to the employer and to other employees, the need to complete a job in hand, respect for seniority and superiority and for superiors and in an assortment of other attributes. Each of these serve a young person well. By pursuing further education at college, university or vocational training they are equipped to set their feet confidently on the first rungs of the employment ladder. These young persons are soon shaping up to become wholesome, well rounded individuals who are on the threshold of responsible adulthood. Why does this progression from child to adult not happen in all families? What are the ingredients in the life of some young persons that propel them towards scant respect for the law and a life of criminality?

It is written, that in the USA 70% of black children are born to couples who are not married. Now, this of itself, is not a significant statistic in the sense that it did not contribute to racism nor to the underprivileged status of blacks nor to their poor life achievement. But this figure is reflected in what President Barack Obama said in 2008 - that more than 50% off black children live their lives in single parent households. A similar picture may be seen in Britain today. The absence of a father contributes to other sobering statistics too - children from these families are about four times more likely to live in poverty and to engage in crime, children are also more likely to drop out of school and a staggering 20 times more likely to be sent to prison. However, the implications implicit in these figures are challenged by Josh Levs, *'Buy All In: How Our Work-First Culture Fails Dads, Families, and Businesses—And How We Can Fix It Together'*. Black fathers, when present, are deeply involved in the care of their children. Joseph Harker wrote in *'Safe: On Black British Men Reclaiming Space'*, how he acquired his stepfather when his genetic father walked out on his mother when she announced being pregnant with him. He describes the comfort of his home and the security and guidance provided by both his parents. The figures for other ethnic groups show that five times more Asian homes and twelve times more white homes have a resident father. The 2006 film

'*The pursuit of Happyness*' starring Will Smith it's a remarkable tale of a father's devotion to his son, despite considerable and almost insuperable odds. What a child can gain from home is beautifully and succinctly captured by the words of Abraham Lincoln in a letter to his son's teacher where he talks of the importance of honesty, ' it is far more honourable to fail than to cheat'. And goes on about seeking the truth when he writes 'Try to give my son the strength not to follow the crowd when everyone else is doing it. Teach him to listen to every one, but teach him also to filter all that he hears on a screen of truth.'

It is increasingly recognized that the absence of a father in the home has reached crisis proportions in the USA. It is, as has been written. that the affected communities have been hit 'with the force of 100 hurricane Katrinas".

The words of Auma Obama, President Barak Obama's half-sister are telling – 'I'm proud of our name because my brother has really carried our name up there...it's made its mark in the world, …. And it's special for us and for our children and for our communities because it tells every child that if you work hard you can do whatever you want in this world. You can make you future.'

The story of a black boy born with autism and global development delay in the UK, should be an inspiration to all, not only to blacks. As if autism is not enough of a disability, for any parent to be told that their child has global developmental delay is synonymous with a life sentence of dependency and care. The word 'global' implies delay in all parameters of growth and development – physical and mental. But this was no ordinary little boy with disabilities; Jason Arday could not read or write – skills he acquired much later than most children, talking at 11 and being able to write at 18 years. Take a moment and imagine how much Jason had lost in those first 18 years. But he was determined and he had an all-supporting mother. He became a teacher of physical education by day after getting a degree in the subject from University of Surrey. At night he would study. At the age of 22 he wanted to do post-graduate studies and had the support of his mentor, Sandro Sandri, who told him 'I think you can do this - I think we can take on the world and win'. That was precisely what Jason wanted to hear; he got a Masters and a PhD in educational studies. He worked at Roehampton University followed by the post of associate professor in sociology at Durham University. In

2021 he became one of the youngest professors in the UK when he was made professor of sociology of education at the University of Glasgow's School of Education. Jason is working on neurodiversity and is soon to be a Professor in Cambridge University; he is now 37 years old. This story is not the stuff of dreams – it is the stuff of grit, determination and drive which set a young disabled boy on the path to remarkable achievements. Herein lies a lesson for all. One is reminded of the words of the poet, Henry Wadsworth Longfellow – ' The heights by great men reached and kept were not attained by sudden flight, but they, while their companions slept, were toiling upward in the night' – literally and metaphorically speaking!

To return to the vexed subject of reparations, one needs to begin with what is meant by the term 'reparation'. If one uses a basic understanding of the term as paying back or compensating or the act of righting in some manner or form the wrongs done, it makes eminent sense to use the term. But in the context of slavery the term has a complex meaning given that slavery was an accepted process centuries ago, not least by those countries that were actively involved in the process and especially by those persons and businesses which dealt with the capture and delivery of slaves. Some fundamental aspects of reparations in respect of slavery need to be appreciated. Slavery was not one group of persons capturing enslaving, transporting and forcibly working another group of persons. This is a simplified and almost stylized narrative of what, with hindsight, was a dreadful business that reduced people to saleable objects devoid of any humanity. Of course, people were transported across the ocean and forced to work on plantations etc. and others were conveyed to the Middle East. One cannot escape the primary and simple basic question of where these people came from and how did they come to be on the ships that transported them across the Atlantic, that transported them across the continent and transported them to slave markets in Africa from whence they reached the Middle East? The active cooperation and participation of the African man himself, at various stages in this sordid business, was a necessary prerequisite for success of slavery. In the absence of these inputs to the process it is difficult to imagine slavery ever reaching the proportions that it did. Much has been written about why the African man chose to enslave his own kind. Take the slave hunter or slave catcher out of the equation and one can readily imagine how the whole project would not have succeeded to the extent that it did; it is not impossible to even imagine that the whole edifice of slavery outside of Africa would have imploded. Transport oneself for a moment to the horrific lives of ordinary people in the towns and villages in those countries that provided slaves. People going about their normal daily business and running the risk of being captured by those who would make slaves of them, for profit. Children going to school and their mothers not knowing whether they would come home safely or even if they would come out of school at the end of the day! People going about their normal daily lives and being captured by their fellow Africans; even going to seek medical assistance was fraught with the risk of capture. Pregnant women were captured and transported across the African continent. Slavery was endemic to Africa and has been going on for many centuries; various forms of it exist to this day. The risk to an individual was great during those times – one dare not leave home, for at the height of slavery no one was safe. This was the norm that was part of life – amoral and inhuman. But was it or was it seen as such? Human beings were seen as a saleable commodity by other human beings. Ethics and morality did not exist or if it did, was quickly jettisoned. If slavery is evil, what term or phrase would one use to describe people who capture their compatriots and members of their families for slavery and the profits that they bring? The biblical phrase 'twenty pieces of silver' cannot even begin to help understand or compensate for what was occurring in those times.. What part does the African who facilitated the whole edifice of slavery have to say about reparations? Understanding the foregoing are so fundamental to appreciating the clamour for reparations. The words of an unknown writer springs to mind – 'everyone knows that a simple wine must be drunk speedily and in good company; but when one understands wine sufficiently to lay it down, then even the simplest of wines assumes the character of nobility'. This statement graciously captures the gulf between knowledge and understanding. The gulf between knowing about slavery and understanding what happened and its ramifications is wide. As has been noted, slavery is not a simplistic statement of capture and labour – far from it. Those who claim reparations appear not to seek to venture into the realms of its understanding. They remain in the dark like the people in Plato's 'Allegory of the Caves'. The choice to see and yet be blind is the tragedy of modern discussions on slavery. Perhaps the quote by the celebrated American biologist and naturalist Edward Osborne Wilson (1929 – 2021) is relevant here – 'We are drowning in information, while starving for wisdom'. Although written in reference to futuristic data manipulation, it nevertheless remains a useful statement of the need for insight and reflection on the totality of slavery.

Do not the descendants of slave catchers and all those involved in the capture, transfer and sale of slaves have an equivalent or indeed a much greater responsibility for slavery than the white man who transported slaves across the Atlantic? And by deduction, do they not have a responsibility to those whom they enslaved? This is obvious direct compensation, except that it would be near impossible to separate descendants of slaves from those Africans who were active participants in the whole business of slavery. And of course there is calculated and studious silence on trans-African slavery and the much greater slavery that occurred in the east of the continent.

Compare this with the reparations paid by Germany to Israel or even that paid by the British Government to Kenyans following the Mau Mau rebellion in Kenya. In the former, the process of identifying and linkage of crimes committed and those who suffered at hands of Nazi Germany was easy due to the chronological proximity of the holocaust to reparations and compensation. The Mau Mau rebellion occurred in Kenya from 1952 to 1960, prior to that country's independence from Great Britain. Atrocities and abuses of human rights were committed by both sides during the rebellion. The matter was heard in the UK courts and the position of the British government was and continues to be that it is not and continues not to be responsible for the actions of the colonial administration of the time. However, in 2013 the then Foreign Secretary, William Hague, representing the government of the day, agreed a financial settlement of about GBP 20 million with 5228 claimants. William Hague added 'we continue to deny liability on behalf of the Government and British taxpayers today for the actions of the colonial administration in respect of the claims'. This appears, on the face of it, to be an important principle denying responsibility of what happened before, in the case of slavery events of over 200 years ago. More recently the federal Government of Ottawa, Canada has filed notice of an appeal of a court ruling granting $2 billion compensation for its failures in providing child services to First Nations.

It is timely and relevant to consider the descendants of those who were enslaved and transported across the continent of Africa, across the Atlantic and to the Middle East. While their ancestors endured the ordeal of slavery, the descendants of the slaves transported across the Atlantic have grown and progressed in countries which, by the accounts of many, have provided them with better services and the chance of development that has been denied to many people in Africa. While there has been discrimination and attenuated development in comparison to the whites in USA and Europe, their lot has been superior to those in Africa. And now, one has only to look at those descendants of slaves who are in prominent positions to appreciate that they have progressed and accomplished significantly. It is not difficult to conclude that these persons have surmounted various odds on the journeys of their lives and reached the pinnacle or higher echelons of their respective professions.

One invariably returns again to the question of whether reparations need to be paid in respect of slavery and, if the answer is in the affirmative, to whom. The case of paying reparations has not been convincingly made, not least because of the span of centuries from then to now and the impossibility of identifying victims of slavery, as opposed to descendants of slaves. When one recounts the successes of many blacks, one may be tempted to take a hard view of those blacks who have not achieved in life. Why, if not for their failure to run with the chances that life has offered them as much as has and is being offered to all others?

Douglas Murray writes about the need to move away from any discussion about reparations being a matter between 'white' and 'black'. It is much more nuanced than that because reparations are being claimed for the descendants of slaves who have never themselves endured slavery. These are not victims of slavery but victims of racism and other systemic grievances in society. This does not detract from the much greater problems of poor parenting, inadequate education and therefore limited job prospects and high unemployment, poor health care with associated adverse life outcomes etc. Correcting these deficiencies in the lives of blacks are important but should not be confused with reparation.

It is worth looking at, what one may consider, a novel form of reparations. Now, before one goes down this road one must expect howls of horror, screams of selfishness and accusations of abrogation. Be those as they may, it is yet a valid area to consider, namely foreign aid. In basic terms, foreign aid is material that one country gives another country, which it considers to be a deserving recipient. Aid does not have to be money; indeed one may make a cogent case why it should not be money! Aid should not be designed to finance a country but to help it on a path of sustainable development and towards improving the quality of life of all its populations. Implicit in this statement are few important aspects - not to impose the rich man's view on another country, but to use the latter's own resources and the aid provided it to develop in accordance with it's society and values. Aid is provided not to replace that which is there and which is known to be functioning but to help enhance them for the benefit of all. Many countries in receipt of aid are torn apart by ethno-nationalistic and internecine conflict; aid is not provided to support one party or another but for the benefit of all its population irrespective of religion, tribe, class etc. This is a crucial aspect of aid.

In the USA, the current accepted meaning of the term 'aid' may be said to have started with the Marshall Plan in 1948 in Europe. The Marshall Plan helped reconstruct and regenerate Europe, which had been devastated by World War Two. This was followed by the Foreign Assistance Act of 1961 which is the basis of US foreign aid to this day. Only a small amount of aid goes as money paid directly to a government. In 2020 only 3% of foreign aid represented money that went directly to receiving governments. This is an important step which helps avoid disbursement for alternative uses to that which the aid was intended for and most of all to avoid embezzlement of funds by individuals, especially. The bulk of aid is channeled to the recipient countries through the United Nations and other multinational organizations like the World Bank. In 2021 the US gave $32 billion in aid of which $ 1.3 billion went to Ethiopia, $860 million to Afghanistan and $ 803 million to Nigeria.

In 2017 The United Kingdom gave $18 billion in aid of which Nigeria received 420 million dollars. Yemen, South Sudan and Tanzania received in excess of $200 million each. The foreign aid budget of the United Kingdom in 2017 comprised 0. 7% of the Gross National Income (GNI). The ODA (Overseas Development Assistance) : GNI target of 0.7% was agreed internationally in 1970 by the United Nations General Assembly.

The UK incorporated this figure of aid into UK law in 2015 in its International Development (Official Development Assistance Target) Act.

In the nine years from 2013 to 2021, the United Kingdom provided $113 billion in aid.

Ethiopia, South Sudan, Nigeria, Tanzania and Kenya were among the top 15 recipients. It is remarkable that the oil rich Middle East countries do not figure in a list of international aid providers, except for the UAE. However it is known that between 1976 and 1987 Saudi Arabia provided $49 billion in aid, although aid was provided only to Muslim countries. But in 2006, Jack Barton wrote that Saudi Arabia was trying to improve its international image by donating to a South Asian country that had been ravaged by the tsunami in 2004. In 2017 the Saudi charitable foundation, al Walid philanthropies donated 50 million dollars to the UNICEF to help with the eradication of measles. In 2009 the Government Accountability Office (AOA) of the USA published a report accusing Saudi based charities of funding terrorism. However it must be added that these charities are not linked to the Saudi government, which cooperates actively to 'counter terrorism funding'.

When one considers the large amounts of funding that have been provided by the USA and UK to Africa in the form of international aid one must conclude that significant amounts have being sent to Africa. This is important; where has all these vast amounts gone, if not for development of the respective countries in Africa? When one hears that 'black lives matter', one must inquire as to which black lives this statement refers to. Does it refer only to black lives in developed countries or does the phrase extend to those in other parts of the world like in Africa, whose quality of life and survival rates are poorer that those of blacks living in the West. It is sure that black persons living in the developed west need improvements in education, health and so on to bring their quality of life to those of the average white person. But is that all? What about those living in Africa from whence the backs of the west originated?

The UK's Foreign and Commonwealth Development Office (FCDO) allocated £75 million for the Caribbean from 2011 until 2015. Since then it has continued to provide aid to the region. It is opportune recalling the $118 million loan deal by Xi Jinping when he was Vice-President of China and Prime Minister Bruce Golding of Jamaica in 2009. In 2020 it was reported that China had offered Jamaica loans for road construction. In addition China has donated security equipment for use by police forces throughout the Caribbean. It has also constructed several Chinese cultural centres in the region. Given the relatively low degree of commercial activity in the Caribbean, these activities have been a source of concern, especially to the USA. Some have commented that China's apparent benevolence may be a strategy to influence Caribbean nations to move away from supporting Taiwan, which China views an integral part of it's territory. One recalls the construction of a highway in Montenegro by the Chinese, which had to cease because the government of Montenegro was unable to finance the debt involved. This was a proposed 275 mile highway from Port of Bar in Montenegro to Belgrade, the Serbian capital. A former Justice Minister of Montenegro, Dragan Soc, said that the highway would not lead anywhere, commenting that it is ' highway from nothing to nothing' which would also be a financial burden on future generations. What is interesting and particularly worrying is that the contract for the loan and highway construction stipulates the right of the Chinese government owned Export-Import Bank has the right to seize land in Montenegro if the latter defaults on the loan, so long as any such land does not belong to the military or is used for diplomatic purposes. One wonders how such a agreement came about. One does not know the terms of contracts between China and Jamaica but similar onerous clauses would amount to bondage.

The European Union has, over the past 30 years or so, provided several billion euros of aid to Jamaica. These monies have been given in the form of grants to help with education, human rights, security, agriculture, rural development etc. The funds are provided with the conditions of effective expenditure and transparency.

This too is a form of reparations, although not referred to as such.

Trying to correct the supposed injustice of slavery which happened hundreds of years ago is likely to cause more problems than paying blacks to remain silent. As if payment could ever be sufficient recompense for the sufferings endured by slaves. Assuming one could identify those who are to benefit from proposed payments, the result would be to enrich them at the cost of making another section of the community poorer and resentful. One may be sewing the seeds of racism with no net benefit to society.

'Political slavery' is a phrase that may be used to describe China's involvement in Montenegro. A similar situation is developing in the South Pacific. The outgoing President of the Federated States of Micronesia, David Panuelo, alleged that China is engaged in 'political warfare' in his country. The apparent purpose is to ensure that FSM remains neutral in China's battle with Taiwan or remains aligned with China's view on Taiwan. China influenced the Solomon Islands and Kiribati to break their ties with Taiwan. FSM's defence is overseen by the USA. He accused China of including 'bribery, psychological warfare, and blackmail'. The words of Panuelo are of concern to all who value freedom. China, he said has 'demonstrated a keen capability to undermine our sovereignty, rejects our values, and uses our elected and senior officials for their own purposes'. This challenges China's oft repeated cliché of the importance of respecting the sovereignty and territorial integrity of other countries. In this instance, they are apparently being openly accused of meddling in another's sovereignty. 'We are bribed to be complicit, and bribed to be silent. That's a heavy word, but it's an accurate description regardless' said Panuelo.

Not too infrequently one encounters claims that some words in the English language are not politically correct for usage as they are likely to be offensive to some people. One hears about people and words in the English language that have been so called 'cancelled'. In the word 'cancelled' is an implication that such persons are literally 'persona non grata' ie they are not an acceptable person for the purposes that is being considered, for example not an acceptable speaker because their views could be seen or likely to be viewed as being offensive. In a similar vein some words are inappropriate. Take for example the decision of the University of California to avoid use of the word 'field'. Apparently this word is offensive to some persons; why one would ask? The justification given for excluding 'field' is because it apparently, painfully, refers to working in the fields, which is what slaves did. It has not crossed the minds of the staff in the university. that working in the fields is also what a vast majority of people do - working in the fields for eg for all the produce that come to the table and which feeds the world. If it chooses to obliterate the word field from the lexicon of the English language, would a black military officer who has been promoted to the position of Field Marshall, decline the commission because the adjective 'Field' is offensive. It is as ridiculous as it is hilarious to learn that the alternative word chosen to replace 'field' is the word 'practicum'. In their wisdom the University has chosen a word which has connotations of superiority, being Latin, and they imagine it conveys a feeling of inclusivity. The absurdity of this choice is that no other word conveys better the impression of being superior to the plebs of this world, let alone blacks and other non-white persons. One can think of many other words that could be, as it were, unused. 'Boat journey', 'sailing', 'crossing', 'ship' etc. These are all words relative to the Middle Passage. Natural progression of cancelling would be to avoid use of these words. Taken to the ridiculous extreme many words in the English language could have connotations in respect of slavery. After all the English language was a commonly used means of communication then as it is now. Much of the English language cannot be used if one were to proceed down this path. This is reducing the pristine English language to an absurdity. But more than this, it is pandering to 'snowflakes'. These are persons who are offended or think that they are offended or likely to be so about anything that refers to the suffering of or offense likely to be endured by others. Descendants of slaves have not suffered directly as a result of their ancestors in the slave era; they have not suffered because slavery occurred many generations and centuries before their time. Yet some of them choose to be offended and the liberal minded 'wokerati' see offense on behalf of them. If genuine offense is felt by a person, avoidance is seldom the answer. It is far better and indeed noble to encounter that which appears to cause offense, critically appraise and make one's own judgment. There is something sinister about a third party recognizing offense on behalf of another – what may be described as ' surrogate or secondary offense'. Offense to the individual or 'primary offences' may not have occurred. If one were to allow secondary offense, one soon migrates into the world of the 'word police' who appear to have no hesitation in reducing language to a set of words devoid of emotion and meaning. All in the name of a third party who may not have been offended at all! It is the solemn duty of all who use the English language to choose the most appropriate words to express themselves. If genuine offense is caused, one needs to recognize and understand it; explanation and apology shall surely follow. But when third party offense is claimed, there is an overriding need to ignore it. The cancel culture and word police are sinister encroachments on freedom of speech and debate. That they originate from universities speaks much about those who teach in those institutions. A university is a place for open debate of that which is fact, that which is fiction, that which is unpalatable, and that which is likely to cause offense. A university should represent an 'abridgement of the universe'. Human progress follows from debate and discussion. The world would still be flat if not for debate of ideas and opinions, unpalatable though some may have been at the time. And what about the so-called 'snowflakes' in society; those who are easily offended or think that others may be offended. Such persons are not likely to develop because they choose to inhabit a closeted world free of offense and pain. This is a dystopian concept. Life is full of joy and unhappiness, pain, success and disappointment. Universities are culpable in failing to inculcate resilience in the younger generation. One may conclude that the rise in mental illness in the young is at least partly related to a lack of resilience. The same may be said of the victim culture in society.

The ease with which offense was taken was seen recently when the Russian Foreign Minister, Sergei Lavrov, visited Africa. During Lavrov's visit in January 2023, the German Foreign Ministry tweeted with an emoji of a leopard in apparently making fun of him. The tweet was in reference to the decision by Germany to send its Leopard battle tanks to Ukraine. The degree of misunderstanding in Africa is clear in some of the ensuing comments. The chairman of the African Union Commission thought that the tweet gave the impression that Africa was only about animals. While some others wrote - 'you continue to disrespect Africa' and 'some colonialist tendencies here'. Reviewing these comments displays an inability to take a joke and/ or failure to read it in the context of the political situation at the time in Europe. This was not about the leopards of Africa or even about Africa! That the German Foreign Ministry apologised only added weight to the impressions of those who commented on the original tweet. A joke it was and it should have stayed that way – and the joke was certainly not on or about Africa. This case is relevant for the erroneous impressions caused or conveyed when history or the spoken word and written works are taken out of context. The response to the joke also exposes the low level of tolerance of anything said or done that even remotely impinges on race. Could this, of itself, be a form of racism by the black towards others – in this case the German Foreign Ministry?

Continuing in the same vein one reads that the wonderful children's author, Roald Dahl, has had his works altered by 'sensitivity readers'. Roald Dahl's children's works transports children into a magical world of make believe. Imagine for a moment that the 'word police' do not like the gluttonous Augustus Gloop, from the book *Charlie and the Chocolate Factory*, being described as fat. No, he must be described as 'enormous'. But, what discernible difference is there between enormous, fat, obese, overweight? All mean the same and convey the same impression in reading. Would someone who is likely to be offended by the word fat, be less likely to be offended by usage of the word 'enormous'? One may even imagine the word 'enormous' describing a person being much larger than a fat person! What is particularly interesting is to know what the actor Michael Boliner, who acted as Augustus Gloop, had to say about the developing fuss. He does not think that the book is politically incorrect or cruel. And here is the crucial point – 'I think the story is very good…there is nothing harmful….it shows you bad things and bad behaviours…that like kids should not eat too much, and it shows you that the good guys who do the right thing, they win in the end'. In eating chocolate, as in the story of slavery, concealment or alteration of information does not help the reader. By reducing access to alternative views, one significantly impairs critical thinking which is essential to arrival at a satisfactory conclusion. The result is that one is corralled into sharing the monocular intellectual vision of one party.

Roald Dahl had a remarkable ability to use the beauty of the English language to describe not only the niceness but also the naughtiness of children. The publishers of his works could not see it that way; in effect they have changed his most beautiful works. And in so doing they have deprived generations of children of the joys of his works, something that the publishers and the 'sensitivity readers' have themselves enjoyed. The author Salman Rushdie tweeted – ' Roald Dahl was no angel, but this is absurd censorship. Puffin Books, the publisher, and the Roald Dahl estate should be ashamed'. And all of this wokery of Dahl's works underestimates the resilience of children and their sense of curiosity to be as happy as being frightened and shocked. These are attributes to be promoted in abundance in children.

Even the Prime Minister of the UK, Rishi Sunak, weighed in on the controversy with his spokesman saying ' When it comes to our rich and varied literary heritage, the PM agrees with the BFG that you shouldn't 'gobblefunk' around with words. I think it's important that works of literature and works of fiction are preserved and not airbrushed. We have always defended the right to free speech and expression.'

'Sensitivity readers' come out with some amazingly ridiculous suggestions. The award-winning author Kate Clanchy was advised to remove the word 'Taliban' in one of her works as the Taliban are no more a terrorist organization but the government of Afghanistan. What one may ask is wrong in referring to them as having been terrorists? Irgun was a terrorist organisation in Israel in the 1940's. It bombed the King David Hotel in Jerusalem in 1946. By far one of its worst atrocities was the Deir Yin massacre in 1948 where it killed 107 Palestinian Arabs including women and children in the village of Deir Yin, 600 miles out of Jerusalem. Irgun was the predecessor of the right wing political party Likud which has been in government, as a coalition partner, several times. Kate Clanchy said - 'I was told comparing Scotland bings to boils might be offensive to acne sufferers'. She left the publisher and quite rightly so. One is justified in questioning the qualifications and competencies of 'sensitivity readers'; for what they are doing is destroying initiative and in the case of Kate Clanchy's work, interfering with historical fact.

Clarissa Ackroyd who works in children's publishing said that it is Orwellian to have 'update version forced' upon readers. Dahl's biography, Matthew Dennison, wrote that in his works Dahl 'championed the bullied against bullies' and that changes were being made without consideration of the author himself. It is therefore appropriate to learn that the publisher, Puffin Books, will produce the original version of Dahl's books after all, in response to the adverse reception of readers of the sanitised versions of his books. It is thought likely that the original writings would be preferred by readers.

One sometimes wonders what 'sensitivity readers' would do with the phrase 'black market'!

Some of the examples of offence occasioned by the use of words would be considered ridiculous and indeed laughable, if it was not serious to some readers. Adam Habib, director of a School of Oriental and African studies in London, used the 'N' word, which was found to be offensive and drew protests from students. He is a South African of Indian descent and replied that in South Africa where the 'N' word is used, it added context to what is being said. However this was insufficient an explanation; students demanded his resignation. Habib drew a distinction between using the word and mentioning it. The former would be considered offensive as the 'N' word is now derogatory. But mentioning it would not be considered offensive by most persons. If one were to quote literature from the past, the 'N' word would be frequently encountered. However, in this book the word, when found in quotations, has been replaced with 'black'. This is extreme sensitivity without due regard to context and is an extension of the persistent and recurring g lack of context referred to elsewhere in this book.

The downside of all this would be to gradually convert writers; to stunt their imagination and limit the conversion of their thoughts into their written works. 'Sensitivity readers' also seem to want to air-brush history that they do not find acceptable and which probably does not align with their views of the world. Publishers are doing better than the KGB or the Stasi or similar organizations in oppressive countries, ever did. The attenuation of thought and the accompanying reduction in the quality of written works leads to only one outcome- generations deprived of the ability to be free thinking individuals which is an essential ingredient for development and human progression. But, most importantly it deprives readers and the public at large of the imaginations of authors, the bases of their thoughts and impressions, the freedom to analyse, accept, repudiate etc. Does any good come of these acts of literary vandalism? Perhaps, the words of Ikonnikov from another time, a more violent time, may yet be relevant here – 'those who most wish for the good of humanity are unable to diminish evil by one jot'.

It is hopeful too that the New York Times which hitherto had ignored gender dysphoria has now allowed its journalists to publish about the topic, to general dismay but also relief. It is the right to publish that is respected here, especially with the rise in the USA of private gender clinics which are subject to limited or no scrutiny of their work.

The logical extension of the work of sensitivity readers is to remove from established and celebrated works, anything that is likely to offend or even more perversely cause any degree of distress in the reader. Violence, murder, warfare are subjects that may cause pain to some readers and discomfort to most. Often on television, violent news is accompanied by a prior warning of the distress it may cause in some viewers. Is society intending to prevent future readers from access to the original great works that have preceded us? For example some of the most painful, yet riveting reads are the works of authors from the previous Soviet Union- *'War and Peace'* by Leo Tolstoy, the novel *'Life and Fate'* by Vasily Grossman, *'The Gulag Archipelago: An Experiment in Literary Investigation'* and *'One Day in the Life of Ivan Denisovich'* by the Noble prize-winning Soviet writer and dissident Aleksandr Solzhenitsyn etc. Humankind has progressed throughout the centuries, not in a small measure, by violence. It is therefore, no surprise, that the German philosopher Friedrich Wilhelm Nietzsche (1844 – 1900) described history as of three types - historical history, monumental history, and violent history. The value of being acquainted with unadulterated history is to provide an insight how each generation managed the perennial questions of priorities, power, 'hubris, and the battle for resources and respect ' as was written by Jenni Russell. If future generations are to read history devoid of the violence that contributed to progression, they are likely to grew up in a rather sanitized and confused world. When confronted with reality it would not be a surprise if they ask themselves what they see and / or hear was not supposed to happen or why were they not taught or not learned the lessons of history. They are likely to be ill equipped for the vicissitudes of life and most importantly not appreciate that violence achieves almost nothing but causes the loss of much more.

Wokeism and the denial of free speech is a present danger and a threat to society. Dictators and tyrants of all sorts, throughout history, have curtailed free speech. This denies public the right to question and demands from them supine acquiescence.

The apparent fear of the spoken and written word is reaching worrying proportions. One is witnessing nothing less than 'iconoclasm of language'. The English language is one of the world's greatest possessions. It has bound generations of peoples over the centuries, irrespective of ethnicity, colour, religion etc. It has brought the world's people closer together in a great global community and has torn down the veritable 'Tower of Babel'. No other means of communication has achieved so much as the English language. To see it being reduced to a means of communication without affect, emotion and sometimes meaning, is something all lovers of the language should stand up against.

The awards system in the UK is not the best in the world – which country could possibly claim to have the best system of national awards? But the system in the UK recognizes those who have made a significant contribution in their roles either to the UK or to humanity in general. It is often difficult for those of black or coloured ethnicities to accept awards because doing so tears at the heart of their feelings and views about colonialism, and the role of the British Empire. Many blacks and coloured persons have accepted awards and are comfortable with the decisions they have taken; they have critically analysed their often conflicting views and have rationalized before coming to a settled decision to accept an award. One of these persons is Adebusuyi (Ade) Adeyemi, who works on Global Health at Kings College in London and for the National Health Service in the UK. He was awarded a MBE (Member of the British Empire) and was perplexed by the award. He describes what one may call the 'schizophrenic duality' of being Nigerian and now a respected and acknowledged member of British society – from the land of slaves, to be acclaimed for his achievements on behalf of society, in the slave master's house, as it were!

Many persons in the UK decline honours. Some have written to the government asking that the word 'Empire' be extirpated from awards like OBE and MBE because of their reference to British Empire. Some want awards to refer to 'Excellence' instead of 'Empire'. One black who declined an award is the poet Benjamin Zephaniah. His words betray a sense of horror at being chosen for an award, with the words 'Empire' – 'Up yours, I thought. I get angry when I hear that word 'empire'; it reminds me of slavery, it reminds of thousands of years of brutality, it reminds me of how my foremothers were raped and my forefathers brutalised... Benjamin Zephaniah OBE – no way...' said Zephaniah. On the other hand, Ade Adeyemi describes the difficulty he had in understanding the reaction of his father, who is Nigerian by birth, to the news that his son was being awarded a MBE. The Health Services Journal named Ade Adeyemi as one of the 'rising stars' of the NHS. In many respects his father had moved from the colonial mindset and had integrated conceptually into the multicultural society that is the Britain of today. Adeyemi accepted the award having himself crossed the Rubicon. What this event shows is what black people need to do; while retaining their cultural roots and links with their homeland they have to, in effect, integrate in a multicultural society and help break down the barriers between 'us' and 'them'. Become 'we'. Undoubtedly the word 'Empire' conjures memories of painful ancestral history. To many who can definitely identify as being descendants of slaves, it must be extremely painful indeed knowing that they have progressed well while their forefathers were subjected to unmentionable horrors. On the other hand to many blacks there is, at best, a tenuous link with slavery. Yet, the thought that their kith and kin were slaves, will continue to be painful. Against this must be seen the opportunities provided in Britain, the USA and other places and which they have grasped to help progress. They could be wholesome in accepting an award for their achievements but also on behalf of all blacks and other minorities and in the process pay homage to their slave ancestors. This is different to the stance adopted by Benjamin Zephaniah - he has not moved from the linkage to slavery and towards a more inclusive modern, integrated society. One accepts and respects his point of view as it is the prerogative of any individual. But one has to ask what and how long would it take for him and his descendants to move towards a more integrated society and what can be done to facilitate that journey, without adverse reverberations in the rest of society; this is undoubtedly an important journey. The superficiality of removing the word 'Empire' is, in effect, papering deep emotional cracks and attachments. It therefore is incumbent that society, collectively and individually, works towards breaking down barriers. Every street that is renamed, every statue that is pulled down reinforces the gulf between then and now, between 'us' and 'them'. Every statue that is pulled down, is one mor educational icon that would have brought people together. Statues, road names and the like are perpetual reminders of events long gone by and in the words of Nelson Mandela, 'never, never and never again' to be repeated. Take down a statue or re-name a road and one has subtracted empathy from society.

That highly acclaimed and versatile black African American actor, Chadwick Boseman of 'Black Panther' fame, died of colorectal cancer at the young age of 43 in 2020. His death raised awareness not only of colorectal cancer but also of healthcare amongst blacks and ethnic minority persons. Black people are disproportionately affected by colorectal cancer which appears at a young age and unfortunately in a more advanced stage of the disease. His death highlighted the socioeconomic disparities between blacks and whites in American society - poverty, poor housing, poor nutrition, poor education etc. These factors are known to be determinants of poor health and adverse outcomes. If there is one message to come from the death of Chadwick Boseman, it is that blacks and others from ethnic minorities must avail themselves of health services and especially preventive services like screening for diseases that are yet to appear.

African Americans are living longer, with death rates having declined by 25% over 17 years. This reduction is seen mainly in those over 65 years of age. However, despite these improvements in mortality rates, many young blacks are dying of conditions that occur in older whites. There is evidence of mistrust by blacks of the medical profession. Despite the known benefits of screening from bowel cancer, which may help to prevent the disease, blacks still have an underlying mistrust of the profession and of the preventive procedures that are available. In a paper by Leslie Adams, Jennifer Richmond and others in 2017, on mistrust in relation to screening for bowel cancer, they found that not only the intrusiveness of colonoscopy but also the worry about experimentation may be contributing to African Americans not taking part in bowel cancer surveillance programs.

To try to understand medical mistrust one may need to go back to the 1930s and the Tuskegee syphilis experiment. It's real name was the Tuskegee Study of Untreated Syphilis in the Negro Male. The study was set up in 1932 by the United States Public Service department and the Center for Disease Control and Prevention in association with Tuskegee University. The study involved 399 men with syphilis and 201 men without syphilis, which latter formed the control arm of the experiment. All the men received usual medical and mental health care but treatment for syphilis was denied the 399 with the disease. Penicillin was available at the time as the only treatment for syphilis - it was denied to the patients with the disease. On the other hand they were given various pills and potions for what was described as 'bad blood'. The experiment continued until 16th November 1972 when it had to cease following leakage of details of the experiment to the press. At the end of the experiment the results available make horrifying reading - 28 of the trial patients had died from syphilis while hundred died from complications of syphilis, 40 of the wives of patients were infected with syphilis and gave birth to 19 children with congenital syphilis. That the experiment lasted for almost 40 years, hidden away from scrutiny, is surprising. It was on a scale of medicalization and experimentation akin to the drugs used by East German athletes at Olympic Games. From about 1976 East Germany excelled at three Olympic Games and two World Championships. 'We were a large experiment, a big chemical field test," said former sprint record holder, Ines Geipel. She continued ' The old men in the regime used these young girls for their sick ambition. They knew the mini-country absolutely had to be the greatest in the world. That's sick. It's a stolen childhood.' One may even go so far as to compare the Tuskegee experiment with the evil human experiments conducted by Josef Mengele under Nazis during World War Two. It is therefore no wonder that blacks view medical intervention with suspicion.

That the Tuskegee medical trial continued after the Nuremberg Code was accepted by the USA speaks volumes to the inherent racism in the medical establishment of the time that allowed the trial to continue. The Doctor's Trial which was the legal case prosecuted on 9th December 1946 as United States of America v Karl Brandt and others was the first of 12 trials against German industrialists and high-ranking German officials at the end of Word War Two. Twenty -three medical doctors were accused of human experimentation under the Nazis. Several of the accused used as their defence the claim that the experiments they conducted or participated in were no different to those done by German and American doctors. What was even more significant was that there was no international law at the time to define what illegal human experimentation was. This was a cause for concern to the American doctors – Andrew Ivy and Leo Alexander. So concerned was Dr. Alexander by the defence used by the accused, that on 17th April 1947 he submitted a proposal to the United States Counsel for War Crimes setting out basic principles for the conduct of experiments on humans. These eventually became the Nuremberg Code with the basic need for consent, autonomy of the individual, non-maleficence and especially the need to cease any experiment or trial if there was a risk to the health and / or survival of the participants in the trial. Also in 1964 The World Medical Association produced its Declaration of Helsinki which formed the cornerstone of human research ethics. That Tuskegee continued to 1972 when these statutes were evolving in the USA and elsewhere is nothing short of surprising and more so frightening..

But progress is needed. Health care providers must reassure blacks of the benevolence of and lack of malevolence in what is being done. The death of Chadwick Boseman must help raise awareness not only of colorectal cancer but also of the value of preventive health care. Leaders and opinion formers have a major part to play, in taking the message of preventive healthcare to their communities.

It is not uncommon to criticize the Commonwealth of Nations as a colonial club perpetuating the mentality of years gone by, when member states were colonies or Dependent Territories of Great Britain. Most commentators would agree that it is an association of equals who are under no obligation to remain as members of the Commonwealth. Zimbabwe withdrew from the group in 2003; that is how it should be as no nation is under any obligation to remain in the Commonwealth. It is an organization based on the principles of fairness, equality and the rule of law. Similarly, Commonwealth may seek to exclude a member as it rightly did when South Africa was excluded from the Commonwealth during the apartheid era. The Commonwealth is hardly a group of dependent countries. Some like Myanmar (Burma) for e.g. chose not to join the group. Nigeria joined the Commonwealth in 1960 after it gained independence from Great Britain. However in November 1995 it was excluded from the Commonwealth after having breached the Harare Declaration of 1991. This decision was made by the Commonwealth Heads of Government. Following the election of a civilian President in 1999 the country was readmitted to the Commonwealth. The Harare Declaration sets out the core principles and values of the Commonwealth which all member states are obliged to abide by. There is no requirement for allegiance to the reigning monarch in the UK. All policies and decisions are made by the constituent heads of states that comprise the Commonwealth. The reigning monarch may be seen as a titular head devoid of any powers or influence in decisions of the Commonwealth. It certainly is not what Ms Afua Hirsch said: "I sometimes call the Commonwealth 'Empire 2.0' because that is what it is'. One cannot be more wrong in describing the Commonwealth as such and betrays a misunderstanding of what it currently is and what it represents.. One can hardly call the Commonwealth a vestige of colonialism, let alone a continuation of Empire. It is a free association of sovereign, independent, self-governing nations. It was therefore a considered decision of for e.g. Gabon to choose to join the Commonwealth in 2022 and became its newest member. Gabon, a West Africa country was a French colony and mainly French speaking. It became the Commonwealth's 55th member state. The decision to join was obviously criticised by many. This prompted the High Commissioner for Gabon in the UK to state - We are a small nation but we are a proud one...."To think we would sign up blindly to be vassals to another empire is to suggest we are foolish. This is why many in Gabon would feel patronised by these remarks'. Gabon became the third non-English speaking country to join the Commonwealth; with Mozambique having joined in 1995 and Rwanda in 2009. Why, one is bound to ask, would a country that has at most, tenuous links with the UK and is not even an English speaking one would choose to join the Commonwealth?

Review of the progress of some Commonwealth nations may shed some light on differential national development. Ghana, a country on the West African coast gained independence from Great Britain in 1957. It has a population of about 32 million people. It had a nominal GDP (Gross Domestic Product) of $ 81.6 billion and a per capita income of $2,374. Malaysia in Southeast Asia also gained independence from Great Britain in 1957 and has a similar population of about 32 million people. In 2022 it's GDP was $434 billion with a per capita income of $13,108.

White Crocodile, Black Crocodile, New Slavery for Old

Both countries had charismatic leaders for whom nation-building were priorities. Ghana had Kwame Nkrumah (1909-1972) who, by gaining independence for Ghana, made it the first Black African state to do so. He was also a pan–Africanist who believed that Africa needed to rise up, shed the yolk of colonialism and move forwards. Ghana should not be enticed by either the West or the East, during, what was then, the period of the Cold War. He led the creation of the Organisation of African Unity (OAU) in 1963 in Addis Ababa, Ethiopia. Ruthless at times, Nkrumah may have been for eg when he cracked down on unions. Industrial modernisation was his aim and he felt that some in opposition parties would hinder progress. This led to repression with laws passed to curb opposition to his policies like the Deportation Act of 1957 and the several Detention Acts. He veered towards a one–party state. Interference with due legal process occurred when the accused in the court case, related to the assassination attempt on his life in 1962, were discharged. Only for Nkrumah to dismiss the judge, appoint a new one and, most contentiously, a new jury which found the three accused guilty and sentenced them to death. The judgement was commuted to 20 years in prison. Additionally, corruption and nepotism grew. Nkrumah was overthrown in a military coup in February 1966. The military coup of 1979 brought Jerry Rawlings (1947-2020), a military officer, to power.

Ghana is endowed with natural resources – vast quantities of minerals including diamonds and gold.

Malaysia too had a determined leader in Mahathir Mohamad (1925-) for whom Malaysia and its development came first. He too was an internationalist and Malaysia was a founding member of the Association of South East Asian Nations or ASEAN. Its major natural resource is petroleum products and crude oil. In addition it has minerals like gold, tin copper etc.

Both Ghana and Malaysia have invested in agriculture. While both countries have progressed since independence there is yet a difference in attainment of the two. Both countries have progressed despite claims from many quarters that slavery and colonialism have held back countries in the Commonwealth. The lack of even greater progress in Ghana may be attributed, among others, to poor governance.

In both countries colonialism did not have adverse effects on national advancement. A recent television program showed the views of Malaysians who applauded the British who had governed Malaysia. The same may be said of say, Sri Lanka (previously Ceylon), where at independence from Britain in 1948, the systems of government were well established- parliamentary democracy, impartial judiciary etc. The education system and the continuing commitment to education was good enough to allow it to reach a youth literacy rate of 98% and an adult literacy rate of 91%. One can proudly claim, as many Sri Lankans do, that colonialism and British rule was good for the country. What has happened now in the country is due, among other events, to poor governance.

The clamour of the residents of Hong Kong for greater democracy and accountability and away from the control of China is evidence, if it were needed, of the power of good that British rule brought.

Colonialism cannot be blamed for the ills of society, at least where the British Empire is concerned.

The current narrative on slavery appears to point to an apparent antipathy of whites towards blacks. While there has been racism, there are also examples of successful association between people of different colours and ethnicities. One case stands out as an illustration of the friendship between races - the story of Sarah Forbes Bonetta. Sarah was born in 1943 to the Yoruba tribe in the Kingdom of Dahomey, which is now Benin. She was born to Egbado (now Yewa) royalty in the Yoruba tribe. She was five years old when captured following a raid by a rival king. In 1850 the British captain, Frederick E. Forbes visited the country on behalf of the Royal Navy to persuade King Gezo to cease participation in the Atlantic slave trade. The King gifted captain Forbes with Sarah, whom he brought with him to England. Upon our arrival in England, Forbes gifted the child to Queen Victoria who adopted her as a goddaughter. The Queen described Sarah as 'sharp and intelligent'. Captain Forbes also described her as being 'far in advance of any white child of her age in aptness of learning, and strength of mind and affection.' Queen Victoria paid for Sarah's education in Gillingham and in Sierra Leone, while taking an interest in Sarah's family. A lover of music, Sarah spoke fluent English and French and was a part of Brighton's social circle. In 1862 Sarah married James Davies who was a rich merchant from Sierra Leone. They had 3 children – one daughter was named after Queen Victoria. Sarah died of tuberculosis in 1880 at the young age of 37 years in Funchal, Portugal. The historian David Olusaga wrote in 2019, that the story of Sarah Bonetta 'was widely viewed as a symbol of "the perceived accomplishments of Britain's civilizing mission'.

That this story has dual connotations is readily apparent; the benevolence of Queen Victoria is a given but what about Sarah? Here was a little child who at that moment was instantly dehumanized. She was objectified, deprived of any feelings and became like an inanimate gift to a strange person. That Sarah had feelings of her own and even some morality is without question. Of course she must have known the difference between right and wrong and good and evil. And she must have had a deep foreboding of what was about to happen to her, coupled with extreme sorrow to leave the terrain that she knew and the people and their customs familiar to her. Not for her was The Middle Passage but a passage nevertheless, northerly to England - a strange land with strange people and their customs. What about the morality of King Gezo? Had he no morals - if he had any, they were overwhelmed and submerged by the exigencies of the situation. And finally the morality of captain Forbes. If he had any, one never knows whether he subscribed to them or whether it was something he acquired from his authorities in England. This story captures the inherent nature of slavery in Africa, which was universal on the continent. And it was a practice devoid of any ethics or morals; he who was in power called the tune- might was most certainly right at the time.

The ambivalence of Africans towards the white man is seen very clearly in the readiness with which they would accept, for example, a Rhodes scholarship. They would benefit, they should, from the educational opportunities provided by such programs. But at the same time, while in England to protest about Rhodes, speaks to the confusion in the minds of those who accept such educational opportunities. Like other similar facilities, the Rhodes scholarship is an opportunity to enhance knowledge and understanding which can be brought to bear in the home countries of recipients. It is without doubt a form of reparation which would be best served when the recipient returns and plays an active part in their countries of origin. Educational opportunities in England are not means of enforcing British values on recipient countries. Nothing could be further from what is intended; they are means to appreciate systems, processes etc which may be used in different cultures according to local customs in a kind of hybrid manner for the benefit of all in society.

One of the myths of the narrative of slavery is that the empires of Europe developed because of it. This could not be further from the truth; the European empires were developing and progressing while slavery continued and had been continuing for many centuries in parallel with it. The two met at economic crossroads and the white man saw an opportunity for cheap labour. What needs to be emphasized is that the whole sordid venture of the transportation of slaves to foreign lands would not have occurred without the complicity and active participation of the African man. He too saw an opportunity for profit, even if it meant selling his fellowmen. He was crucial to the whole edifice of slavery. The development of the various European empires – Spanish, Dutch, French, German, British continued apace and would have done so irrespective of slavery. The black man was cheaper than the white man and economics of the time dictated that the former was preferable. This was hard nosed economics in practice. It went hand in glove and was no different to the pecuniary interest the African man and African kingdoms had in slavery. This was Adam Smith's (the Scottish economist) economic principles at play. The Industrial Revolution that started in Britain around 1760 would have happened and was inevitable as natural progression from manual labour to mechanised working. The Iron Bridge made of cast iron and spanning the Severn River in Shropshire, England was the first bridge in the world made of cast iron; construction finished in 1781. Handel and Beethoven, to name but a few would have continued to compose and Caravaggio would have painted. The Enlightenment of the 17th and 18th centuries, that period of profound philosophical and intellectual development that gave birth to human thought, reason, liberty and the pursuit of human happiness, would have occurred. Prior to this was the Renaissance in Europe – a period of intellectual and moral awakening with advances in art, science, humanity etc. These events, among many others in Europe, would have happened irrespective of slavery. So the claim that slavery contributed to progress does not stand up to scrutiny, save to say that cheap labour helped accentuate the profits of companies at the time. Had morality been a factor, one can imagine that the extent of slavery would have been much diminished. One comes back to why morality or the basic human feeling of one person towards another was absent. And one returns to the words of Tidiane N'Diaye who wrote 'Veiled Genocide' and those of Zora Neale Hurston. Hurston wrote ' My own people had exterminated whole nations and torn families apart for a profit before the strangers got their chance at a cut.' This statement is crucial in three aspects – that slavery is not what is being portrayed, as an unimaginable evil perpetrated by the white man on the hapless African. Secondly, is the considered silence or even wilful blindness of the much greater horrors of other aspects of the African slave trade. And thirdly one returns to why and how reparations today would help for the supposed wrongs of the past. Descendants of slaves are hardly victims of slavery. They may be victims of, often deep-seated, racism but not of slavery per se. And no amount of compensation to individuals would make any tangible positive impact. This does not take away the crying need to address racism and its effects in society. The legacy of slavery, wrote Hurston, is to be alive in a land of opportunities and not worrying about the past. 'Slavery is the price I paid for civilization' she wrote. Slavery brought people from the destitution that was Africa to a developing modern world. Booker T Washington implied much the same when he wrote 'Notwithstanding the cruelty and moral wrong of slavery, we are in a stronger and more hopeful condition, materially, intellectually, morally, and religiously, than is true of an equal number of black people in any other portion of the globe'. This must surely be the enduring legacy of slavery and puts to rest discussion about reparations and even racism. Here is a call to join in society as equals and to move away from victimhood – become 'we'. And do not let 'us' see 'them' ; rather see us in them and them in us.

Much has been written about the intentions of the Founding Fathers of America in regard to equality. Did they mean all persons were equal ie. white sand blacks in America including indigenous blacks? Or were they, at the time, referring to all white people as being equal? One may never know their individual and collective impressions which they brought to bear on their final decisions. One could conclude that they brought a unique insight to the problems of different people inhabiting the same land and trying to endow the country with equality of persons irrespective of colour, heritage, religious persuasion etc. The Founding Fathers may have proposed a template for a truly integrationist society which was far ahead of its time. In the process they launched the nation on the path towards a vibrant, multiracial society which has continued in its building to this day and would continue henceforth. This may be the finest contribution of Thomas Jefferson (1743-1826), who is claimed to have had the best intellect at the time. The USA remains a beacon of freedom to the world despite its internal and external opponents. The vast numbers who seek America as their home are testimony to the power of freedom espoused by the USA, the same freedom that remains a thorn in the side of those who seek authoritarianism.

Slavery was not recognised in English law. The celebrated case of Somerset v Stewart (1772) illustrates the law at the time. James Stewart was an African slave in Boston, Massachusetts, USA who was brought to England in 1769 by a customs officer by the name of Charles Stewart. But in 1771, Somerset escaped and applied to court for freedom. Lord Mansfield, the judge sitting in the Court of the King's Bench, set Somerset free as there was no law on slavery at the time.

The abolition of slavery in Britain started with William Wilberforce's Slave Trade Act of 1807 which set out to abolish slave trade in the whole of the British empire. It took until the Slavery Abolition Act of 1833 for slavery to be completely abolished.

The West Africa Squadron or the Preventative Squadron of the Royal Navy was established to enforce abolition and eliminate the Atlantic slave trade. It was a costly exercise that patrolled the Atlantic coast of Africa to deter transportation of slaves by force of arms, if needed. The squadron had extensive powers to intercept not only British vessels but also ships from the United States, the Ottoman empire, Europe and the slave ships of Barbary pirates. However, this was no easy task. Africans protested, as Mohamed Mbodj wrote ' Africans felt that the rules of their traditional life had been called into question, by initiatives which destabilized the bases of their society.' The historian, Paul Davidson, wrote that the African was far from being a passive bystander in this lucrative business, rather 'they exploited its opportunities'. When one considers the 'traditional life' in African society at the time, one is bound to question what this amounted to. Given that slavery was always part of African society, one is now invited to encounter a different concept to what happened in the three major slave trades that afflicted the continent. Slaves sometimes became integral parts of the slaving community and even rose to positions of significance in those societies. This was the 'traditional life' of slavery. What is referred to in the statement by Mbodj is something different – the commercialisation of slavery which was not a significant part of historical slavery. Therefore the African himself had seismically moved the traditional goal posts of slavery – from enslavement in capturing communities to capture, sale and transport of slaves to distant lands. One may conclude that the African changed their traditional slavery which had been a way of life for centuries to what was a new normal, a 'new tradition' in slavery which brought with it a significant financial aspect to it. Was there a moral change- one may never know.

The abolition of slavery by Britain may be viewed as a natural evolution from the Renaissance and the Enlightenment, with the desire for human freedom and happiness. This was the birth of morality regarding slavery. Until then nether the nations of Africa from where slaves originated nor the Americas and West Indies had a functioning notion of morality or if they did, they were superseded by the needs of business.

The Haitian Revolution of 1791-1804 resulted in the end of slavey in Haiti. It thus became the first country in the world to see the end of slavery. Slavery was nominally abolished in the United States of America at it founding in 1776. However the slavery states of the south continued with slavery until the passage of the Thirteen Amendment in 1865, at the end of the American Civil War.

While all this was happening in Britain and the USA, the Arab slave trade continued apace. Arabs were important middlemen in the transatlantic slave trade while continuing their own trade in humans. It is said that, on the basis of research, 14 million blacks were transported across Africa as slaves between the 7th and 19th centuries. This is in comparison to the approximately 12 million transported through the Middle Passage.

That Great Britain at the height of its power found the morality to end slavery is difficult for most to acknowledge; it does not sit well with the current selective story of African slavery. That the great institution of slavery, deeply seared in the culture of Africa and a source of wealth to its rulers, was ended by the British is hardly acknowledged because it is at odds with the narrative of the white man being at the root of the evil that was slavery. It is relatively easy to complain about slavery, but one is bound to ask why those who find it an abomination are unable to move towards confronting the slavery of modern times. While there are many examples of modern slavery, one recent incident sheds light on the evil business. In February 2023 it was reported in the UK that a Nigerian politician and his wife travelled to the UK with their daughter and a poor street trader from Nigeria. The politician's daughter apparently has kidney failure and needed a kidney transplant. The trader was coached to act and talk as if he was a cousin of the patient and that he was willing to donate his kidney. This arrangement was made with the promise of the intended donor being paid £7000 and a better life in the UK. In hospital, it was soon apparent that the young man in question had no appreciation whatsoever of what he was there for or what was to become of him. At the time of this writing a legal case continues. History may judge those who now talk of slavery, as not having had the conviction of their words.

The spoken word is not infrequently identified as racist. Why, one would ask? The example of Lady Susan Hussey who had worked for the Royal Family for over 60 years is a pointer how volatile even a simple and innocent question could be. She was at a reception in Buckingham Palace to which the charity worker Ngozi Fulani had been invited. Lady Susan asked Fulani a question she must have asked others many times over in the 60 years she worked in the Palace. What is wrong with the question 'where are you from?' People like to know where other people are from. There is nothing racist in this innocent question except a desire to understand others. Most people would have asked the same question of their friends, colleagues, associates etc. But as Esther Krakue wrote it was a genuine question in this instance. Here is a person of British birth from a Caribbean family whose name was originally Marlene Headley. She changed her name to Ngozi, which is from the Igbo tribe and Fulani is from a different tribe. She has acquired an African name when she clearly is not African. And her attire is unusual with Krakue quoting her own Ghanian mother who thought Fulani was dressed as a 'fetish priest'. It would be an obvious question asked of Fulani if she visited Africa. Krakue states that she herself would have been easily offended to see Fulani having appropriate her own culture West African. Therefore, it was a right and proper question, unless of course one was easily offended or sought offence with a racist mindset. Most people, including blacks, do not think there was any racism in this matter. And here lies the problem – calling out racism when it does not exist and acquiescence with a claim of racism.

The interpretation of slavery from a position of certainty does not acknowledge that it is a generational phenomenon fashioned by the views of the time. Every era has had its certainties only for them to be bypassed with time. The views of today would be blown away by winds of change. It is universally accepted that slavery was uniquely evil; if only it had not happened. But this selective view does not accord with history – slavery has been present from time immemorial ; every race has enslaved others and have been enslaved themselves. But at the same time there were good people who were capable of amazing acts of kindness. The two existed together as again it is in the nature of civilisation that good and evil coexist. The current time is hardly an example of greater kindness despite the advances of civilisation; brutality towards fellow humans continues as if progress had not occurred. The wars in Syria and Ukraine are but a few instances of violent human convulsions, not to mention the evils of shootings and stabbings at community level. There were in excess of 25 million people recently held in slavery around the world. Some would put the figure at 35 to 45 million worldwide. Where, asks Thomas Sowell, is there indignation about this painful fact? Then again, what about the appalling condition in which people live in Africa today? For example over 22,000 malnourished children received life-saving help at a centre run by Medecins Sans Frontières (MSF) in Nigeria's Zamfara state and over 7500 people needed emergency medical treatment in Bentiu Hospital run by MSF in South Sudan. Some of these people too, are descendants of slaves or are slaves themselves. But violence is commonplace at home too - in Britain, 1425 females were killed by men between 2009 and 2018.

Two aspects in the UK need mention here. In 2022 a report was produced by Dr. Tony Sewell, the chairman of the Commission on Race and Ethnic Disparities and his team. It concluded that while there undoubtedly is prejudice in society, there was no evidence of this being structural. The team comprised eminent persons grounded in the assimilation, analysis and interpretation of evidence. This was as scientific in its approach as was possible. The report concluded that black children were doing better than some sections of the white community and that multi-racialism in Britain is a model to the world. But this did not prevent opponents calling the report a 'whitewash'. Dr. Sewell stated that various groups hate 'black success' and are practising a from a racism of their own. The report does not sit well with the accepted view among sections of the black community even though it was evidence based. One shudders to think if the same conclusions were reached by a committee of white persons! The imperative to maintain the status of black victimhood against all evidence is as worrying as it serves to perpetuate the myth of racism and encourages divisiveness in society.

The second event is the case of Ernesto Elliott. He was one of about 23 serious criminals who were due to deported to Jamaica on a charter flight in December 2020. This was prevented at the last minute by an appeal to the courts. About 60 so-called famous persons signed a letter opposing the deportation. The names included the historian David Olusaga, the actresses Thandiwe Newton and Naomie Harris and the model, Naomi Campbell. Fast-forward to June 2021, Ernesto and his son Nico were involved in a fracas which led to the death of Nathaniel Eyewu-Ago in Greenwich in broad daylight. Ernesto Elliot was sentenced to 26 years and his son to 22 years in jail. The attack which was witnessed by the public was reported to have 'caused significant trauma to innocent members of the public who witnessed it'. One wonders if the 'famous persons' have apologised to the victims of this vicious attack. They could choose to emulate the late King Hussein of Jordan. The King knelt before the parents of children who had been murdered and asked for forgiveness saying – 'Your daughter is like my daughter. Your loss is my loss'. This is humanity at its finest.

These two anecdotes appear to describe anything that happens to a black person as being an example of victimhood and that relieves them from responsibility. This needs to change and blacks, like all, need to move towards responsibility and accountability. They should not see racism in all adverse events. All actions have consequences and blacks need to appreciate and take ownership of their responsibilities to themselves and to society. By acting as they did, so called 'famous persons' have set back race relations. Racism and victimhood, even if real and existent, should not and must not be permitted to make inroads to personal responsibility.

Tearing down statues has almost become a fashion, increasingly devoid of meaning because of the almost primitive instinct to destroy the past and re-write in a manner that is acceptable to the narrative of today. But the person whom the statues depict were individuals who functioned at a given time in history without recourse to the morality of today, and they were not in conflict with the law of the time. They were benevolent as seen from their contributions to all in society. The toxic combination of iconoclasm, wokery and imagined racism would reduce British history to what Dominic Sambrook called 'a cartoonish caricature of cruel imperialists and saintly martyrs'!

Claims of racism, wokeism and iconoclasm combine to form a toxic amalgam which could destroy the fabric of society and set back race relations in UK. Society needs to be aware that it may be sleepwalking towards a racial calamity.

Black lives smatter wherever they may be, not only in the developed world or in the consciousness of those who see the evil of our times. Racism is evil too and has no place in an apparently civilised world. Indeed all lives matter.

Madam Tinubu in Lagos, Nigeria

Elmina Castle, Ghana

Colin Kaepernick taking the knee

Printed and bound by CPI Group (UK) Ltd, Croydon, CR0 4YY